Dear friend,

Anyone who wants to delve into the book of Hebrews is someone I'd like to meet for coffee. It's ideal for those who are ready to grow, to know Christ better, to let go of the "try hard" life and figure out how to run this marathon with grace and grit.

Hebrews contains some of the most beautiful passages you'll find in Scripture. It will comfort you and challenge you. Every word of it has a treasure to mine, and those who are willing to make the effort will be richly rewarded.

Never have I been more convinced of the importance of women being grounded in hope. There is much in the world that discourages us, but frankly, there are just as many things within our families that wreck our hearts. Most of us are doing the best we can to love, serve, and take care of the people close to us, but heartache and despair still steal in through a crack in the door. I don't know about you, but I can get pretty tired from the effort to hold things together.

Hebrews reminds us that it isn't all up to us. Yes, we have our part to play, but ultimately, God has got a grip on those things that feel out of control. I know this, you know this, but this study of Hebrews will give us a bigger view of God that will help us *believe* it. Hope springs up when we see that all the threads are being woven together by the master artist. We are not disintegrating. We are being built.

We need to be grounded in truth as well. Our postmodern culture works like carbon monoxide; we don't notice that we're breathing it in, yet it's slowly but surely killing us. We need to put on the oxygen mask of God's Word to keep our head straight in the midst of total confusion.

So let's dive into this rich and dense book and see what God has to say. We will not be disappointed.

Grateful to be running beside you,

Lisa Brenninkmeyer
Founder and Chief Purpose Officer of Walking with Purpose

Dedication

This study of Hebrews is dedicated to my dad, Denny Harris. I have watched you run your race of faith, seeing not just the tremendous impact you have had on the world around you but also your integrity behind the scenes. You have taught me that following Christ requires being sold out—giving everything you have for the sake of the One who held nothing back from us. I have never seen your equal in terms of perseverance and tenacity. As you have quietly sacrificed, served, led, listened, and guided, always doing the hard thing, consistently and without complaint, I have been watching. I've been doing this my whole life and I have never seen you shrink back. You press hard into the Lord, never content with where you are, always asking Him to keep molding you and shaping you. There have been so many times I have wanted to quit, Dad, and take an easier path. But you have always been up ahead of me, showing me that if I just press on, if I do not give up, it will be worth it. Thank you for running your race and passing the baton to me. I promise to carry it with God's grace and hand it to the next generation. May they treasure the legacy you have given us.

"Therefore, since we are surrounded by so great a cloud of witnesses, let us rid ourselves of every burden and sin that clings to us and persevere in running the race that lies before us while keeping our eyes fixed on Jesus, the leader and perfecter of faith." (Hebrews 12:1–2)

Grounded in Hope

A Study of the Letter to the Hebrews

www.walkingwithpurpose.com

Authored by Lisa Brenninkmeyer
Cover and page design by True Cotton
Production management by Christine Welsko

IMPRIMATUR　　　+ William E. Lori, S.T.D., Archbishop of Baltimore

The recommended Bible translations for use in Blaze and Walking with Purpose studies are: The New American Bible, which is the translation used in the United States for the readings at Mass; The Revised Standard Version, Catholic Edition; and The Jerusalem Bible.

Any internet addresses (websites, blogs, etc.) in this book are offered as a resource and may change in the future. Please refer to www.walkingwithpurpose.com as the central location for corresponding materials and references.

Printed: November 2018

ISBN: 978-1-943173-25-9

Grounded in Hope

TABLE OF CONTENTS

INTRODUCTION

LESSONS

APPENDICES

Welcome to Walking with Purpose

You have many choices when it comes to how you spend your time—thank you for choosing Walking with Purpose. Studying God's Word with an open and receptive heart will bring spiritual growth and enrichment to all aspects of your life, making every moment that you've invested well worth it.

Each one of us comes to this material from our own unique vantage point. You are welcome as you are. No previous experience is necessary. Some of you will find that the questions in this study cause you to think about concepts that are new to you. Others might find much is a review. God meets each one of us where we are, and He is always faithful, taking us to a deeper, better place spiritually, regardless of where we begin.

The Structure of *Grounded in Hope*

Grounded in Hope is a seventeen-week Bible study that integrates Scripture with the teachings of the Roman Catholic Church to point us to principles that help us manage life's pace and pressure while living with calm and steadiness. It is designed for both interactive personal study and group discussion.

If you're going through this study either on your own or in a small group, you are welcome to order the DVDs, but you might find it simpler to watch the talks online. The URL for each talk is listed in the Talk outline within the study guide.

Study Guide Format and Reference Materials

The three parts of *Grounded in Hope* are divided into three sections:

The first section comprises seventeen lessons. Most lessons are divided into five "days" to help you form a habit of reading and reflecting on God's Word regularly. If you are a woman who has only bits and pieces of time throughout your day to accomplish tasks, you will find this breakdown of the lessons especially helpful. Each day focuses on Scripture readings and related teaching passages, and ends with a

Quiet Your Heart reflection. In addition, Day Five includes a lesson conclusion; a resolution section, in which you set a goal for yourself based on a theme of the lesson; and short clips from the *Catechism of the Catholic Church*, which are referenced throughout the lesson to complement the Scripture study.

For the talks in this study, accompanying outlines are offered as guides for taking notes. Included are questions to use either for personal reflection or for additional small group discussion. URLs are also provided for those who would like to view the talks online.

The second section, the appendices, contains supplemental materials referred to during the study, and includes an article about Saint Thérèse of Lisieux, the patron saint of Walking with Purpose (Appendix 1). Appendix 2, "Scripture Memory," gives instructions on how to memorize Scripture. Memory verses have been chosen for *Grounded in Hope*, and we encourage you to memorize them as you move through the Bible study. An illustration of the verses can be found in Appendix 2, and a color version and phone lock screen can be downloaded from our website.

The third section contains the answer key. You will benefit so much more from the Bible study if you work through the questions on your own, searching your heart, as this is your very personal journey of faith. The answer key is meant to enhance small group discussion and provide personal guidance or author's insight where needed.

At the end of the book are pages on which to write weekly prayer intentions.

Walking with Purpose™ Website

Please visit our website at www.walkingwithpurpose.com to find supplemental materials that complement our Bible studies; a link to our online store for additional Bible studies, DVDs, books, and more; and the following free content:

WWP Scripture Printables of our exclusively designed verse cards that complement all Bible studies. Available in various sizes, lock screens for phones, and a format that allows you to email them to friends.

WWP Bible Study Playlists of Lisa's favorite music to accompany each Bible study.

WWP Videos of all Connect Coffee Talks by Lisa Brenninkmeyer.

WWP Blog by Lisa Brenninkmeyer, a safe place where you are welcome, where the mask can drop and you can be real. Subscribe for updates.

WWP Leadership Development Program

We are here to help you take your leadership to the next level! Through our training, you'll discover insights that help you achieve your leadership potential. You'll be empowered to step out of your comfort zone and experience the rush of serving God with passion and purpose. We want you to know that you are not alone; we offer you encouragement and the tools you need to reach out to a world that desperately needs to experience the love of God.

Links to WWP Social Media

Twitter, Pinterest, Facebook, Instagram

NOTES

Lessons

NOTES

Lesson 1: Talk

THE RADIANCE

Hebrews 1

You can view this talk on the accompanying DVD, or please visit our website at walkingwithpurpose.com/videos and select the *Grounded in Hope* Bible Study, then click through to select Videos.

I. Why Hebrews?

II. Differing Worldviews

Depending on your worldview, you're going to have a very distinct way of approaching the big questions of life.

- What is really real—what I see or the spiritual realm?
- What happens when I die?
- Who is God?
- How do I know right and wrong?

A. Postmodern Worldview

B. Christian Worldview

The core question of Hebrews is:

III. The Importance of Knowing Our Story

"The world does not know where it came from, what sustains it, or where its destiny lies, although it assumes that it knows all these things." —St. John Paul II

A. Our Story Fits into a Larger Story

B. Jesus as God's Final Word

We live in a postmodern culture that is repelled by the idea of God having the final word. Jesus is fine as long as He is on the shelf along with all the other gods and truths out there. But the minute He is put forth as the final word, people are offended. This is the one place where Jesus refuses to stay. He will not sit on a shelf as one option among equals.

C. Jesus as the Source of Our Hope

"He is the image of the invisible God, the firstborn over all creation. For by him all things were created: things in heaven and on earth, visible and invisible, whether thrones or power or rulers or authorities; all things were created by him and for him. He is before all things, and in him all things hold together." (Colossians 1:15–18)

And if He can hold all things together, He can hold *you* together.

D. Jesus as the Pioneer of Our Salvation

The word *pioneer* comes from the Greek word *arche*—and can also be translated "captain" or "champion."

Discussion Questions

1. In which area of life do you need hope? When you face choices in terms of where to anchor your hope, who or what competes with Jesus?

2. What is your reaction to the statement "Jesus is God's final word"? Does the finality of who He is and what He teaches feel restrictive? In what way is He calling you to bend your will to His right now?

3. Do you see evidence of the postmodern worldview around you (no such thing as absolute truth, God is irrelevant, emotions take center stage, strong emphasis on individuality and tolerance)?

Looking for more material? We've got you covered! Walking with Purpose meets women where they are in their spiritual journey. From our Opening Your Heart 22-lesson foundational Bible study to more advanced studies, we have something to help each and every woman grow closer to Christ. Find out more:

www.walkingwithpurpose.com

Lesson 2

GREATER THAN THE ANGELS

Hebrews 1

Introduction

Is there a sweet season in your life that you would love to revisit? Do you have memories of a time that seems less complicated—when expectations weren't overwhelming and you felt carefree?

I can remember the season when I was just beginning to wake up to the deep spiritual needs in the hearts of women. The discovery that I might play a part in seeing those needs satisfied by Christ was invigorating. Dipping my toe in the water of ministry, I experienced the thrill of seeing lives changed. That being said, I was certain that God would never expect me to serve Him to the point of real discomfort. I figured the minute things got hard, He'd want me to quit. It was blissful ignorance. A little farther down the road to maturity, I see things differently now. I feel a heightened sense of responsibility, and I know that following God and serving Him actually *guarantees* that life will get uncomfortable. Sometimes I think about heading back to that easier road—the one where you get to quit when things stop being fun. It's a real temptation when the spiritual battle heats up.

The readers of the book of Hebrews stood at a similar crossroads, looking for a way to get to an easier place without a full-on compromise. They were being persecuted for their faith in Jesus, and needed encouragement and instruction. The author of Hebrews set out to offer them both.

Some background information will be helpful as we begin:

Who: Sorry to disappoint, but we don't know who wrote Hebrews. Saint Paul, Barnabas, Apollos, Aquila, and Priscilla have all been credited with the crafting of this letter. But in the words of Origen, "As to who actually wrote the epistle, God knows

13

the truth of the matter."[1] We know a little more about the recipients. Hebrews was clearly written for people who had a thorough knowledge of the Old Testament—especially the events recorded in the Pentateuch (the first five books of the Bible). The author jumps right into discussions about Abraham, the nation of Israel, Moses and Mount Sinai, the Torah and the covenants, priests and sacrifices, and the Israelite Exodus with little to no explanation. We know that the readers were facing persecution (Hebrews 10) but hadn't yet suffered to the point of shedding blood (Hebrews 12).

The name Hebrews comes from the title "To the Hebrews," which was attached to the letter in the earliest manuscripts. New Testament scholar Luke Timothy Johnson explains that this title reveals the attempt to give clarity to "an anonymous text with no addressees as one written to the Jews . . . [although] we cannot determine with full certainty the ethnic makeup of the intended readers (or hearers). There is certainly more internal evidence to support the position that they were Jewish rather than Gentile."[2]

While the name of the book is Hebrews, in Scripture, that word is also used to describe the Jewish people. You'll also hear them referred to as Israelites. The two terms can be used interchangeably. You can say "the Hebrew nation" or describe a Jewish person's nationality as Hebrew.

Where: Most scholars believe Hebrews was written to a community in Rome or another place in Italy.[3]

When: Hebrews was likely written before the Jewish temple was destroyed in AD 70. During that time, the Roman armies destroyed Jerusalem, killing or enslaving hundreds of thousands of Jewish people. According to the historian Josephus, the army killed the elderly and the armed, and enslaved the rest. Thousands were forced to become gladiators; others had to build the Colosseum and the Forum of Vespasian. Children were sold into slavery. It is unthinkable that the author of Hebrews would have written about the temple and sacrifices as he does throughout the letter without referencing this catastrophic historical event.

Why? The core message of the book of Hebrews is twofold.
1) The supremacy of Jesus Christ (No one and nothing is greater than He is.)
2) The importance of perseverance (Keep going. Don't give up. Press on.)

---

[1] Quote taken from Origen's homilies on Hebrews (no longer in existence) in Eusebius, *Ecclesiastical History* 6.25.14.

[2] Luke Timothy Johnson, *Hebrews: A Commentary* (Louisville, KY: Westminster John Knox Press, 2006), 33.

[3] Mary Healy, *Hebrews* (Grand Rapids, MI: Baker Publishing Group, 2016), 21.

As we study together, we'll see that Jesus is compared to angels and the Torah, Moses and the Promised Land, priests and Melchizedek, sacrifices and the covenant. The reason He is contrasted with these particular things is because they represent the best and most solid aspects of the old way of relating to God. As the Hebrews faced persecution, it was tempting to return to "safer" beliefs that were less likely to land them in trouble. The author of Hebrews is determined to show his readers the superiority of Christ so that they don't abandon Him.

It's my prayer that as we read through this brilliant book of the Bible, we, too, will be reminded that Jesus is the greatest and best, and that no sacrifice is too high to pay as we endeavor to faithfully stay the course.

Day One
THE BACKGROUND

One of the aims of the author of Hebrews is to show that Jesus is God's final word, our only hope, the eternal priest, and the perfect sacrifice. Arguments to that end are made throughout Hebrews in hopes that Jesus will be elevated to the place that He deserves in the readers' hearts, which is the highest place of honor and priority.

But the author of Hebrews has his work cut out for him. Most of our lesson this week will be spent looking at things that competed for that place of honor in the hearts of Jewish Christians, but before we do that, it's helpful to take a look at the pagan culture that the Jewish Christians were living in.

It is highly likely that Acts 17 was written around the same time as Hebrews, and we can learn something about the cultural climate of Hebrews through that text. In it, Saint Paul was in the midst of his second missionary journey. He was speaking in Athens, which was the cultural center of the ancient world.

1. Read Acts 17:16. What was frustrating Saint Paul?

Everywhere Paul turned, there was another statue, shrine, or temple to an idol. It was no different in Rome, where there were hundreds of statues to various gods. The Greeks and Romans weren't anti-religious; they were open to all sorts of deities. But convincing people to choose one above all others would not be an easy sell.

Read Acts 17:22–31.

2. In what way did Saint Paul attempt to win over the Greeks in verse 22?

3. How did he build a bridge between his theology and their religion in verse 23?

4. How did Saint Paul's description of the one true God differ from that of the gods that were honored throughout Athens in verses 24 and 29?

5. How did Saint Paul describe God in Acts 17:25–31?

Both the Greek and the Roman cultures were polytheistic—worshipping many gods. Other religions were tolerated for the most part, as long as they were willing to worship the emperor and didn't cause trouble with other religious groups. Judaism and Christianity, both monotheistic religions (worshipping one God), could be problematic.[4]

Because Christianity was a brand-new religion and was spreading like crazy, many found it threatening. Christians referred to their faith as the "One Way," which lacked the tolerance these cultures valued. In addition, many thought the Christians were

---

[4] Sam O'Neal, "Earliest Days of the Roman Christian Church," ThoughtCo., .https://www.thoughtco.com/the-early-church-at-rome-363409.

practicing cannibalism when they spoke of eating Christ's body and drinking His blood.

The recipients of the letter to the Hebrews were experiencing the heat of persecution from two places. They felt it from the Romans, who were becoming increasingly uncomfortable with the Christian religion, and from the Jews, who viewed them as defectors from the true religion, Judaism.

6. The author of Hebrews understood the perils of persecution, and was urging his readers to remain faithful even if they were afraid. But he didn't do it by focusing on their emotions. A deep thinker and gifted writer, the author of Hebrews organized his appeal and presented it as a compelling intellectual argument.

Because of its rich vocabulary, the letter to the Hebrews is considered a literary masterpiece. But this wasn't the author's purpose in writing it. He wanted to see his readers transformed, not just inspired and informed. How did Saint Paul describe this process of transformation in Romans 12:2?

This means we have to do the work of engaging our minds if we really want to see permanent change in our behavior. We need to change the way we look at the past, think about our current circumstances, and view the future. The renewal of our minds takes place as we saturate ourselves with Scripture. Instead of trying to guess what God thinks, we're able to study His own words. If we're going to be true disciples (which means being a follower of Jesus), we'll have to be disciplined about what we feed our minds. This is exactly what you are doing right now, and it is such a game changer in life. You are filling your mind with truth, and are storing up treasure that you'll be able to draw from in all sorts of situations you'll face. What you read today may not apply to your current circumstances, but just wait. Isaiah 55:11 promises us that when God's Word is sent out, it never returns empty handed– it always achieves the purpose that God had for it. The benefit of deep, disciplined Scripture study will pay dividends year after year.

Quiet your heart and enjoy His presence. . . . Let Him renew your mind.

"Yet just as from the heavens the rain and snow come down and do not return there till they have watered the earth, making it fertile and fruitful, giving seed to the one who sows and bread to the one who eats, so shall my word be that goes forth from my mouth; It shall not return to me empty, but shall do what pleases me, achieving the end for which I sent it." (Isaiah 55:10–11)

No time spent listening to God speak to you through His Word is ever wasted. As you take in these Bible passages, wrestle with what they mean, and then seek to apply them to your own life, transformation will come. Reject the lie that things will never change, that you are stuck, that there is no hope. God is doing something new right now in your mind and heart.

Dear Lord,

As we begin this journey through Hebrews, we are ready to drink deeply of Your truth. We long for it. So much of the information we encounter comes at us with lightning speed; it changes every second. We don't always know what we can trust—is this fake news or real? Yet we long to be grounded in truth that doesn't change.

Thank You so much for remaining the same. In You "we live and move and have our being" (Acts 17:28). You not only can be known, You long to be known. When so much in our lives is new and in transition, it's such a comfort to come to You and know that You are steady. You are the rock we can stand on and cling to. Please help us to stop gravitating toward poor substitutes for You. We are unlikely to turn to "an image fashioned from gold, silver or stone" (Acts 17:29), but we often choose things like trying to be in control, performing, or building a life on people's approval instead of reliance on You. We need Your help to choose You, because it's such a well-worn, familiar path back to the cheap substitutes.

Day Two
THE PROLOGUE

Read Hebrews 1:1–4.

1. A. Referencing Hebrews 1:1–2, compare how God communicated to His people in times past and in these last days.

B. What are some of the ways in which God spoke through the Old Testament prophets? See Exodus 3:1–10, 1 Kings 19:11–13, and Numbers 12:6, 8.

As we learned in the opening talk, the phrase "in these last days" holds real significance. It's putting down a marker in history—a significant before and after. It's saying, before this point, this is how God communicated with us. His voice and will was revealed to the prophets in visions, dreams, and sometimes face-to-face. As amazing as that communication had been, it was nothing compared to this new way that God was speaking. Hebrews 1:1 tells us that "in these last days," as in, from that point until the end, He has spoken to us through His Son.

This means that Jesus is God's final word. He is it. There isn't a plan B coming or an alternative way of understanding what God has to say. Jesus is it.

The finality of Jesus also means that we can't change Him—we just need to accept who He is, as He has revealed Himself. When you think about it, it's totally ridiculous to try to have a relationship with someone based on who we think they should be. This isn't grounded in truth, there's no intimacy, and there's no trust. This doesn't work with people, and it doesn't work with Jesus, either. Instead of starting with what *we* think about Jesus, let's look at how He has been revealed to us in Scripture.

2. A. How is Jesus, the Son, described in Hebrews 1:2?

B. What additional insight do you gain from John 1:3 into Jesus as the creator?

C. What additional insight do you gain from Psalm 2:8 into Jesus as the heir? (Note: In the New Testament, this psalm is interpreted as being about what Jesus will gain or accomplish.)

3. What four things do we learn about Jesus from Hebrews 1:3?

4. What did Jesus do after He accomplished purification from sins? See Hebrews 1:3.

Why is it significant that Jesus sat down? Sitting down signifies completion—that one's work is done. When Jesus sat down at the right hand of the majesty in heaven (a place of authority and honor), it communicated that "it is finished" (John 19:30)—that our sins had been paid for.

5. Verse 4 goes on to say that Jesus is superior to whom?

Whether we are talking about an Old Testament prophet, an angel, or a dynamic modern-day religious leader, God's messenger is never higher than the One who sent and embodies the message.

6. A. How is wisdom described in Wisdom 7:26? (Note: The book of Wisdom is only found in Catholic Bibles.)

B. Read Wisdom 7:26 again, this time changing the word *she* (wisdom) to *Jesus*. This verse describes wisdom in much the same way Jesus is described in Hebrews 1:3. The early Church taught that "God's wisdom" in the Old Testament was the preexistent Christ. Wisdom is infinitely more practical than knowledge. In fact, one definition of wisdom is the ability to take what you know to be true and good and apply that in your day-to-day life.

In what area of your life do you need the rays of God's wisdom to penetrate? Are you at a crossroads where you need to make a decision? Are you seeking

God's direction in a challenging relationship? Do you need insight into how to handle an issue at work or with disciplining your children? Write a prayer asking Jesus, the source of all wisdom, to help you to see what you should do.

Dear Lord,

Quiet your heart and enjoy His presence. . . . He will uphold you with His righteous right hand (Isaiah 41:10).

*Hebrews 1:3 describes Jesus as "sustaining all things by his mighty word." This fact is reiterated in Colossians 1:15–17: "He is the image of the invisible God, the firstborn of all creation. For in him were created all things in heaven and on earth, the visible and the invisible, whether thrones or dominions or principalities or powers; all things were created through him and for him. He is before all things, and **in him all things hold together.**"*

This is a truth we can stand on: If He can hold the whole world together, He can hold us together. If His Word is powerful enough to sustain the entire world, then His Word and presence in our lives is powerful enough to keep us from sinking, to pull us back from the brink, to strengthen us to hold on when we desperately want to quit. Jesus doesn't sustain the world from a distance. He is a God who draws near, who comes close. He is closer than our breath—behind us, before us, within us. Take a moment to quiet down and name the things that are making you feel at loose ends. Ask Jesus to take all those things and breathe order and peace into the chaos.

Day Three
SUPERIOR TO ANGELS

Read Hebrews 1:5–6.

This next section of Hebrews 1 draws a comparison between Jesus and the angels, making the point that He is utterly superior to them. For those of us who have been taught about Jesus and His greatness, this section may seem unnecessary. We might wonder if this was seriously a temptation to the people receiving the letter of Hebrews. Were they actually more likely to worship an angel than Jesus?!

To understand why this was indeed a temptation, it's helpful to remember the words that were often spoken before angels appeared to people throughout the Bible: Fear not. The depictions of angels that we see in art make us think of something beautiful, ethereal, and cherubic. But when actual angels appeared in Scripture, people's reactions were to draw back or hide.

Let's delve into the Bible to broaden our understanding of these created beings—creatures that struck fear in the hearts of those who saw them.

1. Read the following passages, recording anything you learn about angels.

   Daniel 10:4–15
   (Note: This passage is a description of an angelic vision that Daniel received. Many consider this vision to be of the angel Gabriel.)

   Isaiah 6:2–4, Revelation 5:11–12
   (Note: According to the *Catholic Bible Dictionary*, the seraphim are "a class of heavenly angels."[5])

---

[5] Scott Hahn, ed., *Catholic Bible Dictionary* (New York: Doubleday Religion, 2009), 827.

Acts 7:37–38, 53

(Note: In Exodus 24, we read of God inviting Moses up to Mount Sinai to receive the stone tablets of the Ten Commandments. It's the giving of that law that is referred to in these verses in Acts.)

Psalm 34:8 (be sure to use the NAB version), 91:11–12

Matthew 1:19–24; Luke 1:26–38, 2:9–12

2. There was no need to explain to the readers of Hebrews that the angels were worthy of awe. That wasn't the problem. The concern was that they would lapse back into comfortable Judaism to avoid the persecution that came with putting Christ first. What does this have to do with angels? If they just saw Jesus as an angel—a powerful, heavenly messenger—that wouldn't be such a deal breaker. A *little* elevation of Jesus wouldn't cause the readers of Hebrews to be kicked out of the synagogue. But putting Him above all others? That was too much.

Most of us can relate to this temptation because we know that saying Jesus is a great messenger, teacher, or prophet rarely causes any trouble. People tend to agree on that point. But professing a belief that Jesus is God and provides the only means for us to be saved? A statement like that will divide the room in an instant.

Can you relate to this temptation? Are you experiencing pressure or discomfort because of your faith and your desire to give Jesus His rightful place in your life?

3. According to the rhetorical question posed in Hebrews 1:5, what are the angels *never* called?

4. The two quotations in verse 5 referring to Psalm 2:7 and 2 Samuel 7:14. Both those verses were originally written in reference to the Old Testament King David. God had promised David that one of his descendants would always be on the throne of Israel. When the Davidic monarchy collapsed, it seemed as if those promises would never come true. But with time, the passages came to be correctly interpreted as prophecies referring to the son of David (as in one of His descendants)—the Messiah (the Savior who was to come and redeem Israel). Read Luke 1:30–33 and 1:68–69 in light of this commentary. What was fulfilled with Jesus' birth?

5. According to Hebrews 1:6 and CCC 333, what is the angels' relationship to the firstborn, Jesus? (Note: When Jesus is referred to as the "firstborn," it's intended to remind us that He is the preexistent, eternal Son.) Please note how the angels interacted with Jesus throughout His time on earth.

When do we first see this occurrence in the New Testament? See Luke 2:8–14.

As we read earlier, we also see that the angels continually worship Jesus in heaven. See Revelation 5:11–13.

6. One of the purposes of the book of Hebrews is to make the point that nothing and no one can compare to Jesus. He alone is worthy of our trust and worship. As we move through the book, He will be compared to the angels, Moses, and the Old Testament priesthood and will always prove superior. Few people today are elevating angels or Moses above Christ, but the tendency to anchor our hopes in

someone other than Jesus still remains. What are some modern things or people we tend to give the place of honor and worship that should be given to Christ alone?

Quiet your heart and enjoy His presence. . . . His name is above all names.

When Jesus is called the Son, *it truly is the name above all names. Angels are God's servants and messengers, but are never referred to as* the Son. *We are called sons and daughters of God, but that is different from being* the Son. *None of us should lose sight of the truth that "the name [Jesus] has inherited is more excellent than theirs [and ours.]" (Hebrews 1:4).*

But may that never make us feel devalued or insignificant! The One whose name is above all names, the Son, *the Beloved, shares His very divine nature with us. He invites us to share in all that He is and all that He has. At the cross, He takes all our inadequacies, failures, and messes, and trades them—exchanges them——for Himself. As He fills our souls with His very presence, we become* the beloved.

Angels are servants of God, but the Son, the ruler of the universe, is superior. And the Son loves you, adores you, and pursues you. Can you take a moment now to thank Him for descending from heaven to earth to convince you of that truth?

Day Four
THE ANGELIC SERVANTS AND THE SON

Read Hebrews 1:7–12.

1. How are angels described in Hebrews 1:7?

The quotation here is from Psalm 104:4, and it shows that angels are *"servants* of God rather than *living embodiments* of him."[6] They may be involved in natural phenomena, but it's always at God's request and in response to His sovereign rule, not whatever they feel like doing.

2. A. Which words from Hebrews 1:8–9 draw attention to sovereignty or royalty?

> This passage, quoting Psalm 45:6–7, was originally addressed to a king at his wedding feast, but later was seen as a messianic prophecy (a prophecy about Jesus). Jesus is the Messiah King; His throne will endure forever.

B. What does Jesus love and what does He hate, according to Hebrews 1:9?

> The point of this passage is to remind us that God longs for real justice (vs. 9), and that the bringing about of justice on earth is to happen not through the angels, but through the Son. They are servants, but He is sovereign. He is the One with the power and control to actually change things.

These verses, showing that God and Jesus are distinct persons yet are one, were later used in the development of the doctrine of the Trinity. What is true of one is true of the other. In this passage, God anoints Jesus with the oil of gladness, above His companions.

The "companions" referred to in Hebrews 1:9 are Christians. Jesus is anointed with the oil of gladness, above us. Yet He loves us so much that He chooses to involve us in His work. We, like the angels, are created beings, below Him but counted on by Him to help carry out His plans and purposes.

3. Notice how Hebrews 1:8–9 links Christ's love of justice with the oil of gladness, or, one could say, joy. When we love what Jesus loves—when we love justice and hate wickedness—we, too, are filled with a joy that comes from knowing we are focusing on what truly matters. This is different than a joy that is dependent on our circumstances. In fact, as we seek justice in a broken and unjust world, we'll

---

6 N. T. Wright, *Hebrews for Everyone* (Louisville, KY: Westminster John Knox Press, 2004), 7.

encounter many situations that are discouraging. But loving justice enough to step out and make what little difference we can will fill us with a sense of meaning, purpose, and fulfillment that is inextricably tied to joy. This is what allowed Jesus to walk forward toward His calling in the midst of unimaginable pain. Jesus, who "for the joy set before him endured the cross, scorning its sham" (Hebrews 12:2).

What injustice breaks your heart? Have you had the experience of stepping out to make a difference and, although it has been difficult, you have nevertheless been filled with the "oil of gladness" as you fight for justice?

4. A. Which phrases from Hebrews 1:10–12 do you think would have been a comfort to the suffering Jewish believers? Why do you think these words would have helped them?

    B. Is there an area of your life where you are experiencing change, and as a result feel unsettled, unsafe, or unmoored? Are you comforted by the truth that Jesus never changes? In what ways can you remind yourself of this truth throughout the day?

Everything we see is finite—it will eventually change and pass away. But Jesus is infinite—He has always existed and will always exist, and He will never change or alter in any way. He can be counted on.

5. When everything feels like it's shifting and changing, the temptation to run back to our old way of doing things is really strong. The book of Hebrews warns us against doing that. It's been said that there is no treading water in the Christian life—you are either moving forward or going backward. In every new challenge and change, there is something fresh that God is wanting to teach us, a way in which He is compelling us onward and upward. Continuing to move forward through those difficulties is how we mature as Christians. Can you think of a time

when growth in maturity was preceded or accompanied by a time of change and transition?

Quiet your heart and enjoy His presence. . . . Expand your view of God.

Could it be that we get overwhelmed by our challenges because we have too small a view of God? Have we become so focused on the finite that we have lost sight of all the power at God's disposal, and the way He dispatches angels to our aid?

Ask God to expand your understanding of how infinite, unchanging, immortal, reliable, capable, and creative He is. Do you feel stuck and unable to come up with a solution? Thank God that it isn't all up to you. The One who is the same yesterday, today, and forever just waits for you to ask Him to extend His scepter over your life, creating calm where there was chaos.

Day Five
THE ONE AT GOD'S RIGHT HAND

Read Hebrews 1:13–14.

The quotation found in Hebrews 1:13 ("Sit at my right hand until I make your enemies your footstool") comes from Psalm 110:1. This passage was widely used in early Christianity to interpret Jesus' messiahship. The early Church considered it foundational to understanding that Jesus is Lord. When it was originally recorded in Psalm 110, it was written by King David for the coronation of his son Solomon. This passage is quoted in the New Testament more often than any other, and Jesus even quoted it Himself in Mark 12:36, revealing that it referred to Him.

Sitting at God's right hand indicates a position of honor and authority. This picture of enemies being a footstool under the honored ruler's feet points to the eventual defeat of those who oppose God. Nothing like this has ever been said about angels. They serve at the pleasure of the Lord, doing whatever He asks to fulfill *His* purposes, not theirs.

Hebrews 1:13 may seem confusing to a modern-day reader, as we don't see enemies made footstools at the end of a war. But in ancient times, it was customary for a defeated king to bend down and kiss the victorious king's feet. The victor would then put his feet on the defeated one's neck so that the captive would become like a footstool for him. You can read an example of this in Joshua 10:24.

1. We can sometimes get discouraged when we see justice thwarted and evil appearing to gain the upper hand. What do Hebrews 1:13 and Psalm 33:10–11 remind us of when we are disheartened by the state of the world?

2. According to the following verses, what will happen one day to Jesus' enemies?

   Philippians 2:10–11

   1 Corinthians 15:24–26
   (Note: The one handing over the kingdom is Jesus.)

3. According to Hebrews 1:14, who are ministering spirits (the angels) sent to serve?

4. This section of Hebrews is meant to encourage, to remind the readers of the help that was always available to them. All that Jesus is and has, He offers to the service of His brothers and sisters. This promise is meant for us as well—when our world falls apart, He comes with His angels and offers us His help and His presence.

Is there an area of your life where hope has worn thin? A circumstance in which defeat has become the norm? Instead of trying to take matters into your own hands, write a prayer in the space provided, asking God to help you trust His plans in your life. Ask Him for the specific things that you need.

5. According to CCC 331, why do the angels belong to Christ?

Quiet your heart and enjoy His presence. . . . Be filled with hope because of His saving plan.

Jesus has made the angels messengers of His saving plan—the messengers of the gospel. And what is at the heart of that message? You are never alone. It is not all up to you. Jesus has come to fill in all the gaps where you are lacking, where you are not enough. God the Father doesn't expect your good works to be so perfect that they connect you to heaven. Only Jesus can bridge that gap between you and the Father. And He doesn't save you from a distance. You may not see Jesus (or His angels), but what is unseen is most certainly real. As we read in 2 Corinthians 4:18, "What is seen is temporary, but what is unseen is eternal." Jesus, the eternal King and Savior, is right with you, closer than your breath. Breathe in His Spirit, and as you breathe out, speak His name, Jesus. It's the name above all names. There is power in the name of Jesus.

Conclusion

"The way Jesus shows you is not easy. Rather, it is like a path winding up a mountain. Do not lose heart! The steeper the road, the faster it rises towards ever wider horizons. May Mary, Star of Evangelization, guide you! Docile like her to the Father's will, take the stages of history as mature and convincing witnesses."[7] —*Saint John Paul II*

The path to holiness will never be the easier one. Temptation to go back to the simpler road will be offered to you in the very moment when you most need to dig in and press forward. But if you refuse to settle for mediocrity, there will be no limit to the impact of your life. God will be able to work in and through you, and the pages of history being written in your lifetime will be changed.

When we are willing to stand as Christians despite the potential unpopularity of our beliefs, we move on to a platform of influence. We are being observed, and a watching world looks at our lives to see if Jesus makes much of a difference. If we refuse to shrink back, if instead we press closer to Christ, then He infuses us with supernatural strength to persevere. People around us will find it hard to deny the power of God when we are able to respond in ways that are not our natural bent.

Are you naturally critical? You evangelize when you stay silent or say something positive.

Do you tend to dominate conversations? You evangelize when you listen well.

Are you typically a worrier? You evangelize when you pray instead of talk about your fears.

Are you naturally timid? You evangelize when you speak up.

Are you often driven toward perfection in yourself and others? You evangelize when you give yourself and others grace.

When we ask God to transform our natural reactions into holy responses, people around us recognize that we are putting Him above our own desires. We are acknowledging the supremacy of Jesus over our own comfort and wishes. Can you see how different it would be if we proclaimed the greatness of Jesus not so much through our words about Him as by our obedience to Him?

---

[7] Pope John Paul II, "Message of the Holy Father Pope John Paul II for the XI World Youth Day," Libreria Editrice Vaticana, November 26, 1995, https://w2.vatican.va/content/john-paul-ii/en/messages/youth/documents/hf_jp-ii_mes_26111995_xi-world-youth-day.html.

He is higher than the angels and higher than our best thoughts and plans. Instead of running back to the easy path when obedience is costly, let's answer the call of Jesus in Luke 5:4, to "put out into deep water" and let down our nets for a catch. May our radical obedience draw a watching world to the Savior.

My Resolution

"My Resolution" is your opportunity to write down one specific, personal application from this lesson. We can take in a lot of information from studying the Bible, but if we don't translate it into action, we have totally missed the point. In James 1:22, we're told that we shouldn't just hear the Word of God, we are to "do what it says." So what qualities should be found in a good resolution? It should be **personal** (use the pronouns *I, me, my, mine*), it should be **possible** (don't choose something so far-fetched that you'll just become discouraged), it should be **measurable** (a specific goal to achieve within a specific time period), and it should be **action oriented** (not just a spiritual thought).

Examples:

1. When I'm reminded that Jesus holds all things together (Colossians 1:17), I feel convicted about the things that I rely on other than Him. All too often, I have looked at completing the things on my agenda as the key to keeping my life together. To live differently, I will give God the first half hour of my day, ignoring the list of to-dos and putting Him first.

2. The easy, comfortable road is so tempting. But I know that God is calling me forward to know Him more intimately and to follow Him more radically. I will identify one area where God is asking me to obey, and take an actionable step toward that obedience this week.

My resolution:

Catechism Clips

CCC 331 Christ is the center of the angelic world. They are *his* angels: "When the Son of man comes in his glory, and all the angels with him." They belong to him because they were created *through* and *for* him: "For in him all things were created in heaven and on earth, visible and invisible, whether thrones or dominions or principalities or authorities—all things were created through him and for him." They belong to him still more because he has made them messengers of his saving plan: "Are they not all ministering spirits sent forth to serve, for the sake of those who are to obtain salvation?"

CCC 333 From the Incarnation to the Ascension, the life of the Word incarnate is surrounded by the adoration and service of angels. When God "brings the firstborn into the world, he says: 'Let all God's angels worship him.'" Their song of praise at the birth of Christ has not ceased resounding in the Church's praise: "Glory to God in the highest!" They protect Jesus in his infancy, serve him in the desert, strengthen him in his agony in the garden, when he could have been saved by them from the hands of his enemies as Israel had been. Again, it is the angels who "evangelize" by proclaiming the Good News of Christ's Incarnation and Resurrection. They will be present at Christ's return, which they will announce, to serve at his judgment.

Verse Study

A verse study is an exciting Bible study tool that can help to bring the Scriptures to life! By reading, reflecting on, and committing a verse to memory, we open ourselves to the Holy Spirit, who reveals very personal applications of our Lord's words and actions to our daily lives.

See Appendix 3 for instructions on how to complete a verse study.

Colossians 1:18

1. Verse:

2. Paraphrase:

3. Questions:

4. Cross-references:

5. Personal Application:

Note: There is an answer key at the back of the study that provides additional insights and teachings. That being said, I encourage you to complete the lesson first, before turning to the answer key. This is critical if you are going to wrestle the material into your heart.

Lesson 3

OUR SUPERHERO BROTHER

Hebrews 2

Introduction

When I was scrolling through Pinterest (instead of making dinner), I found these sibling quotes:

"If you mess with the little sister, there is probably a crazier older brother who taught her how to fight."

"A five-year-old asked her big brother to describe love. He replied: 'Love is when you steal my chocolate from my school pack every day . . . and I still keep it in the same place.'"

Then there was this darling picture of four little boys standing behind their baby sister (dressed in a pink tutu). They each held a chalkboard that created the sentence: DON'T MESS WITH HER.

There's just something irresistible about an older brother coming to rescue his sister. I came from a family of two daughters, so one of my favorite things about mothering a brood of seven kids has been the ways my sons watch out for their sisters (even though there are times our family looks more like this quote: "Older brothers . . . the only people who will pick on you for their own entertainment and beat up anyone else who tries to do the same").

A few years ago, the boys definitely came through for their little sister. After a move from another state, she had gone through months of being bullied at school. She never told us what was going on, until one day everything exploded in a torrent of tears. I went to the headmistress immediately, and told her in no uncertain terms that it needed to stop or we'd be leaving the school. Imagine my surprise when I got the following report from the headmistress the next day. She had called the bully and my

35

daughter into her office, and accused the bully right in front of my daughter. Not surprisingly, the other child denied it all. My daughter totally panicked, knowing that everything was going to get worse now that the bully knew she had told on her. My daughter retracted her story. The headmistress called me to say that I needed to come to the school immediately because my daughter had been lying, and she took that seriously. (Join with me in saying, "What?!")

I couldn't get to the school right then or even at pickup because of something another child needed, and I had to ask my high school sons to go get their sister. And here's the point of my story: Those two boys showed up ready to *take that bully down.* They didn't know which child she was, so they just walked up and down the line of fifth-grade students, occasionally saying to their sister, nice and loudly, "Which one is she?" And that's all it took. The possibility that her big brothers might show up again provided a shield for my daughter that lasted the entire year.

This is what Jesus does for us. He shows up as the Lion of Judah and fights the evil that threatens to take us down. He always comes for us. He also teaches us how to fight the spiritual battle so that we can stand firm.

And that image of a brother leaving his chocolate in the same place, knowing his little sister will take it, that's a lot like Jesus, too. He knows we're not always going to treat Him the way we should, but He never leaves. We can always count on Him to be steadfast and faithful. We couldn't have a better big brother than Jesus.

Day One

WARNING TO PAY ATTENTION

Read Hebrews 2:1–4.

1. We are encouraged to "attend all the more to what we have heard" in order to avoid something. What is it that we must avoid? See Hebrews 2:1.

The phrase "be carried away" in the NAB version of the Bible can also be translated "drifting away." Picture a ship without its anchor firmly connected to the seabed, moving in one direction, slowly but certainly. That's what we're being warned about.

Throughout Hebrews 1, the focus is on the divinity of Christ and His superiority to the angels. Chapter 2 points to His humanity. But before the author delves into this, he pauses and urges us to respond to what we have heard. This entreaty is not an interruption—it's actually the whole point. We're challenged to listen and engage, and do something with what has been revealed to us.

Why is this warning necessary? Because it's so easy to enter the dangerous spiritual territory of apathy and complacency. It can happen without us realizing it. Remember that the author is writing to Christians—those who have heard and accepted the gospel message. This is an in-house conversation with followers of Christ who are beginning to drift away from Him. Their former passion is starting to cool, and persecution is making following Jesus less appealing.

2. A. Drifting away from Jesus can happen without our realizing it. How is it described in Revelation 2:4?

   B. Have you experienced this spiritual drifting in your own life? If so, what has caused it? Time? Overfamiliarity? Busyness? Hurt?

Regardless of what causes us to drift away from God, we can be assured that He has not moved. God's perpetual stance toward us is one of closeness, with arms wide open. His compassion and steadfast love for us always translates into action, and is never dulled or diminished by time or circumstance.

3. A. In Hebrews 2:2–4, an argument is made for why we should take the message we've received seriously. Put that argument into your own words.

These verses are using a rhetorical device, arguing that if something is true that is of lesser importance (a message imparted by angels), then it must be more so when it's of greater importance (a message imparted by Jesus).

B. This argument is built on a certain assumption about the mediation of angels in our world. According to the following verses, what significant role did angels play on Mount Sinai when the law (the Ten Commandments) was given to Moses? See Deuteronomy 33:2, Acts 7:38 and 53, and Galatians 3:19. (Note: The phrase "myriads of holy ones" is considered a reference to angels.)

Father Daniel J. Harrington, S.J., explains it this way:

> If the Mosaic Law given through angels punishes each and every transgression, how much more will God punish neglect of the salvation given through Christ. The logic is that the greater revelation (the gospel) given through the greater revealer (Christ) will exact greater punishment from those who fail to attend to it.[8]

God has offered us a way to be saved from eternal punishment. This was and is the greatest display of mercy ever known to mankind. But ignoring it has consequences. The author of Hebrews begs us to make a decision. Many people just float down the river of life without paying attention to where they are going. This passage tells us that we do this at our own peril. In the words of biblical scholar Luke Timothy Johnson, "The 'more' of the present reality will be seen to demand a 'more' in the response of those who are being offered 'so great a salvation' (2:3). Such a response is 'necessary' because *the penalties for disobedience correspond to the magnitude of the gift being offered*"[9] (emphasis added).

This is heavy language, and it feels especially so because we live in a culture that insists there is no absolute truth, and no hell. "Feel-good" theology is prevalent and popular.

---

[8] Daniel J. Harrington, S.J., *New Collegeville Bible Commentary: The Letter to the Hebrews* (Collegeville, MN: Liturgical Press, 2006), 15.

[9] Johnson, *Hebrews: A Commentary*, 86.

C. How does Saint Paul predict people will respond to sound doctrine and truth? See 2 Timothy 4:3.

The postmodern worldview claims that there is no such thing as absolute truth—there is only your truth and my truth. By contrast, the Christian worldview says that absolute truth exists and is determined by God, not by what the majority of people are currently thinking. Even though we are living during a time when most people are resistant to sound doctrine and prefer to follow teachers who just tell them what they want to hear, we can choose to be humble pursuers and accepters of truth—as God defines it.

4. A. The message of salvation that has come from Jesus has been delivered in three ways. What are they? See Hebrews 2:3–4.

The message came from Jesus Himself; He delivered it in person. Then it was passed on to others through the testimony of eyewitnesses, and finally, miracles of God and gifts of the Holy Spirit given to the believers confirmed that it all was real. When Jesus' followers experienced their gifts being infused with supernatural power, achieving things beyond what they could have done in their own strength, the truth of the message was verified.

B. How is the Holy Spirit described in Romans 8:15–16? What truth does He confirm in our hearts?

The Holy Spirit's confirmation in our souls that *we are God's children* is at the heart of the gospel. The message of salvation is an invitation to be enveloped in the embrace of family—a supplication to come home to the place where you fully belong and are able to become your truest self.

5. A. Hebrews 2:4 encourages us to attend all the more to what we have heard so we don't drift away, neglecting the generous gift of salvation. According to Hebrews 6:19, what can keep us from drifting?

    B. What guidance does Deuteronomy 6:5–9 give us if we want to be anchored in our faith?

Quiet your heart and enjoy His presence. . . . Instead of drifting away, turn and embrace Him wholeheartedly.

"You shall love the LORD, your God, with your whole heart, and with your whole being, and with your whole strength." (Deuteronomy 6:5)

One alternative to loving God wholeheartedly is to reject Him outright, but even wavering has consequences. But the singleness of heart that we know is the goal can be hard to achieve in our own strength. God understands our weaknesses; He doesn't stand over us with a condemning glare. In fact, according to the promise of Philippians 2:13, "God is the one who, for his good purpose, works in you both to desire and to work." This means that when we lack the desire, we can ask Him to both create desire in us and actually do what's needed in and through us. When a civil war starts to rage in our hearts—one side pulling for the easy, drifting way and the other for the narrow road that leads to God—that's when we need to cry out to God to step in and help us. He will never fail to do so.

Dear God,

Please free me from my waverings. Help me to have an undivided heart—one that desires You above all else. As I bring my desires to You [prayerfully tell God what they are], I ask You to purify them. Help me to not want so much the desires that ultimately will not bring me joy. The path that leads to

You sometimes looks boring, hard, and unappealing, so please strengthen my will to take the first step toward it. Thank You for working in me to create both the desire and ability to do what you ask—I am so grateful that it isn't all up to me. Self-reliance is a trap that leads to pride and feeling discouraged. But dependence on You leads to peace and satisfaction. I choose depending on You, so that when I am weak, I am strong (2 Corinthians 12:10).

Day Two
REIGNING IN GLORY

Read Hebrews 2:5–9.

This next portion of Hebrews is intended to help us to see just how much God cares for us. It gives a glimpse into the plans He has in mind for us, "plans for [our] welfare and not for woe, so as to give [us] a future of hope" (Jeremiah 29:11).

1. What does Hebrews 2:5 say that God has *not* done for the angels?

As powerful and amazing as angels are, as much influence as they have on this present world, they are not going to rule the world to come.[10] So who will have that role? Whom will God choose for this privileged task? We're about to find out. But first we need to head back to the Old Testament for a minute.

2. A. Hebrews 2:6–7 is taken from Psalm 8. Read Psalm 8, and record what the psalmist is contemplating (vs. 4). What is causing him to be amazed (vs. 6–9)?

The psalmist is looking at the night sky. He can't believe that God values him so much that He would give him a position just a little lower than an angel's, to crown him with glory and honor, and give man authority, putting everything under his feet.

---

[10] "The world to come" refers not to our current world, but to a future one—the heavenly realm that Jesus has entered, inviting us to follow Him.

B. As you read that passage and reflect on it, do you feel you are experiencing that position of "glory, honor, and authority" in your own life?

C. The writer of Hebrews assumes that something in you will read those verses and think, "Wait a minute. This isn't true. Not everything is under my feet. Not everything is nicely under control. In fact, a lot of it feels like disorder and chaos." He responds to this line of thought in the second half of Hebrews 2:8. Record his answer below.

D. At present, we don't see things as they ultimately will be one day. Things are not as God initially planned because of original sin. When sin entered the world by man's choice, everything changed. Despite this, God never fails to keep His promises. While right now we don't see everything "under our feet" (pulled together and in order), what *do* we see? Look at the first part of Hebrews 2:9.

We do not, at present, see everything in our lives pulled together and in order, but we do see *Jesus*. We see *Him* crowned with glory and honor. Keeping our eyes on Him helps us keep our focus on God's promise that one day things will be different.

3. Read Hebrews 2:9 and explain why Jesus is "crowned with glory and honor."

4. Amazingly, one day, we will reign with Christ. Read the following verses, noting what you learn about the how and why of our future reign with Him.

Romans 5:17

2 Timothy 2:12

If you are able to hold on to only one truth from this passage, may it be this:

Things are going to get better. One day, you will be crowned with glory and honor. Your worth has already been determined. And even if the people in your life make you feel insignificant, even if circumstances feel hopeless, know that what you experience today is not the end of the story. Something better is yet to come.

5. We live in a time of "already but not yet." There is a degree to which we can experience order and authority over the chaos in our lives. At the same time, we won't experience the fullness of this state on this side of heaven. How is the concept of "already but not yet" described in 1 John 3:2?

We are experiencing in the now that we are God's beloved children. But at the same time, we have a "not yet" that will be revealed in the future.

Quiet your heart and enjoy His presence. . . . Endure in order to reign.

We read in 2 Timothy 2:12 that if we endure, we will reign with Christ. In order to endure circumstances that cause us to feel out of control, we need to keep our eyes on Jesus, our anchor of hope.

Just think of the paradox of the cross: The very moment when things seemed most out of control was the moment when Jesus was actually conquering death and showing the fullest extent of His power. In the same way, what our current circumstances feel like and appear to be is not a good litmus test for determining whether God is in control. He reigns in heaven, He reigns on earth, and one day, all the wrongs will be made right. One day, it all will be in sync. In the meantime, we're called to trust.

I know, easier said than done. Nevertheless, we need to discipline our minds so that we judge our circumstances by the character of God, instead of judging the character of God by our circumstances.

Who is He? He is good. He is faithful. He never leaves or forsakes us. He proved His love by dying for us—not when we were perfectly cleaned up and worthy, but when we were a mess. His love surpasses anything we could ever earn, and thank God He never asks us to earn it. Instead, He invites us to accept His free gift of grace. He proved worthy of our trust when He tasted death in our place. Can you take a few moments to thank Him for this? Can you ask Him to help you to endure and to trust that what you are experiencing today is not the end of the story?

"At present, we do not see 'all things subject to him,' but we do see Jesus 'crowned with glory and honor' because he suffered death." (Hebrews 2:9)

Day Three
MADE PERFECT THROUGH SUFFERING

Read Hebrews 2:10.

1. What truth do we learn about all that exists from both Hebrews 2:10 and Colossians 1:16?

2. A. In Hebrews 2:10, "it was fitting" means that an act was worthy of His divine nature. Which act being done in this passage was considered "worthy of God's divine nature"?

B. What is the by-product of the author and founder of our salvation being made perfect through suffering?

3. Although this passage says, "it was fitting," a suffering God was a very hard concept for the readers of Hebrews to comprehend. What insight do we gain into this from 1 Corinthians 1:23?

A God who suffered? The God through whom and for whom everything was made? A God who judged or needed to be appeased made logical sense. A God who suffered out of love on behalf of His children in order to bring them to glory was hard to comprehend. This required a complete paradigm shift for the readers of Hebrews.

4. Our familiarity with the story of salvation makes it less likely that we'll struggle with the concept of a God who suffers on our behalf. It's more likely that we'll have trouble with the idea that Jesus "had to be made perfect." What do the following passages say about Jesus and sin? See Hebrews 4:15, 1 Peter 1:18–19, and 1 John 3:5.

Scripture clearly teaches that Jesus was without sin. So why does Hebrews 2:10 say that He "had to be made perfect"? Jesus' suffering allows Him to perfectly sympathize with us. Without that ability to truly understand what it feels like to be human, He would not have been able to perfectly represent us before God as our high priest. We will continue to explore more about what it means for Jesus to be our high priest in subsequent chapters of Hebrews. This is a theme we'll return to often, so don't worry if you feel you don't have a full grasp of it yet.

5. A. Hebrews 2:10 paints a picture of the leader of our salvation—our captain and champion—modeling what it takes for us to be brought to glory. Another way of saying "being brought to glory" is "becoming fully mature." Jesus shows us through His example that Christian maturity comes from being transformed by

suffering. Each time suffering slams into our lives, we are presented with an opportunity to grow more like Christ. This perspective flies in the face of the prevalent way of looking at suffering as something bad that should be avoided at all costs. What additional insights can you find regarding suffering and glory from Romans 8:18 and 2 Corinthians 4:17?

B. In which area of your life are you currently suffering? Can you identify choices in terms of how you can respond to your circumstances—one route that, while easier, might not be the best choice, and the other a harder choice that you sense will lead you toward maturity?

In Day Two, we discussed the "already but not yet" of God's promise for us to reign with Him. We can apply that phrase to our current suffering. The reward of spiritual maturity gained through suffering isn't always tasted immediately. All too often, it appears that the people who manage to avoid suffering or react to it in unholy ways are the ones who are better off. God asks us to take a long-range perspective, without expecting everything to be immediately fulfilled. Patience and endurance are critical qualities in the spiritual life. But be assured, the leader of your salvation is taking you toward something better. The end of the story is not ruin. It is glory.

Quiet your heart and enjoy His presence. . . . He is the perfect pioneer, leading us to heaven.

"For a child is born to us, a son is given to us; upon his shoulder dominion rests. They name him Wonder-Counselor, God-hero, Father-Forever, Prince of Peace." (Isaiah 9:5)

There are times in life when our suffering feels like a bloodbath. The battlefield is a scene filled with heartache, fear, and weariness. We can barely muster the strength to get out of bed, let alone wield a sword and move forward. Often we feel as if we are fighting alone.

It is at these times that we should grab hold of the truth found in Hebrews 2:10. We have not been abandoned on the battlefield. Jesus is the captain and champion, and He fights relentlessly on behalf of us and our loved ones. When He sees the battle heat up around us, does He stick to His area of fighting while shouting that we need to keep going? No. Our captain rushes to our side and covers us with His shield. He tells us to rest in His protection while He wields the sword of the Spirit as only He can. He suffers for, *and He suffers* with.

He is our hero. He is our rescuer. He is our champion. He is our big brother, and He never fails to stand up for us, fighting our battles steadfastly.

"I love you, Lord, my strength,
Lord, my rock, my fortress, my deliverer,
My God, my rock of refuge,
My shield, my saving horn, my stronghold!"
(Psalm 18:1–2)

Day Four
THE MESSIAH AND HIS BROTHERS AND SISTERS

Read Hebrews 2:11–16.

1. A. What is Jesus not ashamed of? See Hebrews 2:11.

   B. Read Hebrews 1:3 and explain why it's mind-boggling that Jesus is not ashamed to call us brothers and sisters.

C. Jesus is not ashamed to call you His sister. Are you ever ashamed of Him?

I love the way N. T. Wright describes what it means to have Jesus as our big brother:

> [This passage] "encourages us to see Jesus not as the kind of older brother whom we resent because he's always getting things right and being successful while we're always getting things wrong and failing, but as the kind of older brother who, without a trace of patronizing or looking down his nose at us, comes to find us where we are, out of sheer love and goodness of heart, and to help us out of the mess."[11]

2. Hebrews 2:12 is quoting Psalm 22:23. Read Psalm 22:1–23, thinking of Jesus as the speaker. Verses 1–22 refer to His crucifixion; verse 23 is what He did after His resurrection. What did Jesus do?

When we read that Jesus will "proclaim your name to my brothers," it's helpful to remember the significance of a name in the Bible—it revealed that person's character or nature. What is being described here is Jesus revealing God's character to His brothers and sisters. Then as Hebrews 2:12 goes on, Jesus joins His brothers and sisters in praising God.

Again, He is providing us an example of how we should live. Worship is the best antidote to our fear of suffering. It shifts our focus from the unknown future and moves it to what we can be sure of: God's unchanging, compassionate, and sovereign nature.

3. Hebrews 2:13 is quoting Isaiah 7—that's why certain verses are indented. Read Isaiah 7:14 and Matthew 1:23, noting how this Old Testament prophecy was fulfilled.

---

[11] Wright, *Hebrews for Everyone*, 19.

Way back in the book of Isaiah, we were promised that Emmanuel—God with us—was going to come. When we read "Behold, I and the children God has given me" (Hebrews 2:13), we should imagine Jesus placing His arms around the sons and daughters of the suffering Church (us), standing with us, and presenting Himself with us to God.

4. A. Who does Jesus destroy in Hebrews 2:14, and how is he described?

   B. How are the people Jesus has set free described in Hebrews 2:15?

   C. Why do you think people fear death?

Dr. Mary Healy unpacks our fear of death with these words:

> We instinctively resist and recoil from everything that reminds us of our mortality—pain, deprivation, weakness, criticism, failure. This paralyzing fear influences many human choices on a subconscious level, leads to various forms of escapism and addiction, induces us to grasp the false security nets proffered by Satan, and keeps us from pursuing the will of God with freedom, peace, and confidence. It is the slavery from which Jesus came to set us free (see John 8:34, Romans 8:15).[12]

   D. Can you identify any areas of your life where you are turning to forms of escapism or addiction instead of pursuing the will of God? Can you see how fear of your own mortality might be underlying this behavior? I encourage you to bring this to the Lord in prayer, asking Him to set you free in these areas of bondage.

---

[12] Healy, *Hebrews*, 65.

5. Read the following verses, noting any insights or comfort they offer regarding fear of death.

Romans 8:35–37

1 Corinthians 15:55, 57

2 Corinthians 5:21

Revelation 1:17–18

Quiet your heart and enjoy His presence. . . . Nothing can separate you from the love of Jesus.

We belong to Jesus, our captain, pioneer, leader, God-hero, big brother, and Savior. When fear of our own mortality nips at our hearts, He is the One we need to cling to. Instead of listening to the what-ifs, we need to focus on His character. He is steadfast and promises us that nothing will separate us from His love. We need to take Him at His word.

The story is told of a woman who went to Saint John Maria Vianney, the pastor of Ars in France. She was desperate and in tears because her husband had committed suicide by jumping off a bridge. Her deepest fear was that he was now in hell. But Saint John Maria comforted her with these words: "Look, between the bridge and the river, there is the mercy of God."[13]

---

[13] Pope Francis, *Dear Pope Francis: The Pope Answers Letters from Children Around the World* (Chicago: Loyola Press, 2016), 19.

Day Five
OUR SHIELD FROM WRATH

Read Hebrews 2:17–18.

1. Whom did Jesus have to "become like"? Why did He need to do this? See Hebrews 2:17.

I know this is a dense verse. Don't give up! We're about to unveil some of the mystery together.

2. A. What qualities are found in Jesus as our high priest?

I love R. Kent Hughes' definition of *mercy*:

> Mercy is more than an emotion. For example, suppose you were driving . . . and came across an accident in which a victim was lying in the road with no one to assist him. . . . you feel a surge of compassion, but you do nothing and drive on. Why? Because you are unmerciful! To be merciful, one must act to alleviate another's pain. Jesus repeatedly modeled this . . . when he had *compassion* on the hungry or the ill or the grieving, and then [showed] *mercy* in meeting their needs . . .
>
> In being our "merciful . . . high priest" Jesus emotionally gathers up our needs to himself and then in mercy does something about them. . . . a God who has personal emotion at our miserable plight and then springs into action. Even more, our Lord's compassion and mercy are sensitized by the fact that he was really one of us and experienced like miseries; he knows how it feels.[14]

---

[14] R. Kent Hughes, *Hebrews: An Anchor for the Soul* (Wheaton, IL: Crossway, 2015), 83.

B. In which area of your life do you need Christ's mercy? List it here, and then write a prayer, asking Him to spring into action on your behalf.

3. A. What is Jesus' job as our merciful and faithful high priest?

Strong's Concordance defines *expiate* (your Bible might translate it as *propitiate*) as having mercy on, showing favor to, forgiving, or pardoning.[15] When the readers of Hebrews heard this word, it brought to mind the Day of Atonement (Yom Kippur). This was the one day of the year when the high priest would enter the holiest part of the temple to sprinkle the blood of an animal on the mercy seat (the place where God dwelled). The sole purpose of the high priest's visit was to say, "We are sorry, we are sorry, we are sorry." This wasn't a time for the high priest to pop in to hang out with God or to tell Him what he wanted from Him. It was an incredibly important point in the year when the Jewish people acknowledged their desperate need of forgiveness.

We live in a culture that does all it can to make excuses and place blame. Talk of sin, hell, and the need for forgiveness is unpopular to say the least, and we are worse off for it. If we don't recognize our desperate need for expiation, for mercy, for pardon, then we are unlikely to turn to Jesus to receive it.

Some people argue that the God of the Old Testament is a God of wrath, while God of the New Testament is a God of mercy and love. This is to suggest that God is inconsistent and changing, and nothing could be further from the truth. We read in the Old Testament about Him commanding the Israelites to destroy surrounding nations, and many of us place Him on trial in our minds, as if it is up to us to determine whether He is of good character. It seems we need a better understanding of God's wrath, holiness, and mercy.

---

[15] James Strong, *Strong's Exhaustive Concordance of the Bible* (Peabody, MA: Hendrickson, 1890), 37.

B. What do the following New Testament passages have to say about God's wrath?

Romans 1:18

Revelation 19:15 (this is a description of Jesus)

What does Romans 3:23 say about our need for forgiveness?

Now, before you completely panic or stop reading, please hear me out. These verses reveal to us how God feels about sin—He hates it. He hates what it does to us and to the world He created. His desire to eradicate evil and injustice reveals His holiness and His love.

So what do we do when we realize that sin isn't something "out there" but something within each of our hearts? We have to decide where we want the wrath to fall. We can deny that we need a savior and take our chances. Or we can turn to our great high priest, Jesus. He offers to shield us from the wrath of God by allowing it to be poured out on Him instead. The choice is ours.

4. As our high priest, Jesus walked into God's presence not with the blood of animals, but with His own blood. He came to represent us, and to ask for forgiveness on our behalf. His shed blood is what ransomed us, setting us free and offering us justification.

A. Read CCC 1989 and 1990 and write the definition of justification below.

B. Justification is further described in CCC 1992. Read it and answer the following questions:

When is justification conferred on us?

What does justification do for us?

What is the purpose of justification?

5. What else was accomplished on the cross, according to Hebrews 2:18?

Quiet your heart and enjoy His presence. . . . He is a merciful and faithful high priest.

In the Old Testament, the high priest represented the Israelite people to God and represented God to the people. Jesus does the same for us. His humanity allows Him to fully sympathize with our weaknesses. He knows how difficult life can be and the cost of obedience to God. He sits at the Father's right hand and continually intercedes for us with a heart of compassion, empathy, and tenderness. Jesus also perfectly represents God's glory and character to us. We see justice and mercy combined in our Savior, and because of who He is, we find courage to draw near to the throne of grace.

What are you facing today? Sit quietly for a moment and thank Jesus for being your merciful and faithful high priest. Meditate on the fact that there is nothing you face that He cannot sympathize with, help you through, and rescue you from. Ask Jesus for what you need. He will come through for you.

Conclusion

"Jesus is God, but he humbled himself to walk with us. He is our friend, our brother." —Pope Francis

To fully appreciate what it means for Jesus to be our hero-brother, we should never lose sight of the fact that He is God. At any moment during His time on earth, He could have called down legions of angels to rescue Him, yet He endured the worst suffering imaginable to come to our rescue. Why was He willing to do this?

He was falsely accused and condemned so we could be declared not guilty.

He was bound so that we could be set free.

He was given a crown of thorns so that we could receive the crown of life.

He was flogged so that we could be embraced and held.

He was stripped of His clothing so we could wear His robe of righteousness.

His arms were stretched open on the cross so that no one would be past the reach of His mercy.

His hands were nailed to the cross so our hands could receive the riches of divine grace.

He was separated from the Father so we could be ushered into the throne room of God.

He absorbed our sin so we could be filled with His divinity.

His side was pieced with a spear so we could draw near to His heart.

The best response to the mercy and faithfulness of Jesus is to follow the path of the spear and connect with Him, soul-to-soul. It's in intimacy with Jesus that we discover there is no enemy He hasn't conquered already. There's no trial we face that He hasn't endured. There is no cross we carry that He doesn't carry alongside us.

You are never alone. You are beloved. You are rescued. You are free. You are saved by your brother, your captain, your King.

My Resolution

In what specific way will I apply what I have learned in this lesson?

Examples:

1. I have noticed a drift in my spiritual life. I want to get back on track, so I'm going to set my alarm half an hour earlier than usual and devote that time to prayer.

2. I am so thankful that Jesus was willing to take the punishment on Himself that was due me. I will go to adoration this week for the sole purpose of offering Him thanks for His tremendous sacrifice.

3. To help me remember what an incredible Hero and Savior I have in Jesus, I will memorize Psalm 18:1–2: "I love you, Lord, my strength, Lord, my rock, my fortress, my deliverer, my God, my rock of refuge, my shield, my saving horn, my stronghold!"

My resolution:

Catechism Clips

CCC 1989 The first work of the grace of the Holy Spirit is *conversion*, effecting justification in accordance with Jesus' proclamation at the beginning of the Gospel: "Repent, for the kingdom of heaven is at hand." Moved by grace, man turns toward God and away from sin, thus accepting forgiveness and righteousness from on high. "Justification is not only the remission of sins, but also the sanctification and renewal of the interior man.

CCC 1990 By giving Justification *detaches man from sin* which contradicts the love of God, and purifies his heart of sin. Justification follows upon God's merciful initiative of offering forgiveness. It reconciles man with God. It frees from the enslavement to sin, and it heals.

CCC 1992 Justification has been merited for us by the Passion of Christ who offered himself on the cross as a living victim, holy and pleasing to God, and whose blood has become the instrument of atonement for the sins of all men. Justification is conferred in Baptism, the sacrament of faith. It conforms us to the righteousness of God, who makes us inwardly just by the power of his mercy. Its purpose is the glory of God and of Christ, and the gift of eternal life:

> But now the righteousness of God has been manifested apart from law, although the law and the prophets bear witness to it, the righteousness of God through faith in Jesus Christ for all who believe. For there is no distinction: since all have sinned and fall short of the glory of God, they are justified by his grace as a gift, through the redemption which is in Christ Jesus, whom God put forward as an expiation by his blood, to be received by faith. This was to show God's righteousness, because in his divine forbearance he had passed over former sins; it was to prove at the present time that he himself is righteous and that he justifies him who has faith in Jesus.

Verse Study

See Appendix 3 for instructions on how to complete a verse study.

Psalm 3:3

1. Verse:

2. Paraphrase:

3. Questions:

4. Cross-references:

5. Personal Application:

Lesson 4

HARDEN NOT YOUR HEARTS

Hebrews 3

Introduction

Her heart was
a secret garden
and the walls
were very high
—*William Goldman,* The Princess Bride

You can't always tell if a woman has a wall around her heart. The most gracious, kind, and vivacious woman may be hiding deep sadness and hurt. When people ask, "How are you?" how many people are ready to hear an honest answer? And what are the odds that they would know the right thing to say in response? So many of us have given vulnerability a try and found it to be messy and scary. We've tasted betrayal and been disappointed by people. Words have gone deep into our souls and left scars. And we have determined never to be wounded like that again. The walls have gone up, vows have been made, and although we don't intend for it to happen, our hearts can grow hard. Hebrews 3 is going to encourage us to do all we can to prevent this.

In *Strong's Concordance*, sin (*hamartanó*) is defined as "missing the mark."[16] We're aiming at something, but we aren't hitting it. What might we be aiming for? Often, it's to protect ourselves or to achieve some degree of happiness and comfort. But when we think that self-reliance, creature comforts, or any person will satisfy our longings—when those are the things that we aim for—we not only end up disappointed, we often fall into sin. We miss the mark.

---

[16] *Strong's Exhaustive Concordance*, s.v. "hamartanó," Bible Hub, https://biblehub.com/greek/264.htm.

God understands this. When He calls us to confession, it's not to destroy us with judgment. It's to restore us and refocus our aim so that it's directed toward Him, the only One who can truly satisfy our deepest desires. When we go to confession, the ice around our hearts melts away under His divine breath. Our hearts soften, and we are able to receive God—His love and His wisdom.

God wants to defend your tenderness. He is fighting for your heart to be soft and fully alive. Your desires, grief, joy, understanding, thoughts, faith, and belief all find their source in your heart. If you want to be unlocked and set free, to experience victory in the areas where you have been stuck, the key is giving God access to your heart. He promises to be gentle. Yes, He'll go to the places where you want to hide. But He will be tender with you there, and apply the balm of His healing presence to those places where you have felt lonely, a lack of belonging, and a desire for safety and a soft place to land.

Because God is a gentleman and will never barge into a heart uninvited, join me in praying, "Probe me, God, and know my heart. See if there is a wicked path in me; lead me along an ancient path" (Psalm 139:23–24).

Day One
SET APART FOR CHRIST

Read Hebrews 3:1.

1. How does the author refer to the readers of Hebrews in 3:1?

2. How can we be called holy when we make so many mistakes? It helps to gain a better understanding of the definition of *holy*. *Vine's Dictionary* defines it as something or someone set apart, "separated from sin and therefore consecrated to God, sacred."[17] This is not something that we're able to do for ourselves; it's

---

[17] W. E. Vine, *Vine's Expository Dictionary of Old and New Testament Words* (Grand Rapids, MI: Fleming H. Revell, 1981), 266.

something that Jesus does *for* us. What insights do you gain from the following Catechism clip and Bible verses in terms of what makes us holy?

CCC 1227

Titus 3:3–5

1 Corinthians 6:11

CCC 1695 teaches that we are made holy—"sanctified . . . called to be saints . . . [and] have become the temple of the *Holy Spirit*." Read CCC 1695, recording four things that the Holy Spirit does in us to help us to live a life of holiness.

3. A. Remember that holiness means being "set apart." God wants us to be set apart for honorable use, not allowing our bodies and souls to be lifted up and offered to things and people that ultimately won't satisfy us and often will destroy us. What do you learn from 2 Timothy 2:20–23 about how you can be a "vessel for lofty use"?

    B. What additional insights can be gained from 1 Peter 1:14–16 regarding being set apart or holy?

4. A. What are the "holy brothers, sharing in a heavenly calling" told to do in Hebrews 3:1?

Theologian R. Kent Hughes explains how to "reflect on Jesus" by fixing your mind on Him:

> How does one fix one's mind? It begins with desire. David . . . did this because he really wanted to see the Lord: "One thing I ask of the Lord, this is what I seek: that I may dwell in the house of the Lord all the days of my life, to gaze upon the beauty of the Lord and to seek him in his temple." (Psalm 27:4) . . . Along with desire, fixing the mind calls for concentration . . . Isaac Newton said the key to his understanding was, "I keep it before me." . . . Concentration, of course, requires discipline like that of an athlete . . . Paul put it this way: "Since, then, you have been raised with Christ, set your heart on things above, where Christ is seated at the right hand of God. Set your minds on things above, not on earthly things" (Col. 3:1,2) . . . Concentrating on Jesus requires an act of the will. Lastly, fixing our thoughts on Jesus requires time, for true reflection cannot happen with a glance.[18]

B. According to Hughes' commentary, what does fixing your mind on Jesus begin with?

C. Along with desire, fixing your thoughts on Jesus requires concentration. What is needed to concentrate?

D. What other two things does Hughes say are needed if we are going to fix our thoughts on Jesus?

---

[18] Hughes, *Hebrews*, 92–3.

E. Which of those things (desire, concentration, discipline, an act of the will and time) is most difficult for you? What concrete decision could you make today to strengthen yourself in that area?

Quiet your heart and enjoy His presence. . . . Offer Him more than a glance.

In our desire to be holy, we can't lose sight of the source of our holiness. It's not us, it's God. It's the Holy Spirit working in us. But that doesn't mean that we just lie on the couch waiting for Him to touch us with a magic wand. We need to cooperate with grace, and that looks a lot like self-discipline. But as we do our part, the Holy Spirit within us is doing His deep, transforming work, even helping us to want the things that God wants. He can baptize our desires. Because He is always at work within us, we can ask Him to give us the desire and power to do what pleases Him. God will never refuse this request, but He will always wait to be asked and invited into the struggle.

If you want to grow in holiness but are struggling to walk away from the sins that feel a bit like comfortable shoes, join me in the following prayer:

Dear Lord,

I know it's an honor to be set apart by You for a holy purpose. I know how often I've allowed my body and soul to be lifted up and offered to people and pursuits that were far from holy. Why did I do those things, and why do I continue to do them? I'm wanting comfort and happiness. They aren't bad things in themselves, but I get led into bad choices when I pursue those two things in the wrong places. So help me find comfort in You. Help me to desire You above all else so that when I gain You, I am happy. Help me to see that those other choices ultimately enslave me. I end up trapped in situations that I've gotten myself into, having mistakenly thought that I would feel more free if I made that particular choice.

I claim Your promise in Psalm 25:15: "My eyes are ever upon the LORD, who frees my feet from the snare." I commit to fixing my eyes on You—to doing this first thing in the morning, before I fix my eyes on my phone. I commit to keeping my eyes on You, checking in with You at least as often as I check social media or text messages. I claim Your promise that if I do my part, You will free my feet from the snare. Please, Lord Jesus, set me free. Give me the desire and the power to do what pleases You. Amen.

Day Two
OUR APOSTLE AND HIGH PRIEST

Read Hebrews 3:1–6.

1. How is Jesus described in Hebrews 3:1?

It would have been remarkable for the readers of Hebrews to hear Jesus referred to as a high priest. This is because all Israelite priests had to be from the tribe of Levi, and Jesus was from the tribe of Judah. The author of Hebrews had his work cut out for him in convincing his readers that Jesus' priesthood was valid. More will come on that in later chapters.

2. Hebrews 3:1 explains that Jesus is the apostle (meaning one who is sent) and the high priest "of our confession." What is meant by "confession"? N. T. Wright unpacks the word in this context:

> The word "confession" today normally means "telling someone you did something you shouldn't have". It means "owning up": "Yes, officer, I was driving too fast" . . . But the early Christians gave it a wider meaning: "telling people what's really true about your belief." This means "owning up", not to having done something wrong, but to believing in the Christian message and to belonging to the Christian movement . . . "Confession" in this sense might get you into trouble, because in the first century, and in many parts of the world still today, believing and belonging like that is seen by authorities as a threat to their power and their system.[19]

How would you respond if someone asked you to tell him or her what's really true about what you believe? What are the core truths of your faith?

Sometimes it's hard to articulate something that feels like it's always been a part of the fabric of our lives. This is why we are given the Creeds of our faith. They supply us with the words—with a summary—of what we are called to believe.

---

[19] Wright, *Hebrews for Everyone*, 24.

While we never want to force our beliefs on anyone, our faith does demand expression. The author of Hebrews would not have understood in the slightest a claim that ones' faith was "personal," "just between me and Jesus," or a "private affair." The early Church knew the stakes were high—far higher than they are for those of us in the Western world today—but they saw anything less than public confession of faith as a betrayal of Christ.

3. A. What character quality is highlighted in Hebrews 3:2 as belonging to both Jesus and Moses?

B. This next section of Hebrews is going to compare Jesus to Moses in the same way that Jesus was compared to the angels in chapters 1 and 2. Why was this necessary? Was it seriously a concern that people would think more highly of Moses than of Jesus? In a word, yes. At that time, there was no man in history more impressive than Moses. Read the following verses about Moses, noting what made him so exceptional.

Exodus 3:1–10

Numbers 12:3

Deuteronomy 34:10–12

4. What argument does the author of Hebrews make in 3:3–6 regarding why Christ is superior to Moses?

5. Hebrews 3:5–6 describes Moses as a faithful servant, but Christ as a faithful son. Read the following verses, noting the ways in which Jesus' faithfulness was greater than that of Moses.

A. Galatians 3:13

What do you think it felt like to become a curse?

B. Mark 15:29–37

What do you think the loneliness of the cross felt like for Jesus? What do you think it felt like to be verbally abused as He suffered?

Quiet your heart and enjoy His presence. . . . Jesus sacrificed everything so you could experience intimacy with God.

May we be filled with humility, gasping at the sacrifice Jesus made to draw us close to the Father. So much in our lives focuses us on what we deserve—what we feel we are owed. This attitude can creep into our relationship with God, and a surefire way to check if this is true is to look at how we respond when He doesn't answer our prayers the way we would like. Do we cry foul? Do we demand better treatment? Or in humility, do we believe that God is for us and only does what is ultimately in our best interest? Do we believe that He proved this to us already as He suffered on the cross?

Dear God,

How can I question Your goodness to me when I look at all You sacrificed for me? Yet so often, I do just that. Help me to take the time to contemplate Jesus on the cross. Give me eyes of faith that look past my own needs and desires to zero in solely on You. May I begin to look at my disappointments differently, accepting them from Your living hand. When things don't go as I want, give me a spirit of expectancy that believes something better is around the corner.

You are a good, good Father. You are not holding out on me. That's the lie from the Garden of Eden. I reject that lie, and embrace the truth of Your goodness, proven once and for all by Your sacrificial love on the cross.

Day Three
HOLDING FAST

Read Hebrews 3:6.

1. What is meant by the phrase "his house"? The Jewish people of that time would have thought of the house of God as the temple. But in this context, the author is referring to something different. What is it, according to Ephesians 2:21–22 and 1 Peter 2:5?

The "house" referred to in Hebrews 3:3–6 refers to both the Church and the family of God's people. That's us. As members of the Church, we are His house. This implies more than Church membership, though. The Holy Spirit longs to build a home *in our hearts*. I invite you to pause and think about what it actually means for us to be the house—the dwelling place—for God Himself. When you stop to think about it, it's truly mind-boggling.

2. A. What fruits should be planted in our hearts to make them a beautiful dwelling place for God? See Galatians 5:22. Which of these fruits do you want to see more of in yourself?

    B. When Jesus makes His home in our hearts, everything changes. We pray, "On earth, as it is in heaven," in the Our Father, and this is exactly what happens when Jesus brings heaven into our hearts through His presence. Do you live with that level of expectancy? Or do you think we just have to gut it out in this life, but we are going to be rewarded in heaven?

    C. A lot changed in my life when I decided to pray, "On earth as it is in heaven," like I really meant it. Jesus wants to draw near in intimacy with you and me, and to infuse the daily struggles and joys with supernatural power. He wants to do that *within* us, teaching us to commune with the Holy Spirit within our hearts. What are we missing when we just rush through life, content with simply getting our to-do list done? We usually miss the most precious, poignant moments. Are you longing for something more? What is a decision you can make today to slow down and savor your one wild, beautiful life?

3. What does Hebrews 3:6 say we must do if we want to be "God's house"?

The Greek word for "confidence" (*parrésia*) can mean "boldness" and "fearlessness."[20] Do you lack this kind of courage? Take heart. Our confidence isn't based on anything we have done. It comes from recognizing the incredible power that's been placed within us by God. The same power that raised Jesus from the dead is within baptized Christians because the Holy Spirit dwells within us. This means that the boldness or fearlessness that is required of us if we are going to hold fast finds its source not in us, but in the Holy Spirit.

Every day, we are asked to persevere and stay faithful, regardless of our circumstances. Whether we drift away or hold fast will be determined by our dependence on the Holy Spirit. If we choose self-reliance instead of dependence on God, we'll likely give up.

4. One of the ways that we can hold fast to our confidence is by stoking the fire of the Holy Spirit within our hearts. What gift of the Holy Spirit is offered to us to help us do this? See CCC 1831 and CCC 1837 for the answer.

Fortitude is a *gift* from the Holy Spirit. It is unearned and freely offered. But this gift will remain unopened if we just keep it on the shelf. We need to receive it, open it, and put it into practice. We do this through prayer when we ask God to do in and through us what we cannot do on our own. When we feel we are drifting away, we can call out to the Holy Spirit, "Give me fortitude! Help me to stay firm and hold fast!" He will always come through and replace our weakness with His power. Always. Stoke the fire of the Holy Spirit in your heart through prayer and then obey straightaway when He directs you. This is making your heart a home for the Spirit.

---

20 *Strong's Concordance*, s.v. "parrésia," Bible Hub, https://biblehub.com/greek/3954.htm.

Quiet your heart and enjoy His presence. . . . Your heart is His home.

According to 1 Peter 2:5, you are being built into a spiritual house. This is a process, a journey. God's hope is that with each passing day, another part of our heart (another "room in the house") will be handed over to Him for some remodeling. Sometimes He needs to remove a wall to make your heart as beautiful as it can be. Other times He knows the fire of the Holy Spirit needs to be lit so courage and boldness will emanate from within you. There will be times when you have a closet you'd really like to keep closed in your heart. It's the last place you want God poking around. He won't force the door open, but He'll remind you that you'll live with much more freedom if you'll allow Him inside. If you open the door, He'll work with you to sweep out the garbage that is cluttering your life and dragging you down. We rarely want *to give Him this access. We prefer to hide the garbage instead. But every time we are brave enough to do it, we'll be flooded with mercy and feel like a new person.*

But here's the amazing thing about God. He doesn't ask you to get your heart all cleaned up before He moves in. He wants your house "as is." In 1 Corinthians 3:17 we read, "The temple of God, which you are, is holy." You are a temple of the Holy Spirit. You are holy because of God's presence within you. Give Him full access to your heart, and witness a transformation like no other.

Dear Lord,

Give me the courage to throw open all the doors to my heart. I ask You to fill every nook and cranny with Your presence. When You discover sin cluttering my soul, please cleanse and forgive me. When I'm feeling numb or disinterested in You, please kindle a fire in my heart so that the Holy Spirit works in me to desire You more. Forgive me the times I think it's all up to me. Help me to place all my trust in You. Come, Holy Spirit. May my heart be Your home.

Day Four
HARDEN NOT YOUR HEART

Read Hebrews 3:7–11.

Note: This section of Hebrews is taken from Psalm 95. Saint Benedict (c. 480–c. 547) required the monks to sing Psalm 95 as the first psalm of the day, and it has been a treasured psalm in the Christian tradition ever since. It's the invitatory psalm of the Liturgy of the Hours, calling us all to listen to God's voice with tender and teachable hearts.

1. What did the Israelites in the exodus do when they heard God's voice? See Hebrews 3:7–9.

2. How is the Israelites' behavior described in Hebrews 3:10?

3. The "rebellion on the day of testing in the wilderness" (Hebrews 3:8) refers to the Israelites' rebellion in Numbers 14:1–38. At that point, the Israelites had been rescued from slavery in Egypt and brought to the edge of the Promised Land[21] by Moses. Before embarking on the battle to gain this new territory, Moses sent twelve spies to check it out. When the spies returned, ten of them sowed seeds of fear and despair, describing the inhabitants as huge people who made them feel like grasshoppers by comparison. Only two spies, Joshua and Caleb, felt that they should go up and seize the land.

    A. How did the Israelites respond to the spies' reports? See Numbers 14:1–10.

    B. What did God say would be the consequence of their lack of faith in Him? See Numbers 14:26–38.

4. The hardening of the Israelites' hearts (Hebrews 3:8) began with unbelief. These were the people who had seen the miracles of the exodus, yet they didn't believe that God would come through for them this time. No doubt they could remember His past faithfulness, but in the present moment, their focus had shifted from God's power to their own resources. Their strength and resolve were woefully inadequate for the challenge of taking over the Promised Land.

    Human thinking and human resources are simply not enough for many of our challenges. Thinking the solution lies in ourselves will cause us to wander away

---

[21] According to the *Catholic Bible Dictionary* (p. 733), the Promised Land is the land of Canaan, promised by God to Abraham and his offspring (Genesis 12:7; 13:14–15; 17:8). The promise was renewed to the later patriarchs (Genesis 26:3; 28:13) and Israel (Exodus 13:5; 33:1–3).

from God and likely fall into the pit of discouragement when our own resources fail to produce the desired results.

This reminds me of my own experience in the spiritual battle. I have gone through many seasons when there seems to be no letup. Just when I think life might be settling down, one more thing slams into me from left field. It's so easy in those moments to let my head and shoulders droop and give in to despair. "I'm all alone," I think. "It's all up to me." These are two of the oldest lies in the enemy's book, but at my low points, they can start to make sense to me. Yet this is faulty thinking, and it's not taking into account God's history with me. How many times has He come through for me? *Every time.* How often has He shown up to the rescue? *Always.* That means this current trial or challenge should not be seen as the exception to the rule.

A. What about you? Have you also experienced God's faithfulness, yet found you struggle with doubt when facing a significant challenge?

B. Unbelief can produce contempt for God. When the Israelites doubted God would fight for them, He responded by saying, "How long will this people spurn me?" (Numbers 14:11) The Hebrew word for "spurn" (*naats*) can also be translated "treat with contempt." Contempt is revealed by negativism, complaining, arguing, and disobedience. Do you experience any of these things when you are afraid that God is not going to come through for you?

5. We obviously don't want to show contempt for God. But sometimes the things we are facing are so terrifying, we don't know how to get rid of the fear. What does 1 John 4:18 tell us will help us in those times?

Only God's love is utterly perfect, and that is what we need to immerse ourselves in when we are facing our giants. Instead of looking at the challenge or the cause of our fear, we can choose to shift our gaze to God and contemplate His love for us. This restful posture may sound impossible when we are in the midst of a crisis. But it is always a choice on offer to us. It's counterintuitive to stop relying on ourselves, to stop problem solving, brainstorming, and so on and instead kneel in prayer, but that is the only way we will be able to experience the promised rest and peace that God has for us.

Quiet your heart and enjoy His presence. . . . He will not fail you.

"Today when you hear his voice, do not harden your hearts." (Hebrews 3:7–8)

And what does God's voice say? It always reminds us that we are the beloved. Then it tells us the way to walk as beloved children. It warns us away from going down the dangerous path and encourages us to stay on the path to blessing and rest. Sometimes the path He is pointing us toward seems as if it is sure to lead to ruin. No doubt that is what most of the Israelites were feeling in the wilderness. In those moments, it's critical that we shift our focus away from our circumstances and onto God. He is omnipotent—He is all-powerful. He is omnipresent—He can be all places at once. He is omniscient—He knows everything (so obviously more than we do). He has the best mind for coming up with the right plan, He goes before us into the future to prepare the way for us, and He has the power to fight against anything that would harm us. We can count on Him.

Dear Lord,

Please forgive me for the times that I have shown You contempt. Forgive my negativity, complaining, arguing, and disobedience. It's been said that delayed obedience is disobedience. I delay obeying You because I am hoping there's another option. I'm relying on myself to come up with a more appealing plan. Help me to trust You more than I trust myself. Give me the strength, courage, and conviction to obey You the minute I hear Your voice say, "This is the way; walk in it" (Isaiah 30:21).

Day Five
THE DECEITFULNESS OF SIN

Read Hebrews 3:12–19.

1. A. What are we warned against in Hebrews 3:12?

B. This verse brings to mind the seed that fell on the rocky ground in the parable of the sower in Matthew 13:20–21. Based on these verses, how would you describe an unfaithful heart?

C. How do you typically respond when trials and persecution come? What is your attitude when you don't see your work for the Lord paying off? How does your trust in God hold up when one more thing goes wrong, just when you've told God that you can't take any more?

I don't ask those questions to make you feel condemned. But if you feel a little convicted (I know I do), then I encourage you to bring this to the Lord in confession. Not only will you be met with mercy, you'll be infused with grace that will strengthen you to persevere.

There will always be people within the Christian community who are just along for the ride. As long as life moves along as it should, being a member of the Church feels good and some degree of commitment remains. Author Kyle Idleman would describe them as fans, as opposed to followers. He considers "the biggest threat to the church today [to be] fans who call themselves Christians but aren't actually interested in following Christ. They want to be close enough to Jesus to get all the benefits, but not so close that it requires anything from them."[22]

Oh, that we would be different! I pray that we would be steadfast, even in the face of trials, remembering that our loving Father will never leave or forsake us and is worth every sacrifice.

---

[22] Kyle Idleman, *Not a Fan* (Grand Rapids, MI: Zondervan, 2011), 25.

2. A. Why are we told to encourage ourselves daily in Hebrews 3:13?

The deceit of sin tells us that sin will somehow make us happy. The enemy whispers the lie that following God will ruin all our fun and that this particular sin really isn't all that bad.

B. Is there something small that you are playing around with, rationalizing that it isn't that big a deal? Which specific rationalization are you using? Are you willing to stop the progression of sin and break the habit through the power of the Holy Spirit?

3. Hebrews 3:14 challenges us to hold fast to our confidence in God until the end. The alternative is a hard heart of unbelief. What causes a heart to harden? Unconfessed sin is a common cause. The more we sin, the less sensitive we become to the Holy Spirit's convicting work. When nothing is convicting us, we might want to check if we have become desensitized to the seriousness of sin. If you find that certain behaviors used to make you feel guilty but now don't, that isn't a cause for celebration. That is a cause for concern. A woman with a soft and tender heart is sensitive to even the smallest acts of disobedience, and runs quickly to the Lord for mercy and a fresh start when she fails.

Another thing that can harden our hearts is being hurt. Something wounds us and we determine to never feel this way again. All too often, we evaluate the situation and make vows of self-protection and self-reliance that actually build a wall around our hearts. Can you identify any times in your life when you experienced significant hurt? Is it possible that some doubt as to God's goodness or willingness to provide for and protect you crept in? Ask the Holy Spirit to bring to mind any significant memories that need God's healing touch. He was there in your time of suffering, and He is here right now, ready to minister to your heart.

4. Hebrews 3:16–18 is a series of questions intended to drive home the author's point. Answer the following questions and then summarize the point he is making.

A. Who were those who rebelled when they heard? (Hebrews 3:16)

B. With whom was he "provoked for forty years"?

C. To whom did he swear they should not enter into his rest?

D. What point is the author making? Although the Israelites began well, they didn't end well. God was disappointed because although they had seen the miracles of the exodus, they didn't believe He would come through for them this time. Their disbelief led to action, which was disobedience.

The Israelites experienced God's miracles, as well as the trauma of slavery and being pursued by Pharaoh's army. They experienced hunger and thirst. Fear was their constant companion. No doubt their hearts were wounded by all they went through. In the face of trials, their faith in God wavered, and disobedience and unbelief resulted. They chose self-reliance over dependence on God. No doubt this felt like the safer choice at the time, but ultimately, it led to their downfall.

Quiet your heart and enjoy His presence. . . . May you remember His faithfulness.

"I do not want you to be unaware, brothers, that our ancestors were all under the cloud and all passed through the sea, and all of them were baptized into Moses in the cloud and in the sea. All ate the same spiritual food, and all drank the same spiritual drink, for they drank from a spiritual rock

that followed them, and the rock was the Christ. Yet God was not pleased with most of them, for they were struck down in the desert. These things happened as examples for us, so that we might not desire evil things, as they did." (1 Corinthians 10:1–7)

The stories of the Israelites remind us all that no matter how well we start off, staying steady till the end can be really hard. We're warned that we shouldn't desire evil things, as they did. What makes it so difficult is that the evil things are often disguised as good things.

To be on guard against this means we need to start paying attention a couple of steps back. It's critical to continually be checking our lives for "trust leaks." These are the little indicators that we are starting to play around with the question, "Is God holding out on me? Does He really want what's best for me?" Once our mind goes there, disbelief in His goodness can quickly follow.

The minute we start to feel our trust waning, let's run to adoration and kneel before Jesus in the Eucharist. Let's ask the Holy Spirit to encourage our hearts by helping us bring to mind all the times God has come through for us. The enemy will always tempt us to forget. It's our job to remember. Doing this in the presence of Christ in the Eucharist is especially powerful, and His potent grace can chase away the distractions that keep us from focusing on all God has done for us.

This is a spiritual discipline, and it will be strengthened in our lives in the same way a muscle is strengthened—through use. And by use, I don't just mean when it's easy. Just as a muscle strengthens when it's challenged, the spirit within us will become stronger in the discipline of gratitude and trust when we exercise it in the hard times.

Dear God,

I want to eat the spiritual food You offer me and drink from the spiritual rock: Jesus. I know that's what will truly nourish and satisfy me. Yet I keep finding myself turning to the junk food of distractions and self-reliance. Forgive me for my lack of trust.

Holy Spirit, fill me with the gift of faith. I know this isn't something that I can conjure up, so I ask You to grow it in my heart. Be my eyes so that my perspective widens to see all the times God has rescued, sustained, and strengthened me. Be my mouth so that my words are full of hope instead of complaint. Be my feet so that I go to the people and places that will encourage me to remain steadfast and devoted to God. Be my hands so that I pick up the Bible instead of my phone or laptop.

Thank You for being my encourager, counselor, comforter, helper, and strengthener.

Conclusion

When I moved to Europe, newly married at twenty-two, I had the gift of being surrounded by women who were older than I was. It took time to learn a foreign language, and my closest friends were English speakers. Most expatriates had to be older to get an overseas assignment, which meant most people in my social circle were not my age. God knew that this was exactly what I needed. My husband and I started a family quickly, and those women taught me how to mother old-school style.

One of the lessons they shared with me was this: If kids are not taught to obey their parents *the first time they are asked to do something*, then they are actually being trained to disobey God. They challenged me to think about why I was disciplining my kids. Was it to ensure that they would be less likely to embarrass me in public? Was it to give me some relief? They encouraged me to choose a purer motivation—to discipline my kids to get them used to surrendering their will to mine so that one day they could transfer that habit of obedience to their relationship with God. I was taught that the whole "I'm going to count to three" method is actually teaching kids to disobey twice before obedience comes. We're in effect saying, "You don't have to obey the first time I ask you, not the second time either, but the third time, when I'm starting to get annoyed, then you'd better get moving." When we respond to God in that way, there are always consequences. The lessons those women taught me about mothering were lessons I needed to learn in my relationship with God.

I was taught and wholeheartedly believe that delayed obedience is disobedience. The greatest blessing comes when we obey straightaway. True, God doesn't withdraw His love when we don't obey. His love is not conditional. Nor do we stop being His beloved children. But we end up learning whatever lesson He has for us the hard way.

Hebrews 3 is God's voice pleading with us to learn the easy way. He's asking us to keep our hearts soft and open, receptive to the Holy Spirit convicting us of anything that is getting in the way of us experiencing the fullness God created us for. God desires to give us rest, and He knows the best way to get us there. We can trust that He is not trying to spoil our fun when He points us down the narrow path of obedience.

A heart that trusts in God is indomitable. When we trust in His goodness and provision, we can face the giants in our lives, whatever they may be. Anxiety, addiction, fear, suffering—whatever is threatening to take you down, God can bring victory into that very area of your life. The secret is not self-reliance or numbing out so you don't feel the pain. It's turning your focus to your Savior, the One who has and will come to fight for you. He rages against the evil that has hurt you, and He never leaves you to fight the battle alone. When it is the fiercest, He draws the closest. When you can't bear another minute, He will hide you and give you rest. You do not fight alone. He who is in you is stronger than he who is in the world, and that makes all the difference.

My Resolution

In what specific way will I apply what I have learned in this lesson?

Examples:

1. I feel I have a hardened heart due to deep hurt in my life. Instead of just moving forward without dealing with the painful memories, I commit to finding a Christian counselor to help me walk through the process of healing.

2. When difficulties come and my trust in God is waning, I am far more apt to turn to distraction or self-reliance instead of plugging the trust leaks in my heart. Because of this, I am going to find a friend to hold me accountable in this area. I will give her permission to speak truth into my life when my hope is waning and disbelief is beginning to creep in. I will ask her to challenge me to go to adoration at those times, and remember all the times God has come through for me.

3. I am committing to "first-time obedience" with God. Instead of procrastinating when He asks something of me, I will do it without delay. Delayed obedience is disobedience.

My resolution:

Catechism Clips

CCC 1227 According to the Apostle Paul, the believer enters through Baptism into communion with Christ's death, is buried with him, and rises with him:

> Do you not know that all of us who have been baptized into Christ Jesus were baptized into his death? We were buried therefore with him by baptism into death, so that as Christ was raised from the dead by the glory of the Father, we too might walk in newness of life.

The baptized have "put on Christ." Through the Holy Spirit, Baptism is a bath that purifies, justifies, and sanctifies.

CCC 1695 "Justified in the name of the Lord Jesus Christ and in the Spirit of our God," "sanctified . . . [and] called to be saints," Christians have become the temple of the Holy Spirit. This "Spirit of the Son" teaches them to pray to the Father and, having become their life, prompts them to act so as to bear "the fruit of the Spirit" by charity in action. Healing the wounds of sin, the Holy Spirit renews us interiorly through a spiritual transformation. He enlightens and strengthens us to live as "children of light" through "all that is good and right and true."

CCC 1831 The seven *gifts* of the Holy Spirit are wisdom, understanding, counsel, fortitude, knowledge, piety, and fear of the Lord. They belong in their fullness to Christ, Son of David. They complete and perfect the virtues of those who receive them. They make the faithful docile in readily obeying divine inspirations.

> Let your good spirit lead me on a level path.
> For all who are led by the Spirit of God are sons of God . . . If children, then heirs, heirs of God and fellow heirs with Christ.

CCC 1837 Fortitude ensures firmness in difficulties and constancy in the pursuit of the good.

Verse Study

See Appendix 3 for instructions on how to complete a verse study.

Isaiah 30:21

1. Verse:

2. Paraphrase:

3. Questions:

4. Cross-references:

5. Personal Application:

Lesson 5: Talk
THE UNWINDING
Hebrews 4

You can view this talk on the accompanying DVD, or please visit our website at walkingwithpurpose.com/videos and select the *Grounded in Hope* Bible Study, then click through to select Videos.

I. Sabbath Rest

Do you know what the Sabbath is? It's a **declaration of freedom**. Freedom from defining your worth by what you produce. Freedom from relentless task lists that are never completed. Freedom from *doing* so that you can simply *be*. Freedom from constantly inhaling information and demands so that you can slowly exhale.

II. Canaan Rest

Faith was the key to entering the rest of Canaan, and it's the key to experiencing the deep soul rest God promises to each one of us.

III. God's Rest

The third type of rest mentioned in Hebrews 4 refers to God's rest after creating the world.

IV. Soul Rest

When these verses tell us that we need to "cease from our labors," they describe a faith that causes us to stop striving and depending on ourselves. It's a faith that takes self-sufficiency out at the knees and replaces it with dependence on God.

Soul Rest can only occur when we are at peace with who we are, and when who we are is uncoupled from what we do.

V. The Work of the Word of God

For the word of God is living and active, sharper than any two-edged sword, piercing to the division of soul and spirit, of joints and marrow, and discerning the thoughts and intentions of the heart. And before him no creature is hidden, but all are open and laid bare to the eyes of him with whom we have to do. (Hebrews 4:12–13)

We don't have to justify ourselves anymore. It is finished.
We can walk away from our work, because we know who we are.
We know what we are worth.
Jesus says, "You are worth my everything."

Discussion Questions

1. What is your perspective on the command to honor the Sabbath? Have you ever seen the Sabbath as a declaration of freedom? Do you feel that you need permission to rest?

2. What is standing in the way of you experiencing true soul rest? Does your inner voice of self-reproach consistently whisper, "not enough"? If this is a struggle for you, why do you think you are overworking or committing to more things than you have time for?

3. Have you experienced God's Word moving in your life, revealing motives, thoughts, and hurts? How have you responded? What difference would it make if you truly believed the words of Saint Julian of Norwich: "When God sees sin, He sees pain in us"?

Lesson 6

REST AT THE THRONE

Hebrews 4

Introduction

"What is it, then, that this desire and this inability proclaim to us, but that there was once in man a true happiness of which there now remain to him only the mark and empty trace, which he in vain tries to fill from all his surroundings, seeking from things absent the help he does not obtain in things present? But these are all inadequate, because the infinite abyss can only be filled by an infinite and immutable object, that is to say, only by God Himself."[23] —Blaise Pascal

Most women I know would agree that a life of "go, give, do" leaves them with a list of accomplishments but a large dose of weariness. Someone recently said to me that sleep doesn't help if it's your soul that's tired. I relate to this. When I don't rest *internally*, I get fried and overwhelmed. I may be crossing off lots of tasks on my to-do list, but these are quickly replaced by new demands. The result? A depleted soul.

Yet we know that doing good is to be commended, not avoided. So what is the problem with the scenario I just described? In my own life, the root of it is my self-reliance. Instead of beginning with a restful time at the throne of grace, I jump into tasks, often before asking God if this is a need He is calling *me* to fill, or if it's meant for someone else. That sacred pause for prayer is so critical, and when I fail to do it, I find myself caught in the quagmire of self-sufficiency. The result? Exhaustion. Martyrdom. The blame game. Sometimes anger. Always discouragement.

This is disobedience. I know I'm to lean on God and ask Him to work through me, and then stop worrying and instead trust Him with the results. This is a big part of why I need to rest. But far too often, the difficulties of the present moment overshadow what God has promised me.

---

[23] Robert Mayard Hutchins, ed., *Great Books of the Western World*, vol. 33, trans. W. F. Trotter (Chicago: Encyclopedia Britannica, 1952), 244.

God has promised us rest. Amazingly, we can experience a deep soul rest while going through periods of turmoil. The author of Hebrews reminds us in chapter 4 that our lives are a lot like those of the ancient Israelites. Just as they were on a pilgrimage from Egypt to the Promised Land, we're on a journey that leads through a desert but ends in heaven. Along the way, we can experience rest if we listen to God's voice and respond with obedience. The alternative is doing things our own way. But if this is what we choose, we'll never experience rest.

The secret to rest does not lie in finishing all our tasks. If we wait for that, we will never stop striving and will miss the life we were created for. Rest is possible only for those who slow down and listen to the voice of the Father. He asks us to hold up the lie that is keeping us from resting. The lies are varied and formed by the enemy in such a way that they make sense. These are some of his favorites:

"It's all up to you."
"There's no way out."
"If you stop, it'll all fall apart."
"You need to get this right."
"If you work smart it'll all get done."

Here's the thing. It *never* all gets done. Mistakes are always made. You don't need to get this right. There is a way out; it is not all up to you. You are not the savior of the world or of your life; Jesus is. And even He left tasks unfinished when He was here on earth.

Rest is not a cruel delusion. It is possible, but it requires a reboot of the way you have been operating. The desire within you to slow down is God-given, and while perfect balance will only be experienced in heaven, God's presence within and around you on earth promises greater calm in the here and now.

Day One
BELIEF PLUS TRUST

Read Hebrews 4:1–2.

Hebrews 4 starts off with the word *therefore*. Whenever we see this word, it's a tip-off that what we're about to read is going to be an application of the previous passage, in this case, Hebrews 3. As we saw in Lesson 4, "Harden Not Your Hearts," Hebrews 3 addresses the rebellion of the Israelites in the wilderness and the consequence of their disobedience. Hebrews 4 continues to quote Psalm 95 (just as chapter 3 did), but instead of focusing on the Israelites' unwillingness to hear God's voice and their hard hearts, it addresses their forfeited rest.

1. A. Why does the author of Hebrews tell us we must be on our guard?

It's interesting that the author wrote, "let *us* be on our guard." The "us" reveals that we *all* (including the author) run the risk of missing the rest that God has promised. The literal translation of "let us be on our guard" is "let us fear."[24] This isn't saying that we should fear something or someone, but that we should fear stopping short of experiencing what God desires to give us. God isn't looking for an excuse to punish us. He has something more for us, and He longs for us to experience every ounce of the goodness and blessing that He waits to pour out.

B. Experiencing all that God has for us requires the willingness to shift gears and change. We have to stop settling for mediocrity. The rest of what God longs to give us isn't only to be experienced in heaven. He wants us to experience an abundant life now (John 10:10). This doesn't mean He promises a life free of sorrow; it means that even in the midst of the pain, we can live in abundance. But we can so easily miss it. **Are you willing not to just do things the way you've always done them?** Are you willing to grasp hold of hope—a hope that says what has been lost, what seems beyond repair, what feels dry and barren can be made new? Write out Hosea 6:3, and follow it with a heartfelt prayer, committing to a new beginning if you are able. If that is not where your heart is today, can you ask God to grow hope in you, to strengthen your belief that when the Lord comes, things will change?

2. A. According to Hebrews 4:2, what did both the Israelites in the wilderness and the readers of Hebrews receive?

---

[24] Healy, *Hebrews*, 85.

B. Hebrews 4:2 can also be translated, "For we also have been evangelized just as they were."[25] This is a fascinating statement, because it reveals that the salvation that was promised in the Old Testament is the same message as the Gospel that is proclaimed in the New Testament. They were looking forward to the fulfillment of the promise of salvation, while we look back at what Christ's death and resurrection accomplished.

The point being made here is that we have no excuse if we follow the Israelites' example of unbelief. We can't claim that we never heard the good news. *They* heard it and *we* have heard it, but whereas they just had the promise, we have actually seen the promise fulfilled. But is that where our perspective remains? What do we think about more often—the promises God has fulfilled, or our current discontent? Gratitude is a discipline, a decision—one in which we choose to spend more time focusing on our blessings than on the things we wish were different. Which of your lists is longer, your blessings or your complaints?

C. Why did the word that the Israelites heard not profit them? See Hebrews 4:2.

"Those who listened" were Caleb and Joshua, the two spies who measured the challenge against God's limitless supply instead of their own limited strength. Not only did they believe that God had the means for victory at His disposal, they trusted that He would come through for them, that He'd deploy His strength on their behalf. Both belief in God's ability and trust in His goodness were needed.

3. A. Which circumstances or people in your life are causing you to worry, strive, or stress out?

---

[25] Philip Edgcumbe Hughes, *A Commentary on the Epistle to the Hebrews* (Grand Rapids, MI: William B. Eerdmans, 1977), 156.

B. Do you trust that God is greater and more powerful than what you are facing? Do you trust that *He is able* to work all things for good? Read Romans 8:28 for encouragement.

C. Do you trust that God's love for you means that *He cares deeply* about the outcome of what you are facing? See 1 Peter 5:7 for a reminder of how He feels about you.

D. Do you trust that *He loves the people you are worried about, even more than you do,* as His love is divine and yours is human? See 2 Peter 3:8–9 for insight into God's timing.

We will not be able to experience rest until we hand our concerns over to God and leave them with Him. I know this is easier said than done. All too often, when I hand something over to God in prayer, I snatch it back a couple of minutes later. When this happens, I have a choice. I can give up, dwell on some self-condemning thoughts, or just hand it to Him again. The third choice is the best one. It doesn't matter how many times I have to hand it back. In fact, each time I do is an act of faith, which makes that muscle stronger because of frequent use.

Quiet your heart and enjoy His presence. . . . Hand your concerns to Him because He cares for you.

I love how autobiographies pull back the curtain on the interior lives of fascinating people. But even more interesting is hearing from those who have had a front-row seat to the way a person has actually lived, because aren't we all pretty good at putting our best foot forward and curating our image? To that point, I love the following quote from the son of Protestant missionary Hudson Taylor. Reading this makes me think about the tremendous influence of a life faithfully lived for the Lord. It has been said that faith is caught more than taught. I wonder, who is observing you right now? What can you learn from the example of this humble yet valiant missionary?

> *Day and night this was his secret, "just to roll the burden on the Lord." Frequently those who were wakeful in the little house at Chinkiang might hear, at two or three in the morning, the soft refrain of Mr. Taylor's favorite hymn ["Jesus, I am resting, resting in the joy of what Thou art"]. He had learned that for him only one life was possible—just that blessed life of resting and rejoicing in the Lord under all circumstances, while He dealt with the difficulties, inward and outward, great and small.[26]*

Oh Lord Jesus,

What a witness of trust Hudson Taylor was. I feel convicted that what is often observed in my life isn't trust; it's worry. Help me to grow in trust by meditating on Your faithfulness. When have You ever not come through for me? I can't come up with a single example of a time You have failed me. What I have failed to do, however, it to ask You for help. Give me the wisdom to look to You for help before I try out every other option.

I truly want to get to the place where trust is my natural reaction, but if I'm honest, Lord, some of my lack of trust comes from hurt deep within. There have been times in my life when it seems that You abandoned me. Please heal my heart, and help me to see that You never left me, even if I could not see proof of Your presence. Give me eyes of faith to trust that You have been at work even when there was no evidence of it. Grant me the humility to recognize, each and every day, that just because my mind does not comprehend something, it doesn't mean that Your great plan, presence, and promise is not at work.

---

[26] Dr. and Mrs. Howard Taylor, *Hudson Taylor's Spiritual Secret* (Chicago: Moody, 2009), 213.

Day Two
REST ON HIS HEART

Read Hebrews 4:3–7.

1. A. What do we learn about God's *works* in Hebrews 4:3 and His *rest* in Hebrews 4:4?

Here's something interesting about the account of creation in Genesis 1-2:3. On days one through six, the description of creation always ends with the phrase "evening came, and morning followed." But when the seventh day of creation is described, it simply says, "God blessed the seventh day and made it holy, because on it he rested from all the work he had done in creation" (Genesis 2:3). There was no evening on the seventh day, which biblical scholars say indicates that God's rest is everlasting.

B. Do you make rest a priority in your life? Why or why not?

2. If God's rest is everlasting, does that mean His "work" is over and that He is idle? Read the following passages and comment on whether or not God is at work today.

Lamentations 3:22–23

Psalm 68:20–21

John 5:17

Philippians 2:13

Are these Scripture passages somehow contradicting Genesis 2:3, which depicts God's everlasting rest? No. God's rest *is* never ending. But this rest is not idleness. We can see that God has not been idle since He created the world. He has been at work, but *in a manner that is restful.* And this is the rest He invites us to share; it is available to us as well. This means that there is a way of working, of obeying, and of being productive that does not include stress, worry, or striving. Because of Jesus, it can be done. It *is* possible.

I regularly listen to (and highly recommend) a podcast called *Abiding Together,* and recently heard Sister Miriam Heidland talk about the word she felt the Lord had given her for this year: *rest.* This is what she said:

> It's not just a rest from activity; it's a rest on His heart. And in that moment, I saw that's where I'm going to spend my year. I felt Him say, "You've been working really hard. Let me just take care of you this year. Let me provide for you as your husband. Let me send people that will speak into you and help you. Let me just love you for the year." And I guess for me, someone who is type A, who is not lazy, who is thinking about all the things I need to get done, He is saying, "Those things are going to be accomplished, but *I* am going to do them. And what I need you to do is just rest on my heart." That kind of rest is the intimacy of lovers. That's not just idle time. That kind of rest is the kindling of intimacy—bridegroom to bride, where new fruit is born in that intimacy.[27]

Who knows what the year will hold, but Sister Miriam is keeping these thoughts always in her mind, accompanied by a focus on the reality that God cares for us; He is particularly concerned with a tender, humble love for us; He is solicitous for our hearts and our lives and doesn't miss a detail; and He longs to have us come to Him so He can provide for us and give us rest for our soul. This is the kind of rest that will produce fruit that lasts into eternity.

---

[27] Sister Miriam Heidland, "Our Word for the Year," February 27, 2017, *Abiding Together,* podcast, 28:57, http://abidingtogether.libsyn.com/our-word-for-the-year-002.

3. A. When do you find yourself striving, white-knuckling, or working with a harried heart? What insight do you gain from John 15:4–5 about working in a way that produces lasting fruit?

When John 15:5 says that apart from Christ we can do nothing, it doesn't mean that we can't accomplish anything at all without Him. There are countless examples of people in the world who don't acknowledge or follow Jesus and are accomplishing quite a lot. It's saying that work done apart from Christ won't produce *lasting* fruit. It won't be the kind of work that continues to matter in eternity.

B. What is something concrete that you could do to bring a more restful, God-dependent spirit into your work?

4. What word is repeated twice in Hebrews 4:7?

From God's perspective, it is still today. This means it isn't too late for us to grab hold of His promises and start to experience the more He has for us. But it also means it's up to us to decide how we are going to respond. We can't delay this offer forever. It's a call to us to stop putting off our obedience to Him and get serious about what He has asked of us.

The deep rest described in Hebrews is on offer to us today, but it requires a choice on our part, and a willingness to do things differently. It's been said that the definition of insanity is doing the same thing over and over again and expecting a different result. But isn't this exactly what we do in our stressed-out, too-busy schedules? We complain and lament, but we don't change. Maybe, that's just me. But I have a feeling I'm in good company.

It's time for us to grab hold of this gracious gift of rest—this alternative way of working—and start experiencing the abundant life Jesus has promised us.

Are you willing to kick self-reliance to the curb? Are you willing to come to Jesus, broken and weak, and ask Him to do what you cannot? Are you willing to do this *first*, not after you have exhausted every other resource? Are you willing to prove your seriousness about this by increasing your prayer time and decreasing time spent "producing"? We will only see change when we start living differently. This is what it means to cooperate with grace.

Oh, that today you would hear His voice calling you to stop striving and rest. Harden not your heart with self-reliance. There is another, gentler way to live.

Quiet your heart and enjoy His presence. . . . He's inviting you to depend on Him.

Wouldn't it be great if depending on God required no effort? It seems as if it should be easy, but the reality is, our desire to be in control is so strong that choosing dependence over self-reliance is often a moment-by-moment battle. When I get discouraged by having to learn these lessons over and over again, often the hard way, I am reminded that God is at work within me, both helping me to desire what He wants and giving me the energy to do what He asks. I must do my part, but it is not all up to me. And when I fail, which I inevitably will do, His mercies are continuously on offer. I can always begin again.

Do you need to hit the reset button? Do you feel yourself being called to a deep soul rest? Accepting the invitation will be so much easier if you stop defining your worth by what you do, and embrace the truth that you are loved, have always been loved, and can do nothing to alter that love. As author Amanda Bible Williams writes, "The rest God calls us into is restorative and real. Even when work is left undone and we throw up our hands in another ballad of surrender, He invites us to claim His redeeming love over any anxiety about our mess and feelings of failure . . . He has already assigned you more worth than you could ever create or accumulate."[28]

---

[28] Amanda Bible Williams, "True Sabbath Rest," SheReadsTruth, http://shereadstruth.com/2014/08/09/true-sabbath-rest/, accessed January 15, 2018.

Litany of Trust
by Sr. Faustina Maria Pia, Sister of Life

From the belief that
I have to earn Your love
Deliver me, Jesus.
From the fear that I am unlovable
Deliver me, Jesus.
From the false security
that I have what it takes
Deliver me, Jesus.
From the fear that trusting You
will leave me more destitute
Deliver me, Jesus.
From all suspicion of
Your words and promises
Deliver me, Jesus.
From the rebellion against
childlike dependency on You
Deliver me, Jesus.
From refusals and reluctances
in accepting Your will
Deliver me, Jesus.
From anxiety about the future
Deliver me, Jesus.
From resentment or excessive
preoccupation with the past
Deliver me, Jesus.
From restless self-seeking
in the present moment
Deliver me, Jesus.
From disbelief in Your love
and presence
Deliver me, Jesus.
From the fear of being asked
to give more than I have
Deliver me, Jesus.
From the belief that my life
has no meaning or worth
Deliver me, Jesus.
From the fear of what love demands
Deliver me, Jesus.

From discouragement
Deliver me, Jesus.
That You are continually holding me
sustaining me, loving me
Jesus, I trust in You.
That Your love goes deeper than my
sins and failings, and transforms me
Jesus, I trust in You.
That not knowing what tomorrow
brings is an invitation to lean on You
Jesus, I trust in You.
That You are with me in my suffering
Jesus, I trust in You.
That my suffering, united to Your own,
will bear fruit in this life and the next
Jesus, I trust in You.
That You will not leave me orphan,
that You are present in Your Church
Jesus, I trust in You.
That Your plan is better
than anything else
Jesus, I trust in You.
That You always hear me and in
Your goodness always respond to me
Jesus, I trust in You.
That You give me the grace to accept
forgiveness and to forgive others
Jesus, I trust in You.
That You give me all the strength
I need for what is asked
Jesus, I trust in You.
That my life is a gift
Jesus, I trust in You.
That You will teach me to trust You
Jesus, I trust in You.
That You are my Lord and my God
Jesus, I trust in You.
That I am Your beloved one
Jesus, I trust in You.[29]

---

[29] Faustina Maria Pia, Sister of Life, "Litany of Trust," Sisters of Life, http://www.sistersoflife.org/litany-of-trust.

Day Three
NOW AND THEN

Read Hebrews 4:8–11.

1. Who is the Joshua referred to in Hebrews 4:8? Skim Numbers 13:1–14:9 (you'll recognize the story) and read Joshua 1:1–3. Interesting to note: The words for "Joshua" and "Jesus" are exactly the same in Greek. The name Joshua/Jesus means "God saves."

2. A. Although Joshua faithfully led the Israelites through many conquests in the Promised Land, what was he unable to do? See Joshua 13:1.

   B. Do you wonder why the Israelites failed to fully possess what God had offered them? No doubt some complacency set in. Many were comfortable with what they had and likely thought to themselves, "Isn't this good enough? Can't I settle for this? Gaining more territory will require reentering the battle. I'll have to muster up trust in God again." Many just stayed put, but in doing so, settled for less than God's best.

   But another major issue was brewing, although it would take time for its consequences to become evident. When God commanded the Israelites to take the Promised Land, He told them to completely drive out the people living there. He warned them that if they failed to do so, they would be tempted to follow their false gods. While some effort was made to drive out the inhabitants of the Promised Land, the Israelites failed to obey completely in this regard. They tried, but their obedience was halfhearted. What was the result? See Judges 2:7–14.

C. What is the application for our own lives? If we do not obey *all the way*, if we settle for mediocrity, there will be consequences. God will not remove His love from us—it is unconditional and doesn't depend on us in any way—but we will not experience His best. The abundant life we were created for? We will forfeit that if our obedience is halfhearted. Is there an area of your life where your obedience is slow or halfhearted? What can you do today to obey straightaway, all the way?

3. According to Hebrews 4:9, what still remains for the people of God?

Although the Israelites did enter the Promised Land, they were not able to experience all that God desired for them. Because of their disobedience, Joshua was unable to lead them to perfect rest. But that is not the end of the story, according to Hebrews 4:9. The new and greater Joshua, Jesus, is now able to do what Joshua could not. Despite the fact that we are just as disobedient as the Israelites, Jesus saves so completely that we can experience perfect Sabbath rest.

4. A. How is Sabbath rest described in Hebrews 4:10?

B. What insight do you gain into how we can "rest from our works" from Ephesians 2:10, Philippians 2:13, and Matthew 11:28–30?

The work we are called by God to do is never to be destructively hard. That is not doing the Lord's work the Lord's way. What would change if we just asked God for our work to be an outpouring of His abundant life within us, instead of working to do things perfectly or to secure our reputations? And could it be that one of the reasons we are feeling heavily laden is because the tasks we are performing are not things that God has called us to do? Or that we are feeling responsible for the results, when all He has asked is that we be faithful, not perfect?

C. Look at the work that fills your day, paying special attention to work that is causing you stress. Are you striving to fill a need? Is there something within you that doubts God can fill that need, that thinks He requires your help (even if that help is currently self-destructive on some level)? Do you trust that God sees the problem as clearly as you do and is working on a solution, even now? Can you write a prayer to the Holy Spirit asking Him to reveal to you any self-sufficiency that could become God dependency instead?

5. What are we told to do in Hebrews 4:11?

At first glance, this can seem confusing. Weren't we just told to lay our burden down and depend on God? But now we need to strive to rest? A deeper understanding of the word *strive* can be helpful here. According to *Strong's Exhaustive Concordance*, the verb translated "strive" means "to use speed . . . to make effort, be prompt . . . be diligent . . . endeavor."[30] This is the opposite of a spirit of complacency or a lack of concern. It's a *prompt* response to God's invitation to rest in Him. It's a call to contend against the human tendency to want to save ourselves through our own efforts. We are being reminded that depending totally on God isn't just going to happen because it sounds like a good idea. It will take effort on our part to choose to live differently.

Sometimes it will mean saying no or letting things go that everyone around you insists are important. It's a choice to move against the current. It's allowing the rhythm of your life to be dictated by your Creator instead of by your friends and family. If we expect the full reward of a life well lived to be experienced here on earth, we'll find it really hard to live in this countercultural way. A *heavenly perspective* is what makes all the difference.

Quiet your heart and enjoy His presence. . . . Catch a glimpse of heaven.

We'll experience rest in our daily lives to the degree that we trust in God. If our trust is wholehearted, we'll experience peace and rest. If we question God's goodness or ability to help us, we'll be inwardly agitated. It all boils down to trust.

---

[30] *Strong's Exhaustive Concordance*, s.v. "spoudazó," Bible Hub, http://biblehub.com/strongs/greek/4704.htm.

There's also a future rest, one we will experience in heaven. But we'd be wrong if we pictured eternity as an infinite calendar of non-activity. We know from Genesis that God rested on the seventh day, and that His rest is never ending. Yet He continues to be active—protecting us, sending us grace, and executing justice, among other things. We will rest in heaven from trials, toil, and sadness, but our days will be full and satisfying. The daily grind will be replaced by joyful service and unhindered worship, all offered for God's glory. It will not be boring; it will be deeply fulfilling and satisfying.

It makes me think about the times in my life when my service for God and worship of Him has been pure in motive, and I have felt the Holy Spirit course within me, doing more through me than I could ever do in my own strength. This rush of being used by God for His purposes is one of the most amazing things I have ever experienced. When we are fully alive in our spiritual gifts and are doing it for God's glory, we are filled with a joy like no other. If that is a taste of what heaven is like, then I can't wait.

"Walk with your feet on earth, but in your heart be in heaven." —Saint John Bosco

Day Four
SWEET SURGERY

"God's word is not a transient and evanescent word which when uttered is immediately diffused through the air and perishes, but it is a permanent word, not carried off, not dispersed, not diffused, but sustaining and binding together all things." —Lefèvre d'Étaples

Read Hebrews 4:12–13.

1. How is the Word of God described in Hebrews 4:12?

2. The Word of God is living and effective. What additional insights into these qualities do you see from Isaiah 55:10–11 and 1 Peter 1:23–24?

3. In reflecting on the role the Word of God should have in our lives, Pope Benedict XVI emphasized the importance of approaching it as a solution to our problems, a place to go with our questions, a way to broaden our values, and the fulfillment of our aspirations.[31]

The Word of God, also known as the sword of the Spirit (Ephesians 6:17), intersects our lives and cuts through our justifications and defenses. There's nothing like it if we want to experience true inner transformation. As theologian F. F. Bruce says, God's Word "diagnoses the condition of the human heart, saying, 'Thou ailest here, and here'; it brings blessing to those who receive it in faith and pronounces judgment on those who disregard it."[32]

A. How would you diagnose the state of your heart? Where is your heart ailing? You might want to ask the Holy Spirit to give you His insight—He sees into the depths of your soul.

B. Are you able to remember the last time a passage you read in Scripture pierced your heart, convicting you of something that needed to change? Did you receive that word in faith or disregard it?

Sometimes we become frustrated because God appears to be silent about something that concerns us. "Why won't He give some direction or fix the problem?" we wonder. Could it be that God has already given some direction, but we have chosen to ignore it?

In my own life, I have found that when God asks me to do something and I ignore Him, He allows me to sit in the mess until I obey the last thing He told me. When I find myself in the same mess repeatedly, His Word gently reminds me that He has shown me how to break this pattern, but I have ignored His direction.

We can receive God's Word in faith or disregard it. One response leads to restoration; the other, to being stuck in sinful patterns. It may be uncomfortable to allow the Word of God to pierce our hearts, but His purpose is always to bring us to a place of

---

[31] Benedict XVI, *The Word of the Lord (Verbum Domini)*, (Boston: Pauline Books and Media, 2010), 38.

[32] F. F. Bruce, *The Epistle to the Hebrews* (Grand Rapids, MI: William B. Eerdmans, 1990), 111.

greater healing. This is the sweet surgery of the God's Word. Whether that purpose is fulfilled depends on our response.

4. According to Saint James, God's Word acts as a mirror, revealing who and what we really are. How does Saint James say we should respond to the Word of God? How does he describe it? What will happen if we respond to it in the right way? See James 1:22–24.

5. What does Hebrews 4:13 say about our ability to hide from God?

6. Are you willing to make a commitment to allow Scripture to penetrate your heart on a daily basis? What decisions do you need to make to fulfill that commitment? What is the best time of day and place for you to do this?

Quiet your heart and enjoy His presence. . . . Allow His Word to perform sweet surgery on your heart.

May we never forget that the doubled-edged sword of the Spirit is an instrument of divine grace. We expose our hearts to the tender lover of our souls. He will never take advantage of us or condemn us. He diagnoses us and heals us instead. God's Word is living and effective. It sustains and regenerates us. As Jesus said, "The words that I have spoken to you are spirit and life" (John 6:63).

Dear Lord,

I pray that the sharp sword of the Spirit would penetrate any hardness in my heart. Cut away my justifications and excuses. Slice through my false self so I see myself as You do. May I have the wisdom and perspective to recognize that "incisions" made by Your Word are an act of love. Although conviction might feel painful in the moment, may I see it as a revelation of truth that ultimately brings healing, not harm.
Amen.

Day Five
THE THRONE OF GRACE

Read Hebrews 4:14–16.

Note: Throughout Hebrews, the author continually shows his readers that Jesus is superior. So far, he has shown that Jesus is superior to angels and to Moses. From Hebrews 4:14–10:18, he will show that Jesus is superior to the Old Testament high priest Aaron.

Here comes the comfort. As we get to know Jesus as our high priest, we will see that there is no one more compassionate, qualified, or effective. He is the One who makes it possible for us to approach the throne of God.

1. A. According to Hebrews 4:14, why should we hold fast to our confession of faith?

   You might be wondering what it means for Jesus to have "passed through the heavens." This is not meant figuratively; He has physically passed through the heavens to stand in God's presence, and He has done this on our behalf.

   B. Describe the way Jesus relates to us based on Hebrews 4:15.

   C. In which area of life are you feeling weak or tempted? Can you think of a time in the life of Christ when He might have felt something similar?

2. A. According to Hebrews 4:15, in what way was Jesus' struggle with the temptation to sin *not* like our own struggles?

Before you assume that resisting temptation was easy for Jesus because He was both God and man, read the following commentary from C. S. Lewis from his book *Mere Christianity*:

> Only those who try to resist temptation know how strong it is. . . . A man who gives into temptation after five minutes simply does not know what it would have been like an hour later. That is why bad people, in one sense, know very little about badness. They have lived a sheltered life by always giving in. . . . Christ, because He was the only man who never yielded to temptation, is also the only man who knew to the full what temptation means.[33]

Jesus was and is fully God and fully man. The fact that He did not sin does not mean He didn't experience weakness and temptation. It means that He continually overcame that weakness and experienced victory over temptation.

B. What does Saint Paul have to say about the times we feel weak in the face of temptation? See 2 Corinthians 12:9.

Jesus experienced human weakness and temptation yet never gave in to sin. In doing so, He showed us that human frailty does not mean we are doomed to be stuck in sinful patterns forever. It actually leaves room for God's power to work within us and help us to resist.

C. According to CCC 2602, what does Jesus offer God the Father when He offers Himself? (Note: This is Jesus in the role of our high priest.) According to this Catechism clip, why does Jesus sympathize with our weakness?

D. Before we delve into Hebrews 4:16, let's learn a little background about the throne of God. If we don't know anything about it, we're unlikely to appreciate that we now have access to it. Read the following verses about the throne of God and record what stands out to you.

---

[33] C. S. Lewis, *Mere Christianity* (New York: Macmillan, 1952), 124–5.

Isaiah 6:1–5

Revelation 4:2–11

Suffice it to say, we would not wander up to the throne nonchalantly, figuring someone should scoot over and give us a place to sit down. Looking at the throne of God would be far more likely to cause us to fall on our knees.

3. A. Because Jesus is our high priest, how are we to approach the throne of grace? See Hebrews 4:16.

   B. What should we expect to receive at the throne of grace?

   C. The word translated "confidence" is *parrhesia* in Greek. How is that same word (*parrhesia*) described in CCC 2778?

   D. Do you feel that level of confidence in your personal relationship with God? In which specific area would you like your confidence to grow?

Quiet your heart and enjoy His presence. . . . Come boldly, with the certainty that you are loved.

Why are we able to approach the throne of grace confidently? Is it based on our merit? Do we deserve an audience with the King of kings?

No, our confidence is not based on anything we have done; it's based on the character, sacrifice, and perfection of our great high priest, who passed through the heavens and now sits at God's right hand. Because of Jesus, we can receive mercy and favor when we approach God's throne. Jesus is always there, praying for us, advocating for us, representing us to the Father.

Jesus is like us in every respect except for sin. He understands how hard life can be. This means that your tears are welcome at the throne of grace. You are not expected to bring your most shined-up version of yourself. He invites you to come as you are. He knows. He knows the pain, the hardship, the temptation, the weakness, the feeling of powerlessness. He invites you to rest at the feet of the Father at the throne of grace, not the throne of condemnation.

You are invited to come and worship your King—who is also your Father, your Abba, your Daddy. He waits to receive you, even now. He is calling you by name. Can you hear Him? He calls you . . . the beloved.

Conclusion

I thought I was going to throw up on my way to the first Walking with Purpose board meeting. Reading *Robert's Rules for Dummies* had helped me to some degree, but a boatload of self-doubt remained. The only part of forming a nonprofit board that seemed doable and appealing to me was having a board retreat. So once the paperwork was completed, I talked four friends of mine into joining me for a weekend away to see if we could get this idea off the ground. We crafted a mission statement and set the audacious goal of launching five new parish groups in the next five years. Little did we know what God had planned. We began to watch Him do "immeasurably more than all we ask or imagine" (Ephesians 3:20).

This journey of serving God through women's ministry has brought some of my life's greatest highs and some of the deepest lows. One lesson that I've learned in my years of ministry is that what we offer to the Lord does not need to be perfect to be good. In fact, when we are weak and imperfect He shows up most powerfully. We bring Him the best we've got. Sometimes it's enough; sometimes all we see is the shortfall. But when God is pursuing His beloved daughters with the gospel of grace, He is never limited by our limitations. He breaks through barriers and gives us just what we need to press on.

In hindsight, it has been during times of brokenness that I have most fully seen God's goodness and blessing being extended to me. This has been the case personally and within Walking with Purpose, and often the two experiences have been interwoven.

But in the middle of a season of disappointment or suffering, it's very hard to see the blessings. It's during times of brokenness that we are most susceptible to lies about the heart of the Father. We question His love, His goodness, His power, and His interest in us.

In his book *Life of the Beloved*, Henri Nouwen writes about the two best responses to brokenness. The first is to befriend it—to "face it squarely instead of trying to stuff our emotions or deny them. The second response is to put our brokenness under the blessing. In his words:

> This putting of our brokenness under the blessing is a precondition for befriending it. Our brokenness is often so frightening to face because we live it under the curse. Living our brokenness under the curse means that we experience our pain as a confirmation of our negative feelings about ourselves. It is like saying, "I always suspected that I was useless or worthless, and now I am sure of it because of what is happening to me." . . . When we have cursed ourselves or allowed others to curse us, it is very tempting to explain all the brokenness we experience as an expression or confirmation of this curse . . . **The great spiritual call of the Beloved Children of God is to pull their brokenness away from the shadow of the curse and put it under the light of the blessing.**[34]

As we listen to God's Word calling us to rest, I pray that we would be able to accept ourselves as the beloved in the very moments when we feel least deserving of it. I pray that Jesus would speak to our hearts, quieting the clamor of the voices that cause us confusion and doubt.

I'm moved by John Steinbeck's words, "And now that you don't have to be perfect, you can be good." When we can rest in God's grace, when our belovedness doesn't feel like it is perpetually on the line, we are free to love. Recognizing that God loves us in our brokenness frees us from the chains of perfectionism and allows us to extend that same grace to others. We can invite our loved ones to exhale and drop the mask. We can become soft places for others' hearts to land because we aren't so busy

---

[34] Henri Nouwen, *Life of the Beloved: Spiritual Living in a Secular World* (New York: Crossroad, 1992), 97.

trying to prove ourselves. The unconditional love we have received is passed on to people who are desperate for a place to belong and call home.

You are a part of a family, a sisterhood, a tribe. You are welcome as is—not the cleaned-up version of you, but the *real* one. In your weakness, in your brokenness, you are called beloved.

My Resolution

In what specific way will I apply what I have learned in this lesson?

Examples:

1. I desire to grow in confidence (straightforward simplicity, filial trust, joyous assurance, humble boldness, the certainty of being loved) in my relationship with God. To help myself to do this, I will pray the Litany of Trust by Sr. Faustina Maria Pia (Day Two) each morning.

2. On Day Four, I identified an area of my life where God has asked me to obey, and I have not responded to His Word with obedience. I will go to confession over this, to ask forgiveness and receive mercy and grace for timely help (Hebrews 4:16). Then I'll move forward in obedience.

3. Rest is hard for me. It's difficult for me to obey the commandment to keep the Sabbath holy. To grow in this area, I will take time this week to plan to rest on the Sabbath. I will begin thinking early in the week of which projects can be done ahead of time so I can use one day to take a break from my work (from specific tasks and social media), and trust that God is in control. I will replace those activities with time sitting with God in prayer and Scripture reading, and activities that truly bring delight to my soul.

My resolution:

Catechism Clips

CCC 2602 Jesus often draws apart to pray *in solitude*, on a mountain, preferably at night. He *includes all men* in his prayer, for he has taken on humanity in his incarnation, and he offers them to the Father when he offers himself. Jesus, the Word who has become flesh, shares by his human prayer in all that "his brethren" experience; he sympathizes with their weaknesses in order to free them. It was for this that the Father sent him. His words and works are the visible manifestation of his prayer in secret.

CCC 2778 This power of the Spirit who introduces us to the Lord's Prayer is expressed in the liturgies of East and of West by the beautiful, characteristically Christian expression: *parrhesia*, straightforward simplicity, filial trust, joyous assurance, humble boldness, the certainty of being loved.

Verse Study

See Appendix 3 for instructions on how to complete a verse study.

Romans 8:15

1. Verse:

2. Paraphrase:

3. Questions:

4. Cross-references:

5. Personal Application:

Lesson 7

CARRIED ON HIS HEART

Hebrews 5

Introduction

"Don't suffer in silence; the liar is counting on you to isolate." —*Shell Rioux Hurrell*

When we are in a season of suffering, we are wise to recognize that we are sitting ducks for the enemy of our soul, the greatest liar of all time, to tempt us to despair. His lies can quickly sound reasonable when we are isolated, tempting us to embrace and believe them. He weaves lies like these:

"I am all alone."
"No one understands me."
"I am powerless."
"Things will never change."

The more we know who Jesus is, the more we will be able to reject these lies and live victoriously, even as we walk through difficult circumstances. As we journey, we are accompanied by One who is committed to our spiritual health and growth. He is our high priest, Jesus.

Hebrews 5 helps us to get to know Jesus better as our high priest. It begins by pointing out the qualities that had to be true of a high priest, and then shows how Jesus had those qualities.

As the bridge between God and man, the high priest carried his fellow Israelites into God's presence. His clothing symbolized this reality. He wore a linen tunic covered by a blue robe, and then an apron called an ephod over the robe. The shoulder pieces of the ephod were embellished with onyx stones, and the names of the twelve tribes of Israel were engraved on them. Over the ephod went the breastplate. This was a tapestry that had four rows of three stones—twelve in total. Each of the twelve stones was engraved with the name of one of the tribes. The high priest literally carried the people of Israel on his shoulders and his heart as he approached God. Representing the people before the Lord, he thanked God for all the blessings given—His mercy and forgiveness especially. He then represented God to the people, reminding them of His mercy, as well as His guidelines for holiness.

What was true of the Old Testament priests is true of Jesus. He carries us within His heart and brings us into the presence of the Father. He wraps us in mercy and love, but also reminds us of the importance of obedience.

Jesus fulfilled everything required of an Old Testament high priest, and more. We'll see that He belongs to a different sort of priesthood, and this is one that we can completely rely on.

Day One
SOLIDARITY AND SYMPATHY

Read Hebrews 5:1–3.

1. How is a high priest described in Hebrews 5:1, and what is he expected to do?

2. Why was a high priest able to deal patiently with the ignorant and erring? See Hebrews 5:2.

3. A. In Hebrews 5:3, what do we learn about the sin offerings a priest made?

B. Leviticus 9:8–9 describes how the high priest, Aaron, made an offering for his own sin. Can you explain the process in your own words?

Keep this image in the back of your mind as we go through our study of Hebrews. We'll learn more about the significance of blood in later lessons.

4. A. The high priest's function was to act as a bridge, or mediator, between the people and God. Who is *our* mediator? In what way does He have the qualities of solidarity and sympathy? See 1 Timothy 2:5.

B. In what sense was the priesthood of the Old Covenant inadequate? See CCC 1540.

The fact that the high priests needed to make offerings for sin over and over again points to the insufficiency of the Old Covenant's system of atonement. The constantly repeated sacrifices could never take away sins (Hebrews 10:1–11).

When Jesus stepped in as our high priest, everything changed. While the old covenant provided no means of ritual forgiveness for sins committed willfully, Jesus atoned for *all* our sins perfectly. In the words of theologian Philip Edgcumbe Hughes:

What we, and they, needed was not a fellow loser but a winner; not one who shares our defeat but one who is able to lead us to victory; not a sinner but a savior . . . By reason of its very inadequacy, the old order awaited the appearance of the perfect and final high priest who would offer up the perfect and final sacrifice—perfect, because, not now the inadequate offering of some dumb and uncomprehending beast, it is the fully equivalent offering of his own unblemished and victorious self, as our fellow man, and final because it avails for all sin and for all eternity.[35]

Jesus didn't just face temptation; He *overcame* temptation. In doing so, He became the perfect sacrifice for sin, and purchased a completely new level of freedom for us that had never before been experienced.

5. Jesus represents us to the Father as a high priest who truly understands what it means to be human. This means that your high priest, Jesus, knows exactly what you are going through right now. When you come to Him in prayer and pour out your heart to Him, He never responds indifferently. He doesn't just sympathize; He empathizes because He knows what it is to suffer. But He doesn't listen from a position of powerlessness. While the priesthood of the Old Covenant was "unable to achieve a definitive sanctification,"[36] Jesus is able to give you exactly what you need in order to move forward with holiness, strength, and courage. You simply need to ask Him. The indwelling Holy Spirit makes all the difference. He will do within you what you cannot do on your own.

Is there an area of your life in which are you experiencing weakness or powerlessness? Record it below, and follow it with a prayer, asking Jesus, your high priest, to carry your request to the Father and infuse you with strength, courage, and power.

Dear God,

Quiet your heart and enjoy His presence. . . . He is able to do for us more than we can ask or imagine (Ephesians 3:20).

Not only can Jesus fully sympathize with our weaknesses, He is able to help us to overcome them, just as He overcame His own. But for this truth to truly benefit us, we need to be willing to move beyond desiring comfort to desiring spiritual maturity.

---

[35] P. Hughes, *A Commentary on the Epistle to the Hebrews*, 177–8.
[36] CCC 1540

We all relish the solace of being understood. Unfortunately, too many of us stop there. God's call to holiness requires us to commit to overcoming weakness and sin. He never asks us to do something He does not also equip us to accomplish.

Dear Lord,

I am so grateful that I live in a time when You don't just speak in "partial and various ways . . . through the prophets" (Hebrews 1:1). You speak directly to my heart through Your Son (Hebrews 1:2). May I never take this for granted. Please create in me the desire to "attend all the more to what [I] have heard, so that [I] may not be carried away" (Hebrews 2:1). When You call me to holiness, I want to respond with a resounding yes.

It would be so much easier if obedience to You felt comfortable, but it so rarely does. Your call to holiness often bumps up against my desire for things to be easy and pleasant. What a gift it is that as You lead me to glory, You haven't left me alone. I can always look at Jesus, who was made "perfect through suffering" (Hebrews 2:10). If Jesus suffered on the road to obedience, why do I think I should be able to avoid it?

Thank You for not leaving me without help. "Because [Jesus] himself was tested through what he suffered, he is able to help those who are being tested" (Hebrews 2:18). Jesus sympathizes with what I am going through, and then takes it a step further and helps me when I ask. I pray that instead of barreling through my days without pausing to think deeply and pray, I would "reflect on Jesus, the apostle and high priest of our confession" (Hebrews 3:1). May I "hear his voice, and harden not [my] heart" (Hebrews 3:7–8).

"[I] do not have a high priest who is unable to sympathize with [my] weaknesses, but one who has similarly been tested in every way, yet without sin. So [I pray I would] confidently approach the throne of grace to receive mercy and to find grace for timely help" (Hebrews 4:15–16).

I am grateful that You "deal patiently with the ignorant and erring" (Hebrews 5:2), and that there is grace for the countless times when my sin is not due to ignorance. Because of Jesus, there is no sin that is beyond the reach of Your mercy.

Thank You, precious Lord. Amen.

Day Two
PRIEST AND KING

Read Hebrews 5:4–6.

1. What do we learn from Hebrews 5:4 about the requirements of a high priest?

A high priest was always appointed; it was never a job someone would choose for oneself. Aaron (the brother of Moses) was the first high priest appointed by God.

2. What happened in the following Old Testament passages when a man decided to appoint himself to this type of spiritual leadership?

Numbers 16:28–33
Background: In this story, an Israelite named Korah accused Aaron and Moses of going too far, suggesting that they had set themselves over all the Israelites. In essence, Korah said, "What's so special about Aaron? Why does he get to draw extra close to God? Why is he the high priest? He's no better than me! And you, Moses, why do you get to be the one in charge?" Moses asked the Lord how to deal with this rebellion, and God asked that Aaron and Korah both take a censer and present it before Him. Those who allied themselves with Korah in the rebellion came and stood with him. Numbers 16:28–33 reveals the consequence of their actions:

1 Samuel 13:10–14
Background: In 1 Samuel 13:8, King Saul got tired of waiting for the priest and prophet Samuel to come and sacrifice the burnt offering. He took matters into his own hands and did it himself. King Saul was not appointed by God to perform the duties of a priest. What was God's response to Saul's presumption and rebellion?

2 Chronicles 26:16–21

Background: This passage describes the actions of King Uzziah. He had a good beginning and "did what was right in the Lord's sight" (2 Chronicles 26:4). Unfortunately, his end was not as good as his start:

3. Who glorified Christ, according to Hebrews 5:5 and John 8:54?

4. The readers of Hebrews would have recognized the phrase "You are my son; this day I have begotten you" as a quote from Psalm 2:7. This psalm was written to celebrate the coronation of an Israelite king and was also considered prophetic, speaking of the Messiah's coronation. Biblical scholars consider this a reference to the royal office of Christ the King.

But the purpose of Hebrews 5 was not to prove that Jesus was a king, but to prove that He was a high priest. To accept this, the readers of Hebrews would need to be convinced that He was appointed by God, rather than "taking this honor upon himself."[37] This was problematic, because priests came from the tribe of Levi, and Jesus was from the tribe of Judah.

Confirmation of Jesus as a high priest would come from Psalm 110:4, another prophetic psalm about the Messiah, quoted in Hebrews 5:6. Record it below:

5. Who was Melchizedek, according to Genesis 14:18?

---

[37] Hebrews 5:4

It's interesting that in Israelite history the offices of king and priest were always kept separate. There was a king and there were priests, but one man never held both offices. The only exception to this was Melchizedek. When Psalm 110:4 (quoted in Hebrews 5:5) says that Jesus was a "priest forever according to the order of Melchizedek," it means that the royal office and the priestly office were being united in Jesus. We'll continue to explore the importance of Melchizedek in Hebrews 7.

6. Perhaps you have gone through today's readings and found them fascinating. But it's also possible that you have wondered what this passage has to do with day-to-day life in the twenty-first century. We are promised in 2 Timothy 3:16 that "All Scripture is inspired by God and is useful for teaching, for refutation, for correction, and for training in righteousness." This passage from Hebrews is not the exception to the rule.

   As I read these verses, what strikes me is how God took care to plant seeds of prophecy hundreds of years before Christ. Things that at the time might have seemed random or senseless were actually replete with meaning and significance.

   In that same way, there are circumstances in all our lives today that not only seem senseless but also might be incredibly painful. We can't see why God is allowing them, and because we don't understand, we assume it's all going terribly wrong. But what if the very circumstances we so desperately want to change are seeds of truly significant things that God is weaving together into His overall plan? Can we just open our hearts a little bit to this possibility?

   What circumstances in your life right now do not make sense?

   Write out Jeremiah 29:11 below, and record your reflections on God's overall plan, timing, and attention to detail.

Quiet your heart and enjoy His presence. . . . Come humbly, come open, be still.

Life has a way of throwing curveballs that make us long for control and peace. All too often, we pursue those things by taking matters into our own hands. This was the choice of Korah, King Saul, and King Uzziah, and we know how that turned out.

The truth is, we are never in control. Even when we feel like we are, it's an illusion, because it is utterly temporary and could be over in an instant. Only one truly holds the world, all our circumstances, and our hearts in His hands. And the supreme controller of all is not a dictator or a tyrant. He is an adoring Father. There is nothing that touches His beloved children that has not first passed through His hands.

That truth may bring you comfort, or it may make you angry or confused. Because if everything passes through His hands, why do we experience such suffering? Is the key to our understanding this to be found in separating out what God permits and what He wills? Not according to Carmelite Father Wilfrid Stinissen:

> *There is no need to distinguish carefully between what God positively wills and what he merely permits. What he permits is also part of his universal, all-embracing will. He has foreseen it from the beginning and decided how he will use it. Everything that happens has a purpose in God's plan. He is so good that all that comes in contact with him becomes in some way good. God's goodness is contagious and even gives evil something of its own goodness.* [38]

This means that we can rest from the relentless pursuit of understanding it all. Our human nature guarantees that we will never be able to make sense of all circumstances that intersect our lives. God's thoughts are above and beyond ours. Our job is not to understand, plan it all out, or control things. Our job is to trust. Trust and release the burden. It is not yours to carry. The One equipped to carry the burden is also carrying you. Rest. Be still.

Day Three
PRAYERS AND SUPPLICATIONS

Read Hebrews 5:7.

---

[38] Wilfrid Stinissen, *Into Your Hands, Father: Abandoning Ourselves to the God Who Loves Us* (San Francisco: Ignatius Press, 1986), 16.

1. What did Jesus offer to "the one who was able to save him from death"? See Hebrews 5:7.

2. A. Luke 22:39–44 describes a critical time when Jesus offered "prayers and supplications with loud cries and tears to the one who was able to save him from death." Describe this event in the space below.

We miss a critical point if we reduce Jesus' agony in the Garden of Gethsemane to a fear of suffering His passion and then death on the cross. Most definitely, the prospect of this was horrifying. But many people throughout history have faced martyrdom with courage and a miraculous level of calm. Theologian Philip Edgcumbe Hughes asserts that to assume this was the primary concern of Jesus at this moment would not be consistent with Christ's character. He explains:

> The agony of Christ at Gethsemane was occasioned by something other and deeper than the fear of physical death; for what he faced was not simply a painful death but also judgment—the judgment of a holy God against sin, our sin . . .

> The "loud cries and tears" which accompanied Christ's supplication are to be understood, then, in relation to the indescribable darkness of the horror that he, our High Priest, was to pass through as, on the cross, he bore not only the defilement and guilt of the world's sin but also its judgment. At Gethsemane and at Calvary we see him enduring our hell so that we might be set free to enter into his heaven.[39]

B. Another way of describing what it meant for Christ to bear our judgment is found in 2 Corinthians 5:21. Write the verse out in your own words, and reflect on what it means to you that Jesus endured "our hell so that we might be set free to enter into his heaven."

---

[39] P. Hughes, *A Commentary on the Epistle to the Hebrews*, 183.

3. According to Hebrews 5:7, why was Jesus' prayer heard? Was it answered?

4. It has been said that the point of prayer is not to change God's mind, but to change our hearts and wills to come into line with what God desires. Think about Jesus in the Garden of Gethsemane. Did He say, "God, this can't be Your will. You love me. So of course You would never want me to suffer"? No. He said, "Not what I will, but what You will."

If we want to experience peace, this is the level of spiritual maturity that we should desire and be moving toward.

In which area of your life do you want to take control?

Have you asked God to remove some suffering? Is its continuing presence causing you to question His power or love?

Can you look to the example of Jesus' passion and death and accept (or wrestle with the idea) that "God makes use of evil in such a superb way and with such skill that the result is better than if there had never been evil"?[40]

---

[40] W. Stinissen, *Into Your Hands, Father: Abandoning Ourselves to the God Who Loves Us*, 15.

Quiet your heart and enjoy His presence. . . . He is listening to you.

". . . he was heard because of his reverence." (Hebrews 5:7)

Jesus was heard. You are heard. There is not a tear you shed, an ounce of pain, or even the slightest loss that God does not see and record. He hears your cry and leans into your suffering. God is never, ever indifferent to His children's needs.

We cause ourselves untold distress when we equate God hearing us and answering our prayers with Him doing what we want Him to do. Far too often, we reduce prayer to a time when we give God our wish list, which is really His to-do list. We wait to see if His love will be proven by His answers to our requests, when all the while it was proven on the cross.

If only we could fully grasp how deep the Father's love for us is, how vast and beyond measure is His care. If only we could stop judging God by our circumstances and instead wait patiently and with confident expectation for Him to reveal the way He is working all things for good.

Dear Lord,

Grant me patience to wait for Your purposes to be revealed, and humility to recognize that just because I can't see something doesn't mean You are not at work. Forgive me for the countless times I am convinced that I know best, even though my perspective is so limited.

Stinissen diagnoses our problem:

> *We often live in the past and the future at the same time, which gives us a feeling of inner division and is perhaps the main cause of our weariness. We have not surrendered our past with its guilt and painful wounds. We carry it with us like a heavy burden. Nor do we dare to surrender our future to God. We are afraid that he will take advantage of our trust. How many there are who do not dare to pray: "Do with me as you will. Whatever you do with me, I thank you. I am ready for everything. I consent to all. May only your will be done with me and with all you have created!"[41]*

Give me the courage to dare to surrender all to You. How can I be afraid that You will take advantage of my trust when You literally laid down Your life for me? May I meditate on Your "loud cries and tears" and think about how You endured my hell so I could experience heaven. May I follow the example of Saint Thérèse of Lisieux and have just a little more courage than fear to say, "I choose nothing. One option over another—they just flit across my soul. What I want is what You want. Nothing more. Nothing less. May Your will be done."

---

[41] Ibid., 62–3.

Day Four
OBEDIENCE AND SUFFERING

Read Hebrews 5:8–10.

1. According to Hebrews 5:8, how did Jesus learn obedience?

It might surprise you to read that Jesus had to *learn* obedience. When we think of Him as sinless (which we are right to do), we can mistakenly jump to the conclusion that obedience was automatic for Him. This was not the case. Jesus had to battle His weak human nature in order to make the right choices and follow God's will.

Having experienced the spiritual battle makes Jesus a tremendous advocate and help when we are finding obedience hard. Is there an area of your life where you need to learn obedience? List it here and ask Jesus to rescue you from the lure of compromise.

2. What happened when Jesus was made perfect? See Hebrews 5:9.

The word translated "perfect" can also mean "completeness" or "maturity." When Jesus learned obedience through His suffering, He went through the process of becoming fully who He already was—our selfless Savior. He resisted the constant temptation to put His own desires first, ahead of what God was asking Him to do. The supreme example of this came "when God called on him to die, [and] Jesus had to overcome the most powerful of all human instincts, toward self-preservation, in order to hear that will and do it."[42]

---

[42] Bruce, *The Epistle to the Hebrews*, 150–1.

3. If we want Jesus to be our "source of eternal salvation" (Hebrews 5:9), what must we do?

4. Obeying God means that we respond to His voice, moment by moment. So often, we don't hear Him because there is so much noise around us. It's up to us to quiet down and create an environment where we can start to discern what He is calling us to do. What circumstances allow you to get quiet and listen to God? Is there a change you can make in your schedule to increase the likelihood that you can hear His voice each day?

5. What did God declare Jesus to be in Hebrews 5:10?

Why is this point repeated in Hebrews 5? For now, it's sufficient to say that the author of Hebrews wanted to make sure his readers knew that being our high priest was not an honor that Jesus "snatched"—it had been God's plan all along. But Jesus was a priest from a different order; He was the same kind of priest as Melchizedek. A deeper discussion of this is postponed until Hebrews 7, and Hebrews 5:11 says it's difficult to explain. It's also difficult to understand, but we'll grow in our understanding as we move through the chapters.

Quiet your heart and enjoy His presence. . . . Let Him refine and mature you.

No one wants to be considered immature, but the path to maturity is a tough one that many people avoid. All too often, instead of pressing on when spiritual perseverance is required, we take a detour to comfort.

Jesus understands this temptation and has not left us to battle it alone. He runs by our side, encouraging us to stay steadfast and faithful to God. He reminds us that anything we suffer or give up on the way will ultimately be worth it.

His time on earth proved the truth of this equation:

Suffering + Obedience = Maturity

When we accept suffering as integral to spiritual growth instead of fighting against it, we, too, are polished and refined. We become truly and fully who we are meant to be. What allows us to live in this way? A spirit of self-abandonment, rooted in the knowledge that we are deeply and extravagantly loved by One who vigilantly watches over us.

May God "grant you in accord with the riches of his glory to be strengthened with power through his Spirit in the inner self, and that Christ may dwell in your hearts through faith; that you, rooted and grounded in love, may have strength to comprehend with all the holy ones what is the breadth and length and height and depth, and to know the love of Christ that surpasses knowledge, so that you may be filled with all the fullness of God" (Ephesians 3:16–19).

Day Five
ARRESTED DEVELOPMENT

Read Hebrews 5:11–14.

1. How are the readers of Hebrews described in 5:11–13?

Those of us who love Saint Thérèse of Lisieux and her little way of spiritual childhood might be confused by these words. We might ask, "Isn't it good to be a spiritual child?" It's important to clarify that being child*like* and being child*ish* are two very different things. When we are childlike, we are abandoned to God's will and full of trust in Him. When we are childish, we are attuned to our own desires and want our own way.

2. These verses no doubt hit readers like cold water thrown in their faces. They were written not to make anyone feel bad, but instead to motivate the Hebrews to change. Will they do the same in our lives? Read Saint Paul's words addressing the same issue in 1 Corinthians 1:3–4. What does he list as symptoms of arrested spiritual development?

It's important to note that the author of Hebrews is not saying that his readers have poor intellectual development or are incapable of spiritual maturity. He is pointing out that they are spiritually lazy. They have all that is needed to display grown-up Christianity, but they are choosing to coast along in immaturity instead.

3. According to Hebrews 5:14, what does the author of Hebrews want to see in his readers?

Having our "faculties trained by practice to discern good and evil" is not just about the ability to make good moral choices. It also challenges us to understand what is good and what is evil doctrine. We do this by studying the Word of God and Church teachings. This means we have put in the time to understand all of the Bible, not just our favorite verses of comfort. It requires digging in and studying the whys behind certain Church teachings that we find problematic. Instead of encountering something confusing and then walking away, we lean in and ask questions, displaying a humble, teachable spirit.

4. Is there a specific Church teaching that you would like to understand better? In what way would you like to grow in spiritual maturity?

5. Do you know the elementary teachings of Christ well enough to help others?

By writing "you should be teachers by this time," the author of Hebrews is not saying every single follower of Christ should be in a classroom or behind a podium. Nor is he suggesting that you need to be able to answer every objection, question, or doubt that people around you might have. He is saying there are some elementary teachings we should be able to articulate. We are to "Always be ready to give an explanation to anyone who asks [us] for a reason for [our] hope" (1 Peter 3:15).

(Note: Are you wondering where to begin? *Beloved*, our six-week young adult study, provides a great overview of the basics—the ABC's of our faith. Is there someone who is asking you to explain your faith and isn't ready for a full-year Bible study such as *Opening Your Heart?* Going through *Beloved* together might be a great way to answer her questions.)

Quiet your heart and enjoy His presence. . . . Open your ears and heart to His wisdom.

"The law of the Lord is his joy; and on his law he meditates day and night. He is like a tree planted near streams of water, that yields its fruit in season; its leaves never wither; whatever he does prospers." (Psalm 1:2–3)

We have been promised in 1 Corinthians 2:16 that we have the mind of Christ. What an astounding statement. This means that if we remain in a state of spiritual babyhood, content with milk when we should have moved on to meat, we are missing out on a treasure trove of wisdom and perspective that could have been ours. It's up to us. Jesus stands at the ready, wanting to fill our minds and hearts with knowledge of His will, instructions about how we are to live, and truths that begin to make sense of the big issues in life that can be so perplexing. But Jesus is a gentleman, and He will never force Himself on us.

We open ourselves up to Him when we are self-disciplined and do the work of meditating on His words, day and night. When we saturate our minds with His truth and His voice (found in the Bible) we begin to think like Him. At the very least, we grow in our ability to recognize God's voice in the midst of a cacophony of other noises.

This means we shouldn't be content with just hearing the truth at Mass once a week. We need to engage with what we hear, wrestle with it, and internalize it. We need to endeavor to maintain it by answering the call to "not conform [ourselves] to this age but be transformed by the renewal of [our] mind[s], that [we] may discern what is the will of God, what is good and pleasing and perfect" (Romans 12:2).

If we want to be mature women of God, we won't stop there. Once we "discern what is the will of God," we'll ask Him for the strength to follow it.

If you want to abandon yourself fully to the will of God, this prayer by Brother Charles of Jesus may give you words to express that desire:

> *Father,*
> *I abandon myself*
> *Into Your hands;*
> *Do with me what You will.*
> *For whatever You may do I thank You.*
>
> *I am ready for all,*
> *I accept all.*
>
> *Let only Your will be done in me*
> *As in all Your creatures.*
> *I wish no more than this, O Lord.*
>
> *Into Your hands I commend my soul.*
> *I offer it to You*
> *With all the love of my heart.*
> *For I love You, my God,*
> *And so need to give myself,*
> *To surrender myself*
> *Into Your hands,*
> *Without reserve,*
> *And with boundless confidence,*
> *For You are my Father.*[43]
>
> *—Brother Charles of Jesus*

---

[43] Charles de Foucauld, "Prayer of Abandonment," https://www.ewtn.com/devotionals/prayers/Abandonment.htm.

Conclusion

Even as the author of Hebrews challenged his readers to press on to maturity, he recognized all that they were up against. Obedience to God was sure to cause them suffering, which could quite likely become acute. At the very least, they would be marginalized and persecuted.

While he acknowledged the hardship, he didn't give them an easy way out. Instead he shared the grand narrative, bit by bit, reminding them that life is a journey. He traveled back to the Old Testament, sharing stories and truths that assured them God was in control and has always had a plan. Now was not an exception. They were running a marathon, not a sprint. There would be seasons of suffering, weariness, and feeling alone on that journey. He acknowledged this, but never suggested that they quit.

His words to them are God's words to us. We, too, can find that the call to obedience feels terribly hard in the midst of our particular circumstances. Instead of being told to quit, we're challenged to look to Jesus, "the author and perfecter of our faith" (Hebrews 12:2).

We are to fix our eyes on Jesus, our high priest who fights for us. He doesn't reside far away, dressed in His liturgical robes, telling us to get our act together. He is a high priest who draws near, who enters into our suffering. He stoops down and joins us on the journey.

Sometimes the journey feels like a battlefield. This image brings to mind the book *The Return of the King*, by J. R. R. Tolkien. In a particularly poignant part, Frodo and Sam, two hobbits, climb up Mount Doom carrying the ring of power. It is up to them to save Middle Earth from the forces of evil by throwing the ring into the fire of the mountain, destroying it. Frodo alone must carry the ring, and the weight of this burden feels unbearable.

The climb is treacherous, their water and food are all but gone, and terrors surround them. The last stage of their journey has come, and the torment is greater than anything they have ever faced. They are in pain, parched, and dizzy. Yet they stagger on.

But eventually the burden of the ring becomes too much for Frodo and he falls. All he can do is groan. In that moment, Sam looks at his friend and reminds himself of his promise to carry Frodo, even if it breaks his back.

"Come, Mr. Frodo!" he cried. "I can't carry it for you, but I can carry you and it as well. So up you get! Come on, Mr. Frodo dear! Sam will give you a ride. Just tell him where to go, and he'll go."

As Frodo clung upon his back, arms loosely about his neck, legs clasped firmly under his arms, Sam staggered to his feet; and then to his amazement he felt the burden light. He had feared that he would have barely strength to lift his master . . . and . . . the dreadful dragging weight of the accursed Ring. But it was not so. Whether because Frodo was so worn by his long pains . . . , or because some gift of final strength was given to him, Sam lifted Frodo with no more difficulty than if he were carrying a hobbit-child pig-a-back . . . He took a deep breath and started off. . . .

"Thank you, Sam," [Frodo] said in a cracked whisper. "How far is there to go?"

"I don't know," said Sam, "because I don't know where we're going."

He looked back, and then he looked up; and he was amazed to see how far his last effort had brought him. The Mountain . . . had looked taller than it was . . . The tumbled shoulders of its great base rose for maybe three thousand feet above the plain, and above them was reared half as high again its tall central cone . . . But already Sam was more than half way up the base . . . As he looked up he would have given a shout, if his parched throat had allowed him; for . . . above him he saw plainly a path . . .

Sam . . . guessed that if he could just struggle on a just a little way further up, they would strike this path. A gleam of hope returned to him. . . .[44]

In those times when the burdens of life become too much for us, Jesus crouches down and invites us to crawl into His arms, close to His heart. He doesn't always take the burdens away; they still remain. But He lifts both us and our burdens, and we are able to continue on, to persevere. As we surrender our will to Him, we progress forward in maturity. We move closer to our destiny of peace and joy in heaven.

Our great high priest passed through the heavens (Hebrews 4:14), and then He came back to rescue us. We do not journey up the mountain to heaven on our own. He accompanies us, He carries us, He absorbs into Himself all that is unbearable, and then redeems it. Look to Jesus. Cling to your high priest. He carries you on His heart.

---

[44] J. R. R. Tolkien, *The Return of the King* (New York: Houghton Mifflin Harcourt, 1994), 919–20.

My Resolution

In what specific way will I apply what I have learned in this lesson?

Examples:

1. Day One, I identified an area of my life where I feel powerless. To increase my faith, I will memorize Ephesians 3:20, bearing in mind that Jesus is my high priest and He lives to intercede for me. He wants me to remember the truth of Ephesians 3:20—that the same power within me is the power that raised Him from the dead.

   "Now to Him who is able to do immeasurably more than all we ask or imagine, according to his power that is at work within us, to him be glory!" (Ephesians 3:20)

2. Day Two, I identified some circumstances in my life that don't make sense. Instead of dwelling on them, I will turn my attention daily to the truth of Jeremiah 29:11: "For I know well the plans I have in mind for you—plans for your welfare and not for woe, so as to give you a future of hope."

3. Day Five, I recognized a specific area where I need to grow in spiritual maturity. I will identify a specific action I can take in order to be stretched, and will write that action on my calendar so I don't forget to do it. I will consider this a divine appointment, one I should give highest priority and not ignore.

My resolution:

Catechism Clips

CCC 1540 Instituted to proclaim the Word of God and to restore communion with God by sacrifices and prayer, this priesthood nevertheless remains powerless to bring about salvation, needing to repeat its sacrifices ceaselessly and being unable to achieve a definitive sanctification, which only the sacrifice of Christ would accomplish.

Verse Study

See Appendix 3 for instructions on how to complete a verse study.

Philippians 1:9–10

1. Verse:

2. Paraphrase:

3. Questions:

4. Cross-references:

5. Personal Application:

Lesson 8

ANCHOR FOR OUR SOUL

Hebrews 6

Introduction

"I am not afraid of my seasons. My seasons bring about my heart; my seasons keep telling my story over and over again. And if you could see my heart, you would see all the moments surrounding it when I gave in to the process of growth." —Melissa Helser

I wonder how you look at the seasons of your life. Do you look back with regret, sadness, joy, or longing? How about your present season? Which words would you use to describe it?

The words of Melissa Helser resonate with me as I reflect on the seasons of my life. Unquestionably, it's been the hardest seasons that have revealed my heart the most. Tough circumstances have brought my attention to places in my heart that have been wounded. While the enemy desired to exploit those wounds, certain that the current difficult circumstances would cause me to question God's goodness, my gentle Father used the opportunity when He had my attention to show me where He wanted to bring healing.

This process of maturing, of growing up, hasn't been easy, but as I look back, I can see that I've been in the midst of stormy seas when my heart has been rescued and revealed. I've experienced deep growth on the soul level. Knowing this to be true gives me hope when my circumstances feel less than ideal.

We're going to look at the importance of hope as an anchor for the soul, although the verses about it come at the end of our passage. It's going to take a little time to build a foundation for hope. We'll look at the basic truths we should embrace and the unchangeable nature of God's promises. It's my desire that as we move through this lesson, we would begin to define our seasons of life with words and thoughts that spring from hope. I pray that instead of looking at difficulties as a source of sorrow, we would see them as opportunities for growth.

With each trial, we are offered a choice. We can lean into despair, allow doubt to rain on our soul, and listen to the whispers that say we do not belong and are unwanted. This will cause us to feel untethered and out of control. Or we can think of Jesus' nail-scarred hands, and how it was in the tearing, the breaking, and the wounding that victory was won. He invites us to touch His wounds, then look in His eyes. Jesus looks into our hearts and tenderly whispers, "I know. I have been there. Your hurt, it is real. I see it. But there is more. Hold on to hope. Hold on to me. I bring resurrection and restoration out of the dead and broken places. That is where I do my finest work. Lean in, not to despair, but into my promises. I will never leave you. I will never forsake you." May we be anchored in that hope, grounded and secure.

Day One
THE BASICS

Read Hebrews 6:1–3.

1. A. What is the author of Hebrews challenging us to do, according to Hebrews 6:1?

The Christian life is a journey best lived moving *forward*. We might think we can just coast for a while, but the truth is, coasting usually means we slide backward. Moving forward is another way to describe the process of maturing as a Christian. It means we grasp hold of the basics and then build on them.

B. Reflect on your spiritual life a year ago. Have you been making progress? Are there areas of your life where you can see victory and a deeper level of surrender?

Progressing forward doesn't mean we tackle a sin and then never struggle with it again. Nor does it mean things that have unsettled or derailed us in the past no longer affect us or cause us to lose our footing. We still sometimes fall and get triggered when we're tempted. But are we getting back up, confessing, going to

God for renewed strength, and getting back into the race? That's the goal—not perfection, but progress. Your seasons—of both failure and victory—are bringing about your heart. Resist the temptation to see yourself as God's workhorse. Instead, remember that you are the beloved. God desires that we grow up and mature, not because He is measuring us against a checklist, but because He simply wants to see us act like who we really are—His precious and holy daughters.

2. The author of Hebrews describes the six "basic teachings about Christ" that his readers should have under their belt by now. List these foundational topics.

3. A. The first two basic teachings (repentance from dead works and faith in God) are the two steps of conversion. According to CCC 1430, "Jesus' call to conversion . . . does not aim first at outward works . . . but at the conversion of the heart, interior conversion." This interior repentance or conversion of heart is explained in CCC 1431. Describe it, specifically noting what we turn *toward* and what we turn *from*. What will we desire if we experience true interior repentance?

   B. When we turn from our sin and repent (step one of conversion), we then turn toward God in faith (step two). We don't place our faith in our own ability to save ourselves; we place it in God's work within us.

   Does that mean our good works don't matter? See James 2:17

Our good works matter, but they do not earn God's approval or our salvation. The only one to be credited with our salvation is God. "Conversion is first of all a work of the grace of God who makes our hearts return to him . . . God gives us the strength to begin anew" (CCC 1432).

C. Read Appendix 4, "Conversion of Heart." Is this something you have experienced? If so, describe it here. If not, what do you think is holding you back?

4. A. The next two basic teachings (baptism and laying on of hands) "are sacramental signs through which grace is given."[45] The phrase "laying on of hands" describes the importance of being infused with the Holy Spirit.

What difference does it make when we are infused with the Holy Spirit?

John 14:16–17

Acts 1:8

Romans 5:5

2 Corinthians 3:17

B. It's been said that the Holy Spirit is the secret of the Christian life. Without the indwelling Holy Spirit, we are stuck on the treadmill of performance. If we try to live a holy life in our own strength, we will not only fail, we will become discouraged and weary in the process. A good understanding of what the Holy Spirit offers us is critical, but just as important is our openness to Him. We need the basic teachings, but even more, we need to open up our hearts and invite the Holy Spirit to have His way with us. He will not force Himself on us. The promised freedom that His presence brings is offered to us, but God will never coerce us into accepting it. If you are a Christian, the Holy Spirit is within you. But if you want to experience the fullness of His work in your life, then you need to fan His presence into flame. How do we do this? We invite Him in. We ask Him to fill us. We pray, "Less of me, and more of you!"

---

[45] Healy, *Hebrews*, 116.

Have you invited the Holy Spirit to fill you? Can you write a prayer to Him now, welcoming Him into your life, asking Him to fill you with His love, joy, peace, patience, kindness, goodness, gentleness, faithfulness, and self-control (Galatians 5:22–23)?

5. The final two basic things mentioned refer to "the last things"—the theological topics that have to do with death and what happens to our soul when we die. What are those remaining "basics" that we are supposed to have under our belt?

What do the following passages teach us about "the last things"?

John 11:25

2 Corinthians 5:10

Quiet your heart and enjoy His presence. . . . Come and sit at His feet.

"Less activity . . . more sitting at my feet." These are the words God impressed on my heart when I asked Him for guidance about what I could be doing for Him. I was reminded that He is less interested in my outward accomplishments—even those done "for Him"—and simply desires that I take up the posture of a disciple with a rabbi. This was Mary's choice in the story of Mary and Martha (Luke 10:38–42). When Martha was doing all the work and Mary simply sat and listened to Jesus, Martha asked Jesus to tell Mary to come help. What was Jesus' reply? "Martha, Martha, you are anxious and worried about many things. There is need of only one thing. Mary has chosen the better part and it will not be taken from her" (Luke 10:41–42).

I don't know about you, but when I hear the author of Hebrews say that those six topics are "the basics," I can feel a little overwhelmed, anxious, and worried. Do I know enough? We can become overwhelmed with regret for starting to explore our faith too late. Discouragement can quickly set in.

This isn't how Jesus wants us to feel. He invites us to come and sit at His feet. He promises to teach us, at a pace we can handle. He gives us the gift of the Holy Spirit, and according to John 14:26, "The Advocate, the Holy Spirit that the Father will send in [Jesus'] name—he will teach you everything and remind you of all that [Jesus] told you." Jesus goes on to say, "Peace I leave with you; my peace I give to you. Not as the world gives do I give it to you. Do not let your hearts be troubled or afraid" (John 14:27).

Listen to His voice. He invites you to sit and rest awhile. He is whispering your name, "Beloved." Keep your heart open to Him and you will learn. He will teach you the basics and more, step by step. Let the lover of your soul lead you, and you will surely progress forward. "Forgetting what lies behind but straining forward to what lies ahead, continue [your] pursuit toward the goal, the prize of God's upward calling, in Christ Jesus" (Philippians 3:13–14).

Day Two
FALLING AWAY

Read Hebrews 6:4–8.

This section of Scripture contains a strong warning. As we read these verses, let's avoid the temptation to think of them in reference to people we know. Reading them could cause us to feel panic about people we know and love who are not in a relationship with God. Resist this temptation. As you study, ask the Holy Spirit to speak to *you* about *you*. Leave the eternal destiny of those you love in the hands of Jesus. Ask Him to convict you of anything that needs correction, confess it if something comes up, and then rest in His grace.

1. These verses contain a warning about falling away from the faith. The official word for this is *apostasy*. How is apostasy defined according to CCC 2089?

2. According to Hebrews 6:4–5, a person experiences five gifts if he or she is a committed Christian. List them here.

3. A. "Those who have once been enlightened" describes the process of going from darkness to light. What do you learn from 1 Peter 2:9 about that gift?

B. Having "tasted the heavenly gift" refers to all our blessings in Christ. Some of these blessings are listed in Ephesians 1:18–19. What are they?

When the author of Hebrews writes about "tasting" the heavenly gift, it should make us think of something being *experienced* rather than *heard about*. God wants us to experience Him intersecting our day-to-day lives, bringing peace where there is strife, direction where there is confusion, and love where there is rejection. His desire is for us to set out on a spiritual journey that travels from our head to our heart.

C. Christians receive the gift of sharing in the Holy Spirit. He dwells within us (unlike in the Old Testament, when He filled someone for a specific purpose, for a specific time). Building on what we learned about the Holy Spirit in Day One of this lesson, read Ephesians 3:16–19 for insight into what we should be experiencing if we are sharing in the Holy Spirit.

D. Committed Christians should also be experiencing how "the good word of God" tastes and satisfies us. The more we study Scripture, the more we'll agree with the psalmist who described God's Word as "more desirable than gold, than a hoard of purest gold, sweeter also than honey or drippings from the comb" (Psalm 19:11). We also are to taste "the powers of the age to come" (Hebrews 6:5). This refers to miracles, healings, and inner transformation, all of which point to the power of the Holy Spirit unleashed in our world.

In what area of your life do you need to see God's power at work? Are you waiting for a miracle? List your need here:

We long for "the powers of the age to come"—for miracles, healings, and inner transformation of our hearts. If we have faith, we will witness some of this happening here on earth. Some of our pleas for a miracle will be answered on the other side of eternity. Even if it appears that He isn't going to intervene, God always comes through for us. Don't give up. But at the same time, let's hold on to humility, recognizing that we don't have all the facts and that God's answer of "no" or "wait" is always based on what will be to our greatest benefit in the end.

4. A. Christians experience the gift of enlightenment, taste the heavenly gift, share in the Holy Spirit, and taste the Word of God and the powers of the age to come. The warning issued in Hebrews 6:4–6 is aimed at people who have had this experience of the Christian life. After truly experiencing these gifts, if a person then rejects salvation, it is very hard for them to journey back. Mary Healy describes it like this:

> Whatever led them to make that choice against Christ is psychologically and spiritually very difficult to reverse. Thus the author of Hebrews warns his readers that if they allow themselves to fall away, there is a good chance they will never return for salvation.[46]

I truly appreciate the recognition that when a choice is made to reject Christ, it's *psychologically* very difficult to reverse. The choice to reject Christ can come out of an experience of emotional wounding or trauma. In those times when we have been hurt, we are especially susceptible to lies about God the Father. The enemy of our soul knows this, and tempts us to equate what we are feeling about God with what is true about Him. We may *feel* abandoned by Him; the enemy whispers that we *are* abandoned by Him. We may *feel* rejected by Him; the enemy whispers that we *are* rejected. We may *feel* God is impossible to please; the enemy whispers that we should give up because He *is* impossible to please.

---

[46] Ibid., 121.

Is there a lie that you believe about God the Father right now?

B. To avoid discouragement, record Mark 10:27 below.

Nothing is impossible for God. No person is beyond the reach of His mercy. That being said, when a person has truly tasted the Christian life and then rejected it, it's going to be extremely difficult for a loved one to reach out and convince him or her to return to God. That is the Holy Spirit's work; only the Spirit can travel into the deepest parts of a person's soul to bring the needed healing to create openness to God.

So when our loved ones have walked away from God, do we just give up? No. What do we do?

We pray.

We love sacrificially.

We battle on our knees, and with our hands and hearts, instead of relying on our words.

We cling to the truth of 2 Peter 3:9, that God is patient and does not wish "that any should perish but that all should come to repentance."

Quiet your heart and enjoy His presence. . . . Let His Spirit pour over you.

"Ground that has absorbed the rain falling upon it repeatedly and brings forth crops useful to those for whom it is cultivated receives a blessing from God." (Hebrews 6:7)

God rains down blessings on each one of His children. What kind of fruit those blessings produce has everything to do with how we absorb what He gives us. The ground of our hearts gets hardened by sin, bitterness, and unforgiveness. Lies of the enemy can convince us that the problem must lie with God and not with us, so we fail to repent.

What is the opposite of soil that is packed and hardened? It's soil that has been broken up. This paints a picture of what can happen with a human heart. We tend to point to things that break our hearts as terrible and to be avoided at all costs. But what if God's plan is for those very things to make our hearts more supple and tender? Evil never originates with God, but He is so loving that when something terrible passes through His hand, it is transformed into an instrument for good. For this to occur in our hearts, however, we need to cooperate. We need to choose to absorb the water. We need to invite the Holy Spirit to pour over our broken and raw places.

"Let us know, let us strive to know the Lord; as certain as the dawn is his coming. He will come to us like the rain, like spring rain that waters the earth." (Hosea 6:3)

He will always come. Our part is to strive to know Him, to know His heart, to reject the lies and embrace the truth of His goodness, mercy, and protection. May we know Him as our good, good Father.

Day Three
HIDDEN BUT FAITHFUL

Read Hebrews 6:9–12.

1. What is the author of Hebrews sure of, and why? See Hebrews 6:9–10.

2. A. The Hebrews' faith had been proven by their works. What had they done? See Hebrews 10:33–34.

I wonder how many times they served and sacrificed while wondering if it was making any difference. Do you think they might have felt discouraged at times when their sacrificial love did not result in life getting easier? These verses remind us that God *does* reward good deeds—He sees what is done in secret and remembers. This truth was spoken centuries earlier by the prophet Daniel. "You remembered me, O God," said Daniel. "You have not forsaken those who love you" (Daniel 14:38).

B. In what area of your life are you offering "hidden" service? Is there someone serving you in this way, someone easy to overlook? What could you do to acknowledge that service?

C. When you quietly care for the people God places in your path, how does He see your service? See Matthew 25:37–40.

3. Genuine faith results in visible fruit. What does Jesus say about this in Matthew 7:16–21?

True salvation will be seen by both inner conversion (see Day One) and outward actions. Both are needed.

4. A. When the author of Hebrews reflects on his readers' faith in action, what does he want to see? See Hebrews 6:11.

B. What does 2 Timothy 4:6–8 teach us about finishing well?

C. What is the secret to finishing the race well? Is it self-reliance? Pulling ourselves up by our bootstraps? See the following advice from Saint Paul for insight.

1 Corinthians 15:10

2 Corinthians 1:9

2 Corinthians 12:9–10

5. A. What quality are we to avoid, according to Hebrews 6:12?

Another word for sluggishness is *sloth*, one of the seven deadly sins. Saint Thomas Aquinas defined *sloth* as "sorrow in regard to spiritual good." Rather than feeling excitement over the things of God, you feel droopy and disinterested. In the Middle Ages, sloth was called "the noon day devil." This is a description of the dip you feel in the day, that time when you want a nap and to binge-watch something on your computer instead of getting the necessary things done. When we experience sloth from a spiritual perspective, we simply don't care. We can't be bothered. We're bored by the things of God, shrug our shoulders, and amuse ourselves instead.

Sloth is the enemy of perseverance and grit. If we want to finish our race well, staying faithful until the end, we'll want to be on the lookout for sloth. A willingness to work, to give our attention to the small and hidden tasks, is the opposite of sloth. The difference it can make is illustrated well in the following story from *Proceedings*, the magazine of the US Naval Institute:

The USS *Astoria* (CA-34) was the first US cruiser to engage the Japanese during the Battle of Savo Island, a night action fought August 8–9, 1942. Although she scored two hits on the imperial flagship *Chokai,* the *Astoria* was badly damaged and sank shortly after noon on August 9.

About 0200 hours a young Midwesterner, Signalman 3rd Class Elgin Staples, was swept overboard by the blast when the *Astoria's* number one eight-inch gun turret exploded. Wounded in both legs by shrapnel and in semi-shock, he was kept afloat by a narrow lifebelt that he managed to activate with a simple trigger mechanism.

At around 0600 hours, Staples was rescued by a passing destroyer and returned to the *Astoria,* whose captain was attempting to save the cruiser by beaching her. The effort failed, and Staples, still wearing the same lifebelt, found himself back in the water. It was lunchtime. Picked up again, this time by the USS *President Jackson* (AP-37), he was one of 500 survivors of the battle who were evacuated to Noumea.

On board the transport Staples, for the first time, closely examined the lifebelt that had served him so well. It had been manufactured by Firestone Tire and Rubber Company of Akron, Ohio, and bore a registration number. Given home leave, Staples told his story and asked his mother, who worked for Firestone, about the purpose of the number on the belt. She replied that the company insisted on personal responsibility for the war effort, and that the number was unique and assigned to only one inspector. Staples remembered everything about the lifebelt, and quoted the number. It was his mother's personal code and affixed to every item she was responsible for approving.[47]

B. Is there an area of service in which you're tempted to cut corners or become sluggish? Is there an area of your spiritual life where the temptation of sloth is strong?

C. Instead of becoming sluggish, what are we to do, according to Hebrews 6:12?

D. Who is a person in your life whose faith is worthy of your imitation?

---

[47] Commander Eric J. Berryman, "Strange Things Happen at Sea," *Proceedings*, US Naval Institute, June 1989.

Quiet your heart and enjoy His presence. . . . Grasp the unseen.

"If then you were raised with Christ, seek what is above, where Christ is seated at the right hand of God. Think of what is above, not of what is on earth. For you have died, and your life is hidden with Christ in God. When Christ your life appears, then you too will appear with him in glory." (Colossians 3:1–4)

God sees what is done in secret. The hidden things are not hidden from Him. Nothing is wasted. Wise women have their treasure in heaven, where nothing can destroy or diminish it. We can have our rewards here on earth when we pursue the things the world says matter most. But make no mistake, just because the world is applauding doesn't mean we have made the right choices.

The life best lived is often the one that is shrouded in insignificance by most standards. But God sees the quiet sacrificial love that is offered out of love for Him: the woman who perseveres in a difficult relationship; the one who faithfully serves in the thankless role; the one who turns the other cheek; the one who, though weary, listens to the hurting heart.

He sees you.

Day Four
HIS RELIABLE PROMISE

Read Hebrews 6:13–18.

After encouraging us to imitate people who, "through faith and patience, are inheriting the promises" (Hebrews 6:12), the author of Hebrews takes a moment to assure us that these promises are unchanging and utterly reliable. Trust in God's promises will help us to stand firm and grow in maturity, but if we doubt them, we'll be "tossed by waves and swept along by every wind of teaching arising from human trickery" (Ephesians 4:14).

1. To help us to understand why we can count on God's promises, we are led to which Old Testament patriarch? What promise was made to him?

God promised Abraham that he would have many descendants. This wouldn't have been such a significant promise if it weren't for the fact that Abraham and his wife,

Sarah, had not been able to have children thus far. God took Abraham outside and said, "Look up at the sky and count the stars, if you can. Just so, he added, will your descendants be" (Genesis 15:5). Then God did something really interesting: He followed up His promise with an oath.

2. A. When God got ready to make His oath to Abraham, He included him in the preparations. What did He instruct Abraham to do? See Genesis 15:9–10, noting that the person talking is God.

B. Following this, Abraham fell into a deep sleep. What happened next? See Genesis 15:17.

To understand the significance of this, we need some background on the way treaties were made in ancient times. The rite described in Genesis 15 was a way treaties were ratified. The animals were cut in half and placed opposite each other. The people agreeing to the treaty would walk between the carcasses, in essence saying that this would be their fate if ever they broke the treaty.

C. The smoking fire pot and flaming torch represented God. What do you think was the significance of this oath?

God passed through the animals *alone*. He passed through their carcasses, essentially saying that He would be torn apart if the oath being made were broken.

Was Abraham able to perfectly keep his side of the bargain? Would he be able to obey God and follow Him faithfully? No. And neither can we. God has always known this would be the case. Did He faithfully keep His promises? Always. Without fail.

Centuries later, it was clear that God's people would not be able to keep *their* promises to Him. But who had walked through the carcasses? It was God Himself. Although the oath had been broken by man, God allowed the body of His Son to be torn in two in man's place. Be assured of this: You have a Father who keeps His promises.

3. A. Let's get back to Hebrews 6:16. Describe what an oath is to a human.

   B. If a human swears an oath by someone greater than themselves, who could God swear an oath by?

   Mary Healy explains the difference between a promise and an oath, and points out why God was gracious to give both:

   > To promise is to give assurance of something that one will do or not do. But an oath is much more solemn: it is to invoke God as witness to a promise, asking for his help to keep it and, in effect, making one liable to his penalty if one does not . . . But God has no need to swear an oath! His word is already absolute truth and completely trustworthy (John 17:17; Titus 1:2). The fact that he did so shows his amazing consideration for human frailty.[48]

4. What are the two immutable (unchangeable) things mentioned in Hebrews 6:18?

God is such a tender Father. He knows how prone we are to doubt. Instead of demanding that we blindly believe, He offers His promise and His oath.

5. Isn't it a relief to know it doesn't all depend on us? The story of Abraham and the assurance of God's promises and oath serve as reminders that anytime we think it's all up to us, we are listening to a lie. There is not a thing we face in life that we must face alone.

---

[48] Healy, *Hebrews*, 125.

Write out the following verses, personalizing them to remind yourself that it is *not* all up to you. God stands with you, doing in and through you what you cannot do on your own.

Exodus 14:14

Isaiah 30:15

Isaiah 43:1–2

Quiet your heart and enjoy His presence. . . . You'll find your strength in quiet and trust.

Be Still My Soul
Katherine von Schlegel; trans. Jane Borthwick
The United Methodist Hymnal, *No. 534*

Be still, my soul: the Lord is on thy side.
Bear patiently the cross of grief or pain.
Leave to thy God to order and provide;
In every change, He faithful will remain.

Be still, my soul: thy best, thy heavenly Friend
Through thorny ways leads to a joyful end.
Be still, my soul: thy God doth undertake
To guide the future, as He has the past.
Thy hope, thy confidence let nothing shake;
All now mysterious shall be bright at last.

Be still, my soul: the waves and winds still know
His voice who ruled them while He dwelt below.

Be still, my soul: the hour is hastening on
When we shall be forever with the Lord.

When disappointment, grief and fear are gone,
Sorrow forgot, love's purest joys restored.

Be still, my soul: when change and tears are past
All safe and blessed we shall meet at last.

How are we able to have a still soul in the midst of life's uncertainties and challenges? We imitate the faith of heroes who have gone before us, people such as Elisabeth Elliot, who wrote, "God included the hardships of my life in His original plan. Nothing takes Him by surprise. Nothing is for nothing. His plan is to make me holy, and hardship is indispensable for that as long as I live in this hard old world. All I have to do is accept it."[49]

Oh Lord, give me the grace to have that level of trust in the goodness of Your promises. May I be able to say, along with the psalmist, "Lord, my allotted portion and my cup, you have made my destiny secure. Pleasant places were measured out for me; fair to me indeed is my inheritance" (Psalm 16:6). I trust in You, knowing that all the promises of God are yes and amen in Jesus (2 Corinthians 1:20).

Day Five
HOPE AS AN ANCHOR

Read Hebrews 6:18–20.

1. A. What are we strongly encouraged to do in Hebrews 6:18?

A Christian's definition of *hope* differs greatly from the way the word is most often used. People talk about hoping for the best, which usually means to be full of wishes. The hope referred to in Hebrews 6:18 is based not in wishes, but in certainty. That certainty is rooted in the certainty of God's promises. "God is not a human being who speaks falsely" (Numbers 23:19).

Hebrews 6:18 tells us to *hold fast* to this hope. The Greek word translated "hold fast" is *krateó,* which means "to be strong, to rule." What do we need to rule over

---

[49] Elisabeth Elliot, *Be Still My Soul* (Grand Rapids, MI: Revell, 2003), 29.

in order to hold fast to hope? We need to rule over the thoughts that run through our minds that are counter to the truth about God. As we saw in Day Two, we can be tempted to fall away from our faith when we believe lies about God the Father during difficult times. We need to rule over our thoughts and emotions, "taking every thought captive to Christ" (2 Corinthians 10:5). How is this done? We start to pay better attention to the thoughts running through our minds. We **become aware** of them, name the emotions or thoughts, and write them down. Then we **seek to understand** by comparing what is in our mind to what we know to be true of God. If the thoughts are consistent with who God is, we accept them. But if they aren't—if the thoughts are worries without the grace of God taken into account, if the thoughts are without hope, if they are condemning—we reject them. We **take action**, ruling over our thoughts instead of letting them run wild in our heads.[50] This process enables us to hold fast to hope.

B. Can you think of a time (past or present) when your hope was waning? What thoughts were running through your mind? Practice the process of ruling over the thoughts in your mind (taking every thought captive to Christ) based on that memory.

Become aware (list the thoughts and emotions):

Seek to understand (Are those thoughts consistent with what you know to be true of God?):

Take action (Circle the thoughts that are consistent with what you know to be true of God, and cross out the ones that aren't. Then write out the truth you are embracing and reject the others.):

---

[50] These three steps (become aware, seek to understand, take action) are based on the Discernment of Spirits, by Saint Ignatius of Loyola. Father Timothy Gallagher, O.M.V., has written an excellent book explaining this process, *The Discernment of Spirits: An Ignatian Guide for Everyday Living.*

2. How is our hope described in Hebrews 6:19?

God asks us to return to Him continually—for our hearts to be anchored in Him. It's inevitable that at times our mind will wander away from Him, but we can develop the discipline of faithfully bringing it back. An anchor lets a boat drift only so far before there is a tug, drawing it back. One of the fruits of growing in spiritual maturity is the shortening of the rope connecting us to the anchor. We start to feel the tug drawing us back to God quicker than it has in the past. We become more sensitive to the things that cause us to wander. This is a gift and an indicator that we are becoming closer to God.

Holding fast to our hope by ruling over our thoughts and returning quickly to God when we feel the tug of the anchor are ways that we live out Jesus' command in Matthew 22:37: "You shall love the Lord, your God, with all your heart, with all your soul, and with all your mind."

3. According to Hebrews 6:19, where is our anchor located?

"Into the interior behind the veil" refers to the Holy of Holies in the temple. This was the most sacred place in the temple: God's dwelling place. It wasn't a place that just anyone could enter. A thick veil separated it from the Holy Place, issuing the message, "Keep out." Only the high priest was allowed in the Holy of Holies, and he was permitted to enter only once a year. He wasn't popping in for a quick hello; he was entering with the blood of animal sacrifices to ask God's forgiveness for his sins and the sins of the people.

The lesson contained here is going to be developed further in Hebrews 9, but to understand the significance of Hebrews 6:19, we need to know that what was seen on earth in the temple was a copy of a heavenly reality. This verse paints a picture for us of God in the Holy of Holies in heaven, and us worshipping Him below on earth. Jesus sits at God's right hand, holding the anchor of our soul to connect us to heaven and keep us steady.

4. Life isn't easy, and circumstances can cause us to feel we're in a free fall. As we navigate stormy seas, we're to hold fast to the rope of an anchor that reaches all the way into heaven, right into the presence of God. What comfort can we find

from Psalm 139:7–10 and Isaiah 41:10 for those times when we feel like we are losing our grip on the rope?

5. A. According to Hebrews 6:20, in what role has Jesus entered into the Holy of Holies on our behalf?

B. The definition of a forerunner is someone who goes before us. He explores what's ahead, making sure it's safe for us to follow. This is what Jesus has done for us. What message does He send back to us? See John 14:2–4.

C. What does Jesus do for us now in heaven, where He sits at the right hand of God the Father? See Romans 8:34 and Hebrews 7:25.

Quiet your heart and enjoy His presence. . . . Hold fast to hope.

When we get serious about growing in spiritual maturity, we step into the boat of God's will and set out. I wish we were guaranteed smooth seas, but the opposite is true. Genuine followers of Christ encounter waves and storms, not because they are rejecting God's will, but precisely because they are embracing it. We are told in 2 Timothy 3:12 that "all who want to live religiously in Christ Jesus will be persecuted." Jesus is our forerunner and He has secured our final destination, but we need to remember that He told us, "no slave is greater than his master. If they persecuted me, they will also persecute you" (John 15:20). The waters will get rocky. When they do, don't assume it's because you've done something wrong. Often, it is a sign that you are on the right track.

But you are never left to navigate the storm alone, and this makes all the difference. Resist the lie that God has abandoned or rejected you. Grab hold of the anchor and run to adoration to soak up His presence. Kneel before Him and claim His unchanging, steadfast promises.

"LORD, God of hosts, who is like you? Mighty LORD, your faithfulness surrounds you. You rule the raging sea; you still its swelling waves. . . . You have a mighty arm. Your hand is strong; your right hand is ever exalted. Justice and judgment are the foundation of your throne; mercy and faithfulness march before you. Blessed the people who know the war cry, who walk in the radiance of your face, LORD." (Psalm 89:10, 14–16)

Conclusion

When I feel hope waning, it is usually because I have placed my hope in the wrong things. A heaviness in my soul is often my first clue that somewhere along the road, I've started equating God's protection over me with the removal of hardship. I have placed my hope not in Jesus, but in better circumstances, certain that this is what I need.

This tiredness inside is not the way God wants me or you to live. There is a promised rest (Hebrews 4) that we do not need to wait until heaven to experience. Jesus invites us to roll all our anxiety, hopelessness, anger, frustration, and grief onto Him. He takes it all, passes through the veil, and intercedes for us before the Father in heaven.

To do this, I need solitude. It takes being alone for me to even figure out what I am feeling and that I need help. Our world is so loud and busy that solitude rarely just happens. Most of us need to intentionally create it.

What changes could you make to your schedule this week that would allow you to carve out this critical time alone with God? Go slower. Exhale and wait on the Lord in quiet and trust. Let the Holy Spirit tend to your needs. Lean into the promised rest. Ask the Lord to teach you how to remain there; ask Him to still the inner voice of reproach (it's not His voice) that tells you that you have to do more to be more.

Commune with Him and reflect on your current season. What is God revealing about your heart right now? Invite Him into the most intimate part of you and ask Him for healing. Then rest in expectation and hope because His promises are sure and will never fail.

My Resolution

In what specific way will I apply what I have learned in this lesson?

Examples:

1. I've realized that I don't feel I really understand some of the topics listed as "basic teachings" in Hebrews 6:1–2. I will take the time for further study in the areas where I feel I need a stronger foundation.

2. I will take the time to search my heart for any places where I have agreed with a lie about God the Father. I will then reject the lie and replace it with the truth that I find in Scripture.

3. I will schedule a "boost of hope" this week—a time when I grab hold of the rope anchored in heaven by sitting at Jesus' feet in adoration.

My resolution:

Catechism Clips

CCC 1431 Interior repentance is a radical reorientation of our whole life, a return, a conversion to God with all our heart, an end of sin, a turning away from evil, with repugnance toward the evil actions we have committed. At the same time it entails the desire and resolution to change one's life, with hope in God's mercy and trust in the help of his grace. This conversion of heart is accompanied by a salutary pain and sadness which the Fathers called *animi cruciatus* (affliction of spirit) and *compunctio cordis* (repentance of heart).

CCC 2089 *Incredulity* is the neglect of revealed truth or the willful refusal to assent to it. "*Heresy* is the obstinate post-baptismal denial of some truth which must be believed with divine and catholic faith, or it is likewise an obstinate doubt concerning the same; *apostasy* is the total repudiation of the Christian faith; *schism* is the refusal of submission to the Roman Pontiff or of communion with the members of the Church subject to him.

Verse Study

See Appendix 3 for instructions on how to complete a verse study.

Romans 15:13

1. Verse:

2. Paraphrase:

3. Questions:

4. Cross-references:

5. Personal Application:

Lesson 9: Talk

THE ANCHOR

Hebrews 6:16–20

You can view this talk on the accompanying DVD, or please visit our website at walkingwithpurpose.com/videos and select the *Grounded in Hope* Bible Study, then click through to select Videos.

I. True Hope

Biblical hope is not based on luck, or crossing your fingers.
Our hope is based on the _____ of God.
It's based on **God's _____.**

II. Our Anchor

Because the anchor for our soul is **hope**, we can count on the fact that nothing in the storm or in the rocking of the boat is without meaning. And this is so important.

III. Hope in Struggle

A lot of the time, we think in response, "I would like to think I was created to be happy."

When we are feeling altruistic, we might think, "I was created to make this world a better place."

"Christ in you, the hope of glory." (Colossians 1:27)

"In my deepest wound I saw your glory, and it dazzled me." —Saint Augustine

The places in our hearts where we are wounded are places where we are most vulnerable to lies.

Two of the most important truths to *always* keep at the forefront of your mind are:

1. You are a beloved daughter of God.
2. There is nothing you can do to earn or lose His love.

God wants to speak truth into those places in your heart where lies have taken hold. There is no one safer than Jesus to invite into the tender places of your heart.

"For we have not a high priest who is unable to sympathize with our weaknesses, but one who in every respect has been tempted as we are, yet without sinning." (Hebrews 4:15)

Dr. Bob Schuchts' description of Jesus' suffering:

> **Abandonment:** Jesus experienced abandonment by His friends and by God.
> **Shame:** Jesus was publicly condemned and humiliated.
> **Fear:** Jesus faced the fear of violence, death, rejection, and abandonment.
> **Powerlessness:** Jesus willingly submitted to powerlessness on the cross.
> **Rejection:** Jesus was despised and rejected by the people.
> **Hopelessness:** Jesus faced His death without giving in to despair.
> **Confusion:** Jesus' identity was totally confounded in the public eye.[51]

Jesus knew He was the beloved Son of God. He knew that His suffering was for the greatest purpose: the redemption of mankind. **He knew there was a great narrative—a great story—and He was the most critical part of it.**

"The sufferings of this present time are not worth comparing with the glory about to be revealed to us." (Romans 8:18)

---

[51] Dr. Bob Schuchts, *Healing the Whole Person Workbook & Journal* (Tallahassee, FL: Dr. Bob Schuchts, 2017), 45.

Discussion Questions

1. Have you ever seen God reveal His glory through your wounds?

2. Can you identify any lies that you have believed about God during times of suffering?

3. Instead of isolating Himself or running away, Jesus faced His suffering by continuing to walk toward His calling, continuing to love, continuing to trust. In doing so, He redeemed suffering. Can you identify a specific way God is asking you to follow Christ's example and suffer purely?

NOTES

Looking for more material? We've got you covered!
Walking with Purpose meets women where they are in
their spiritual journey. From our Opening Your Heart
22-lesson foundational Bible study to more advanced
studies, we have something to help each and every
woman grow closer to Christ. Find out more:

www.walkingwithpurpose.com

Lesson 10

OUR INTERCESSOR AND ADVOCATE

Hebrews 7

Introduction

I am currently walking through a season of motherhood that has required a constant surrender of my deep desire to be in control. My carefully laid plans and checklists have been turned upside down, and each day brings a new surprise, a wrench in the works.

The year had been laid out on our family calendar with the assumption that our middle child would be attending his freshman year of college. But everything changed when a phone call from Katy Perry informed me that he had auditioned for *American Idol* and was headed to Hollywood. We've been riding this roller coaster ever since of flights to L.A., last-minute requests for childhood photos, thrill over victories, and worries regarding the influence of the entertainment industry on the heart of our son.

I've had to tear up the itinerary that I had planned for my journey this year, and as I have rounded each corner, I have been met with something unexpected. The truth is, I like to know what's coming, and I prefer to meet whatever it is with a plan. I think most of us do, but I'm learning that moments of joy can be robbed when my focus is on my desire to be in control.

Mine is not a beaten path, but I wish it was. I can't find another person walking through these same circumstances. Do you feel the same way? What path does God have you on, and do you feel you are groping in the darkness? Do you, like me, long for someone to grab hold of your hand and say that she has been there too and can tell you exactly where to go?

Here's what I have found. God often holds back giving us the friend with the exact set of circumstances so that we turn to Him instead. Not even the dearest of friends can see what is around the corner, but God can. God is the one leading us along the path, and He's taking us in a direction that we never would have dreamed. He isn't afraid, and He asks us to fear nothing because He is by our side.

At first glance, Hebrews 7 seems to have nothing to do with what I have just written, but stay with me. You're about to learn more about Melchizedek, and the thought might make your eyes glaze over with boredom. The Lord knows that I came to these passages with scant idea of how they could possibly be relevant to modern life.

Part of this is because this chapter addresses concerns and assumptions that made sense to first-century Jewish Christians, but they aren't familiar to us. The readers of Hebrews would not have been able to imagine anyone with higher authority than the high priest. Hebrews 7 sets out to prove that Jesus is a priest from a totally different order—that of Melchizedek—and that this is superior. Because Jesus never referred to Himself as a priest, the author has some explaining to do.

I pray that we won't get bogged down or bored by details, but instead will look in wonder at the way God has had all the details of our salvation up His sleeve from the very beginning. I hope that we will be blown away by how nothing recorded in the Old Testament is wasted, and how it all points to Jesus.

Why? Because as we walk through uncertain circumstances, longing for a script or a person who can tell us exactly what to do, God wants us to see that He is enough. He longs for us to place our faith in *His* attention to detail, not our own. He wants our trust in *His* plan to be greater than our fear that ours will be thwarted. May we place our hands in His and let Him lead.

Day One
THE SUPERIORITY OF MELCHIZEDEK

Read Hebrews 7:1–10.

At first glance, it seems bizarre that the author of Hebrews brings up Melchizedek again. Before we make this judgment, let's lean in and debunk the author's theory that his readers have become "sluggish in hearing" (Hebrews 5:11). If we persevere through this dense passage, we'll be rewarded with a deeper understanding not just of Hebrews, but of the Old Testament as well.

1. A. How is Melchizedek described in Hebrews 7:1–2?

It's interesting to note that Psalm 76:2 identifies the city of Salem as Zion, or Jerusalem. This city would later become the center of Israelite religious life. Also, Melchizedek was the first person in the Bible to be called a priest.

B. What did Melchizedek do when he encountered Abraham as he returned from battle? What was Abraham's response? See Hebrews 7:1–2.

C. What do you note is significant regarding which person is giving the blessing in Hebrews 7:7?

2. The first mention of Melchizedek is in Genesis 14:17–20. After reading this passage, note what Melchizedek brought out and shared with Abraham. According to CCC 1333, what does the Catholic Church see prefigured here?

3. What do we learn about Melchizedek's family and his life span in Hebrews 7:3? Whom does Melchizedek resemble, according to this verse? How long does his priesthood last?

This passage is often misunderstood. The author of Hebrews is not trying to make it sound as if Melchizedek was a supernatural being. To make sense of his point, we need to remember what qualified a person to be a priest in the Old Testament. For the Jewish people, ancestry and lineage was everything. Only those who belonged to the Levite tribe could be priests. That meant that no man from any of the other eleven tribes of Israel could serve the Lord in this way. The author of Hebrews is pointing out that somehow Melchizedek was considered a priest, even though he could not claim to be a part of the Levite tribe. This introduces the possibility of a different sort of valid priesthood.

The author of Hebrews is beginning to build an argument that Melchizedek is a "type" of Christ. According to the *Catholic Bible Dictionary*, a type is "any person, place, event, or institution in Scripture that foreshadows a greater reality yet to come. Normally something in the Old Testament points forward to something in the New Testament."[52] We'll be studying other types as we move through Hebrews, all shadows of a greater truth to be revealed.

What is meant by "His priesthood remains forever"? This description of Melchizedek's priesthood was meant to draw a contrast with the terms of a Levite's priesthood. When a Levite became a priest at the age of twenty-five, he spent the first five years serving his brothers. He was then allowed to serve twenty more years, after which he had to retire (Numbers 4:3, 43). There was a limited time of service allowed. By contrast, there was no end date for Melchizedek's priesthood. This is another way Melchizedek pointed to Christ, who also exercises His role as our great high priest forever.

4. A. According to Hebrews 7:5, who was to take tithes from the Israelite people?

    B. Taking tithes (10 percent of a family's income) was the way for the Levitical priests to support themselves (Numbers 18:21–29). What interesting point is made in Hebrews 7:6?

---

[52] Hahn, *Catholic Bible Dictionary*, 928.

5. In what sense did Levi pay a tithe to Melchizedek through Abraham?

People at this time believed that a man's descendants all lived "in him," in his loins. I realize that's a strange thought. The reasoning was that the descendants were going to come from him at some point. Also important, in this culture, a son could never be greater than his father. The implication is that Levi is less than Melchizedek, and as a result, the Levite priesthood is less than Melchizedek's priesthood.

6. These verses are meant to prepare the readers for the conclusion that Jesus, the Melchizedek type of high priest, is superior to the Levitical priesthood. While this may seem like splitting hairs to us, it was a shocking thing to say at that time. It flew in the face of the things the people felt were certain and unchanging. The rest of this chapter will continue to prove this point, but let's pause and try to apply this passage to our own lives. Have you ever experienced the rocking of your faith world—a new teaching or discovery that required letting go of previously held assumptions? If so, describe it here.

Jesus has a habit of staying one step ahead of what we can figure out or put in a box. As hard as it is to let go of past assumptions and open our hearts to something new that He is teaching or revealing, we must be willing to be stretched in this way if we want to grow. In the words of Pastor Charles Spurgeon, "A God whom we could understand would be no God. If we could grasp Him, He could not be infinite. If we could understand Him, He could not be divine."[53]

Quiet your heart and enjoy His presence. . . . Our high priest offers us peace.

"Seek not to understand that you may believe, but believe that you may understand." —Saint Augustine, Tractate 29, 6

---

[53] "20 Amazing Quotes from Charles Spurgeon," Christian Quotes, https://www.christianquotes.info/top-quotes/20-amazing-quotes-from-charles-spurgeon/#axzz5CDIJLJcu.

While we will never totally understand God, He chooses to reveal certain aspects of His divine character. How merciful this is of Him, because it's hard for us to trust someone we don't know. In introducing us to Melchizedek and letting us see him as a type or a foreshadowing of Jesus, God shows us something very special about His character. Melchizedek bore the titles of King of Salem and Priest of the Most High God. The Israelites had no concept of this combination; their kings came from the tribe of Judah, and their priests from the tribe of Levi. You were either one or the other, never both.

In this, Melchizedek pulls back the curtain and gives us a glimpse of our Savior, the "King of kings and Lord of lords" (Revelation 19:16). Jesus is the ultimate priest-king, ushering in peace to a degree that no earthly king or priest ever could.

This passage reminds us that the peace He brings does not depend on our understanding. In fact, if we insist on making sense of our circumstances, peace is sure to remain hard to achieve. But if we surrender control to the King of kings, if we trust that the Lord of lords is protecting and defending us, if we stop insisting on knowing why, peace can reign in our hearts.

What is robbing you of inner peace? What worry is stealing the peace of your soul? Are your circumstances making you feel as if everything is out of the box and your whole world is upset? Pass it all over to the One who can hold it all and bring order out of chaos. "Cast your anxieties on him, for he cares about you" (1 Peter 5:7).

Day Two
THE INSUFFICIENCY OF AARON'S PRIESTHOOD

Read Hebrews 7:11–17.

1. Does the author of Hebrews believe perfection came through the Levitical priesthood? See Hebrews 7:11.

God's plan has always been to draw people into a close relationship with Him. Ever since sin entered the world in the Garden of Eden, God has desired to restore the original intimacy between Himself and man. When we read "perfection," we can understand this to mean a right relationship with God, one of closeness and access.

This is exactly what the Levitical priesthood could not provide. This section of Hebrews is going to build the argument that a new order of priesthood was needed for us to be reconciled to God.

2. There are two different orders of priests mentioned in Hebrews 7:11. What are they?

The "order of Aaron" is another way of describing the Levitical priesthood. Let's start back at the beginning with Abraham to figure out whom we are talking about here. Abraham is considered the father of the Israelites. His son Isaac had two sons, Jacob and Esau. The twelve tribes of Israel were named after Jacob's twelve sons, one of whom was Levi. One of Levi's descendants was Aaron, the brother of Moses. These brothers were quite the dynamic duo. Aaron was chosen by God to be the first priest, a role that would be passed down within his family line through the generations.

A Jewish person reading these passages at the time of the early Church would not have been able to imagine a person with greater authority than a high priest, descended from Aaron and of the tribe of Levi. Melchizedek wasn't Jewish, so they would have assumed he would be inferior. The idea that his priesthood was superior would have been mind-blowing for them to read and accept.

3. A. When there is a change of priesthood, what else needs to change, according to Hebrews 7:12?

    B. How is that change in law described in Hebrews 8:10?

The study notes in the *Ignatius Catholic Study Bible* describe the change in law in this way:

> The Mosaic laws of worship must also give way to the messianic laws of worship (7:18–19). Essentially, this is a change from sacrificial rites that involve

the blood of animals (10:4) to sacramental rites such as Baptism (10:22) and the Eucharist (6:4; 13:10).[54]

What the author of Hebrews is doing here is answering the objection that he assumes is in the mind of his readers. He knows they are thinking to themselves, "Everyone knows a priest needs to come from the tribe of Levi!"

He's setting up an argument that *really* pulls the rug out from under them, by saying, "Not only do we need a new order of priesthood, we need a change in the law!" This required a major paradigm shift for the Jewish readers.

4. Priests came from the tribe of Levi, and kings came from the tribe of Judah. What do we learn regarding this from Hebrews 7:14?

Matthew 1:1–16 lists the genealogy of Jesus, revealing that He was from the tribe of Judah, a descendant of the royal family of David. Accepting Jesus as a king was far easier for the reader than accepting Him as a priest.

5. Jesus was not qualified to be a high priest based on His ancestry, so on what was it based? See Hebrews 7:15–16.

"The power of a life that cannot be destroyed" does not mean that Jesus never died. It means that death could not hold Him—resurrection followed. Jesus is alive, forever. His priesthood will have no end. This is reiterated in Hebrews 7:17: "You are a priest forever according to the order of Melchizedek." (Remember we learned in Hebrews 7:3 that Melchizedek "remains a priest forever." That's one of the unique things about his order of priesthood.)

6. The power of the Resurrection is not something that Jesus keeps to Himself. We are promised in Romans 6:5 that "if we have grown into union with him through a death like his, we shall also be united with him in the resurrection." That resurrection power dwells in us; He has shared it with us. He longs for us to know the "surpassing greatness of his power for us who believe," which is the same

---

[54] Study notes on Hebrews 7:12, *Ignatius Catholic Study Bible New Testament*, 2nd Catholic ed. RSV (San Francisco: Ignatius Press, 2010), 424.

power "which he worked in Christ, raising him from the dead" (Ephesians 1:19–20). What part of your life feels dead? Is it a dream or a hope? Is it something in your heart? List it here, and ask God to release resurrection power into that place that is longing for new life.

Quiet your heart and enjoy His presence. . . . Jesus is sufficient.

The Aaronic priesthood and the old law were insufficient, but thanks be to God, Jesus is not. He *is more than enough to meet all our needs. "Not that we are sufficient of ourselves to claim anything as coming from us, our sufficiency is from God" (2 Corinthians 3:5, RSVCE).*

We all want to be filled with peace and free from worry and stress. What is the secret? It isn't a change in circumstances. It isn't that difficult person in your life behaving differently or going away. It isn't more money in the bank. It isn't your child straightening up. It isn't finding a husband or having a different one. The secret is found when we reject the lie that we need more, and embrace the truth that what we have in Christ, right now, is enough. If God has allowed it, then He is providing the grace to get through it. There is no exception to this. He doesn't just squeeze out the minimum on your behalf. God goes all out for His daughters. *He is a God of abundance and of more than enough.*

James 4:2 says that we have not because we ask not. Can you take a moment now to ask the Lord to meet you in your place of need with His abundant grace?

Dear Lord,

You are the all-sufficient One. Please fill up everything that is lacking in me with Your grace. For the many ways I am not enough, rush in with Your abundant grace and be in me what is needed today. Thank You, Holy Spirit, for dwelling in my soul and never leaving me to fight my battles alone. Help me to remember that there is nothing You ask of me that You don't equip me to do. May I be so attuned to Your Spirit that I say yes to what You ask and no to what You've said is not necessary. Help me to discern the difference between Your best and the good, because when I confuse the two, discouragement results.

"Moreover, God is able to make every grace abundant for you, so that in all things, always having all you need, you may have an abundance for every good work." (2 Corinthians 9:8)

Day Three
INTRODUCED TO HOPE

Read Hebrews 7:18–28.

1. According to Hebrews 7:18–19, why was "the former commandment" annulled?

The author of Hebrews is talking about the Old Testament law that was given to the Israelites by Moses. It's important to note that he is not making a "bad to good" comparison. God is the One who gave the law to Moses. If it came from God, then we know it was good. What the author is saying is that something *better* is coming. The law was weak and useless, not because it was bad, but because it didn't provide a final solution.

2. Because of Jesus, what is introduced to us, and what does that allow us to do? See Hebrews 7:19.

"Drawing near to God" is temple language. It brings to mind the progression of intimacy as one moved from the outer court, to the inner court, to the Holy Place, and then to the Holy of Holies (God's dwelling place). We'll spend time looking at the temple when we study Hebrews 9 and 10. But for now, it's important to understand that no Jewish person assumed that he or she could draw near to God in the Holy of Holies. That was a privilege reserved for the high priest, and he was only allowed to enter once a year, to ask for forgiveness. The reader of Hebrews would find it remarkable to be told that he or she could draw near to God. This was something completely new.

In Hebrews 7:20–21, the author continues to point out the superiority of Jesus' priesthood by focusing on the significance of God's taking an oath to confirm it. Mary Healy explains this in her commentary on Hebrews:

> Unlike the Levitical priesthood, the priesthood of the Messiah was established by God's oath and is therefore unchangeable . . . God, who is truth itself, has no need to swear an oath, yet he does so out of compassion for human

weakness, so that we might be absolutely assured of his purposes and "strongly encouraged to hold fast to the hope that lies before us."[55]

3. How is Jesus described in Hebrews 7:22?

This is the first time in Hebrews that we hear about the covenant, and the author will explain it further in chapters eight, nine, and ten. The *Catechism of the Catholic Church* defines a covenant as "a solemn agreement between human beings or between God and a human being involving mutual commitments or guarantees."[56] The old covenant was made between God and His people through Moses. The people broke that covenant countless times, and one of the duties of the Old Testament priests was to go before God and ask for forgiveness for this by sacrificing animals. But as we'll see in Hebrews 10:4, "it is impossible that the blood of bulls and goats takes away sins."

Hebrews 7:22 speaks of an *even better* covenant. Why is it better? Because Jesus has become the guarantor, the person behind the guarantee. The guarantor is someone who promises to pay the debt if the person who owes it defaults. Just like the Old Testament Israelites, we default on the promises we have made to God. But instead of us having to bear the consequences, Jesus has paid our debt. And His payment for our sins satisfies God completely and perfectly.

4. A. Which people are saved when they approach God, according to Hebrews 7:25?

   B. What additional insight do you gain from Acts 4:12?

5. According to Hebrews 7:25, what does Jesus live forever to do?

---

[55] Healy, *Hebrews*, 142-143.
[56] The Catholic Church, *Catechism of the Catholic Church*, 2nd ed. (Vatican City: Libreria Editrice Vaticana, 2012), 873.

To *intercede* means to "stand between," and this is exactly what Jesus does for us. He stands between us and God, and makes peace. He brings our sins before God and then pays our debt with the sacrifice of His life. He then brings the grace of God to us. This divine exchange is described in 2 Corinthians 5:21. Write the verse below.

Jesus absorbed all of our sin, paid the consequence for it that was due us, and then offered the righteousness of God to each of us. Our sin in exchange for His righteousness.

This generous gift is not one that we have earned. Jesus gives it freely, simply because He loves us and cannot bear the thought of being separated from us throughout eternity. What can stand in the way of us receiving this gift? There is no sin that is beyond the reach of His mercy—not even some colossal moral failing. What stands in the way of us receiving this gift is our pride, our belief that we are basically good people. This comes from the assumption that the good within us outweighs the bad. When this is our belief, we choose to become our own saviors, and God allows us to make this choice. But as we saw in Acts 4:12, there is only one Savior, and it isn't you or me.

Quiet your heart and enjoy His presence. . . . His love is enduring.

God wants us to be grounded in a hope that can never fail us. Our confidence can be so much more than wishful thinking if our hope is in Christ. If you desire proof that you can count on Him, look no further than the cross. We get into trouble when we judge God by our circumstances, faultily assuming that a loving God would never allow hardship. It requires humility to acknowledge that our thoughts are not on par with God's thoughts that our level of understanding does not match His. As He said through the prophet Isaiah, "For as the heavens are higher than the earth, so are my ways higher than your ways, my thoughts higher than your thoughts" (Isaiah 55:9).

There may be moments in your life when you wonder where God is. Perhaps you feel He has abandoned or rejected you. I promise you, He has never left your side and never stopped loving you. Those very memories are likely ones you don't understand. Why did God allow it? Why did He not intervene?

And this is holy ground, these places in our hearts that are wounded, so know that I am trying to tread carefully. But could it be that you have been judging God by those circumstances, instead of holding on to hope and truth and the belief that His love never fails?

What might change if you looked for proof of His love—not at the point of your greatest pain, but at the point of His greatest pain? What if you judged Him by the cross instead of your circumstances?

Day Four
THE INTERCESSOR

Read Hebrews 7:25.

1. A. According to Hebrews 7:25, whom is Jesus always able to save?

   B. Jesus is always able to save those who approach God *through Him.* Far too many of us, however, try to approach God in a different way. Many people approach Him by holding out their good deeds as bargaining chips or a way of justifying themselves. This is the opposite of recognizing one's need for a savior and leads to ungodly self-reliance instead of holy God-dependence. One way to check if you are falling into this trap is to look at how you respond when God doesn't answer your prayers the way you would like Him to. Do you indignantly point out all the righteous things you have done, wondering why He hasn't responded by doing what you have asked? Take time to reflect on your answer, looking back at times when you have felt disappointed in God.

Jesus is always able to save all who turn to Him and acknowledge their need. There is no exception to this rule; it doesn't matter how far we have fallen. What is absolutely critical is a humble and contrite heart that has let go of the delusion that we can save ourselves.

2. As we learned in Day Three, what does Jesus live forever to do? See Hebrews 7:25.

As we journey through Hebrews, we need to continue to remember that this letter was written to a group of people who were facing trials because of their faith and were about to give up. While Hebrews is loaded with theological truths, the purpose of this book of the Bible was not so much to feed the intellect as to counsel and encourage the readers to persevere. The author comes to his main point of chapter 7 in verse 25, where he proposes that we will be better able to remain faithful if we recognize Jesus as our faithful intercessor.

The phrase "to make intercession" does not just refer to prayer. It also has a legal meaning. Picture a court setting and a person on trial. Your advocate in the courtroom would be the person interceding for you.

I was recently talking with a lawyer friend of mine and asked him if he would choose to represent himself in court. He looked at me like I was crazy, which surprised me because he's a great lawyer. "I know you see people do that on TV," he said, "but every lawyer knows that it's disastrous to be in court without someone representing you, advocating for you, interceding for you." His point: You don't want to step into the courtroom alone.

What we don't realize is that when we try to approach God through anyone or anything besides Jesus, it is as if we are entering a courtroom on our own, determined to represent ourselves.

3. How is the "courtroom" that we will enter one day described in CCC 678? What will be brought to light? What will be condemned?

What we learn from Hebrews 7:25 is that we do not need to go into the judgment of the last day alone. We can ask Jesus to be our intercessor there. This does not mean that our conduct and the secrets of our hearts will not be brought to light. It does not mean that there are no consequences for our earthly actions. But whether or not Jesus is your advocate and intercessor on that day will impact whether you receive the full punishment due you for your sin.

4. A. According to Romans 6:23, what is the payment or "wages" of sin? What is the gift of God?

   B. How was that gift of eternal life given? Did God say that sin doesn't matter, that no payment needs to be made? See Romans 5:8.

C. Is this payment for sin automatically made on our behalf, or is there something we need to do? See Romans 10:9–10, 13; Ephesians 2:8; and James 2:14–17.

How will we respond? Will we count "the offer of God's grace as nothing" (CCC 678) and enter the courtroom alone, confident that our good works will be enough? Or will we ask Jesus to be our intercessor, our advocate?

If we ask Him to do that, He will enter the courtroom on our behalf, as our great high priest. Just as the Old Testament priests entered the sanctuary with the blood of animals, our great high priest will enter the presence of God with blood. The significance of that blood will be explored in Hebrews 9.

5. Saint John Chrysostom interpreted Hebrews 7:25 as: "Wherefore He is able also to save them *to the uttermost*"[57] (emphasis added).

How do the following verses describe Jesus saving us to the uttermost?

Romans 8:34

Romans 8:35–39

1 John 2:1

Quiet your heart and enjoy His presence. . . . You don't have to go it alone.

There are thousands of times you have relied on yourself instead of turning to God. Confess it and He will save you to the uttermost.

---

[57] Saint John Chrysostom, *Homilies of Saint John Chrysostom: On the Epistle to the Hebrews* (Oxford, UK: Aeterna Press, 2015), 131.

Your actions have at times rejected Christ and embraced sin. If you turn, He will run to you and will save you to the uttermost.

Despair has caused you to feel that Christ's grace can't reach you. But He can break through every bolt, every barrier, and go to the depths, to save you to the uttermost.

Distress has blanketed you, suffocating you with suffering. But Jesus can lead you to the fresh air of hope, and He will save you to the uttermost.

Temptation lures you, causing you to wonder if you can ever please God. Jesus stands as your strength, your purity, your advocate; He does in and through you what you cannot do alone.

He saves to the uttermost those who approach God through Him, because He lives forever to make intercession for them.

Day Five
THE SUFFICIENCY OF CHRIST

Read Hebrews 7:26–28.

1. A. How is our great high priest, Jesus, described in Hebrews 7:26?

    B. Why didn't Jesus need to offer sacrifices daily the way the Old Testament priests did?

The single sacrifice of Jesus was so perfect that no other sacrifice was needed. He was the perfect, spotless lamb, and because He was fully man, He was able to represent us in a way that an animal sacrifice never could.

Let's go back to the "courtroom" we discussed on Day Four and see how Jesus' sacrifice changes everything there. We learned that Jesus, our intercessor and advocate, represents us in the courtroom. We don't have to go in there alone. But how does this work? Does Jesus take out our case file and lay it all out before God, acknowledging that we have messed up countless times, and then beg for God's mercy?

When we watch courtroom dramas, we see many examples of attorneys manipulating the facts, trying to control the jury, and bending the truth. When the attorney realizes that he is going to lose, he might choose to throw himself on the mercy of the court. But this is not what Jesus does. He actually has a case to present. We find that case in Hebrews 7:27, where we are reminded that Jesus offered the ultimate sacrifice for our sins, Himself. This means that He is able to go before God the Father, not asking for mercy, but asking for justice.

The truth is, we are guilty. But the payment has been made. The debt has been paid. The punishment has been doled out, and Jesus bore it all. Because He did this, He is able to appeal to God's *justice*.

2. Read 1 John 1:9. If we confess our sins, how will God respond? Note both His actions and His character in this verse.

God forgives us not only because He is merciful but also because He is just. If we ask Jesus to be our advocate, our Savior—to stand in our place—then God's justice will be satisfied. We will be accepted.

We should have lived as Jesus lived, but instead, He died the death that we deserved. It's the most incredible exchange imaginable, yet how many of us ignore it, choosing instead to represent ourselves before God, holding up our good deeds with statements like "I'm a good person," "I always try my best," or "I work harder than a lot of people"?

Trying to prove our worth to God by approaching Him with our good deeds gets in the way of inviting Him to heal our brokenness. It's only in the humility of brokenness that we can experience healing and salvation, which is what we so desperately need and desire. Self-reliance just keeps us rooted in pride.

Pride prevents us from becoming who we were created to be by tempting us to put on a false front. Any glimpse of the real self in its brokenness is so repugnant that self-justification becomes the focus of our inner thoughts. There is a constant underlying sense of guilt and inadequacy, however, and we live in fear that we'll be found out and seen as not enough.

If we hide behind our self-justifications, if we insist on representing ourselves in the courtroom where we are constantly trying to prove our worth, we will remain trapped and discouraged. God wants us to be free from this. But it is only as we admit our need that love can intervene.

3. Do you come to God needy and broken, or holding out your accomplishments and deeds, trying to please Him?

4. "The word of the oath . . . appoints a Son who has been made perfect forever" (Hebrews 7:28). Jesus was made perfect forever through suffering (Hebrews 2:10). When "he offered up himself" (Hebrews 7:27), He *redeemed* suffering. He suffered acutely, but *did not sin*, and did not lose His identity as a beloved Son. He is our example in this. A false theology exists that says Jesus suffered so that we don't have to. What does 1 Peter 2:19–24 teach us about our own suffering?

Even with Jesus as our intercessor and advocate, we will find that suffering intersects our lives. How and when that happens is out of our control, but we can choose how we will respond to it. Jesus is our example, teaching us not to respond by lashing out or growing despondent. Instead, He encourages us to hold on to our identity as beloved daughters of God, trusting that our heavenly Father, who judges justly, will one day make all wrongs right.

Quiet your heart and enjoy His presence. . . . Come raw and real.

We've looked at the metaphor of a courtroom to help understand what it means to have Jesus as our intercessor and advocate. But I'd like to close by focusing on the intimacy of His intercession for us. Jesus isn't only concerned about how we will fare at the last judgment. He is interested in how we are feeling right here, right now.

He sees your suffering and the circumstances that have caused your heart to break. Standing beside the Father, He prays for you, for your healing and wholeness. His hope is that you would look to Him, touch His wounds, and allow His understanding to bring you comfort.

When we are in the midst of suffering, we are especially vulnerable to lies from the enemy about the love and faithfulness of God. He tempts us to believe that God has abandoned us, that our faith has nothing to offer us in this moment of crisis, that we are alone. It is in those very moments that we need to wage a battle in our minds, grasping hold of truth and rejecting thoughts that are false. The truth is, you are beloved. Difficult circumstances in your life are not indications that God has left you or doesn't care. He is present, He is at work, and He is making sure that everything happening to you can be transformed into something for your benefit.

I pray that Jesus would be your example as you suffer, helping you to catch a vision of what it looks like to walk through trials without losing sight of who and whose you are.

Conclusion

I have found that what seems logical to me in terms of how suffering should be alleviated or a prayer answered is usually different from God's plan. This is how my current season has gone, and my request for God to wipe away difficulties has seemingly been ignored.

But this I know with all my heart: God does *not* ignore the pleadings of His children. He is entirely tuned in and aware of every heartache. Psalm 56:8 reveals that God keeps each one of our tears in a bottle. I am comforted by this and need to continually remind myself that when He seems slow to intervene, He is actually working out a much better plan than mine.

Is there something that God is asking you to surrender today? What do you desperately want to control? Does letting it go feel as if it will mean sure loss or deprivation? Could you open your heart to the possibility that surrendering will ultimately mean that you win what matters most? With God, when it appears *we* are being conquered, that is often when the things that are hurting us most are being defeated.

There is no limit to the miracles that God can do in our lives. But we hamper His efforts and put the miracle on hold when we are clenching our own plan, our desires, our dreams, and our worries. God works best when our hands are open, vulnerable, and ready to receive.

Each surrender feels like death. Letting go costs us something and makes us feel out of control. God understands this, so for Him, letting go is the greatest gift we can offer. Father Wilfrid Stinissen describes it this way:

If we are subject to trials here on earth, if we must struggle to say Yes to God, it is because in eternity, God wants to say to us: "You have given me something. It is not only I who give, but rather we give to each other. I give myself in gratitude because you have given me something that you could have refused to give. Now you can no longer give me anything, but at one time you did, and it has an eternal value. I never forget."[58]

The time to give these gifts to God is now. In heaven, we'll no longer have the opportunity. Our immediate sufferings, the very things we most want to change, are the perfect opportunity for us to let go and surrender to God's will. Yes, this is costly. I know it's easier said than done. But God is never outdone in generosity. As we are promised in 2 Timothy 2:11, "If we have died with him we shall also live with him." Real life, true freedom, and joy are not found in perfect circumstances. They are found in the release of control, the unclenched fist, the surrender, the fiat.

Let's allow our shoulders to relax. May we surrender to His hands, and let God move our heads and hearts, directing us where He deems best. In the words of Fr. Stinissen, "God is like a specialist in relaxation who works with the patient's head, turning it in different directions. The fact that it causes pain is not the specialist's fault. He does not turn it too far. No, it is because the patient's neck muscles are tense."[59] We tense up when we carry the weight of the world on our shoulders, mistakenly thinking it's all up to us.

It's time to throw off the weight of trying to keep it all in control and release it to the only One who has the power to bring the miracle, raise the dead, and usher in hope.

My Resolution

In what specific way will I apply what I have learned in this lesson?

Examples:

1. Day Two, I identified a part of my life that feels dead. I am going to ask God daily to release resurrection power into that place that is longing for new life. I will pray that He will replace the resignation in my heart with hope.

---

[58] Stinissen, *Into Your Hands, Father*, 74.
[59] Ibid., 85.

2. I have looked for proof of Jesus' love in my circumstances, and when suffering has intersected my life, I've struggled to believe He cares for me as a loving Father. To counter this mind-set, I will go to adoration this week and contemplate His suffering on the cross. I will meditate on the truth that His love was proved to me *there*.

3. I have identified in myself a pattern of self-reliance, of counting on my own goodness to save me instead of the grace of God. I will go to confession and confess the sin of pride and ungodly self-reliance. I will ask for grace to grow in trust and dependence on God.

My resolution:

Catechism Clips

CCC 678 Following in the steps of the prophets and John the Baptist, Jesus announced the judgment of the Last Day in his preaching. Then will the conduct of each one and the secrets of hearts be brought to light. Then will the culpable unbelief that counted the offer of God's grace as nothing be condemned. Our attitude to our neighbor will disclose acceptance or refusal of grace and divine love. On the Last Day Jesus will say: "Truly I say to you, as you did it to one of the least of these my brethren, you did it to me."

CCC 1333 At the heart of the Eucharistic celebration are the bread and wine that, by the words of Christ and the invocation of the Holy Spirit, become Christ's Body and Blood. Faithful to the Lord's command the Church continues to do, in his memory and until his glorious return, what he did on the eve of his Passion: "He took bread . . ." He took the cup filled with wine . . ." The signs of bread and wine become, in a way surpassing understanding, the Body and Blood of Christ; they continue also to signify the goodness of creation. Thus in the Offertory we give thanks to the Creator for bread and wine, fruit of the "work of human hands," but above all as "fruit of the earth" and "of the vine"—gifts of the Creator. The Church sees in the gesture of the king-priest Melchizedek, who "brought out bread and wine," a prefiguring of her own offering.

CCC 1544 Everything that the priesthood of the Old Covenant prefigured finds its fulfillment in Christ Jesus, the "one mediator between God and men." The Christian tradition considers Melchizedek, "priest of God Most High," as a prefiguration of the priesthood of Christ, the unique "high priest after the order of Melchizedek"; "holy, blameless, unstained," "by a single offering he has perfected for all time those who are sanctified," that is, by the unique sacrifice of the cross.

Verse Study

See Appendix 3 for instructions on how to complete a verse study.

2 Corinthians 4:17

1. Verse:

2. Paraphrase:

3. Questions:

4. Cross-references:

5. Personal Application:

NOTES

Lesson 11

TAKEN BY THE HAND

Hebrews 8

Introduction

We are living in turbulent times culturally, politically, and globally. Change comes at us at an unprecedented speed. I don't know about you, but I look at the landscape and long for everything to be defined, mapped out, and settled. There's comfort and a sense of security that comes from living in the black-and-white. But what do we do when so much of what surrounds us seems gray? Where do we turn when we long to feel grounded but constantly seem to be navigating change?

I recently sat with some Catholic middle school girls and asked them why they thought so many people were leaving the Church. One girl talked about how people want to be in control rather than surrender to God (I thought this was amazing insight from someone so young), a lack of relevant teaching that addresses their areas of struggle, discomfort with the way they perceive the Church to be handling the issue of same-sex attraction, and a limited role for women in the Church. The discussion was honest, deep, and engaging. I witnessed them coming alive spiritually as they wrestled. They were engaging in their faith rather than just parroting the "right" answers back to me.

One of the girls asked me, "But what do I do when one person teaches one thing, and then someone teaches me something different? How do I know what is true? How do I know which person I can trust?" This question was prompted by the girls having been taught about their true worth and God's purpose and plan for their lives in our gatherings, but then being told by a religion teacher that while man was made in the image and likeness of God, woman was not—she was taken from the man. This is a doctrinal error (Genesis 1:27 specifically refers to both man and woman being made in God's image), and it's highly likely that they misunderstood the teacher. I don't know; I wasn't there. But a part of me wanted to respond by saying, "Trust *me*. I love you. I am for you. What I am teaching you is truth." But then I paused, knowing that

I am not infallible. I will make mistakes. So where did I tell her to go? I told her to go to the source of truth. We know from Scripture that Jesus is truth (John 14:6). He is the well, the font, the supplier of truth. If we never go directly to Him in relationship, we will build on a shaky foundation. Yes, we can stand on the truth of the teachings of the Catholic Church. I am deeply grateful for them and when we ignore them, it's to our detriment. But good theology is not a substitute for a real relationship. Both are needed.

You have a high priest, Jesus, whom you can run to and count on. Totally trustworthy, truth personified, safe and protective, and your sure guide. He is not a distant high priest, performing His duties methodically and mechanically. Instead, He is a high priest who ministers on your behalf, takes you by the hand, and draws you close. He enters into the gray with you, grasps your hand, and leads you through the murkiness of your life journey. You might long for a shortcut, but from my experience, the way Jesus leads is always *through* instead of *around*. Is the journey clean and without complications? No. It's often through rocky terrain surrounded by fog. But He never, ever lets go, and His presence is enough.

Day One
THE TRUE TABERNACLE

Read Hebrews 8:1–2.

1. According to Hebrews 8:1, what is the main point? (Note: This is the point the author has been trying to make throughout the book of Hebrews thus far.)

Hebrews 7 describes the kind of priest we need, and then chapter 8 opens with the news, "We have such a priest because we have Jesus!"

2. A. What is Jesus doing, according to Hebrews 8:1?

Jesus has ascended into heaven and taken His place at God's right hand. His placement here is significant because it is considered the place of highest honor and authority.

B. Jesus sits in the place of highest authority. His voice rules and is considered the final word. We have many voices in our heads that compete, all wanting to be considered the highest authority. Only the voice of Jesus should be given that place of honor. What thoughts run through your mind when you quiet your heart? When you reflect on your value and worth, what do the voices say?

C. Jesus says the following about you:

Romans 8:17

2 Corinthians 5:17

1 Thessalonians 5:5

1 Peter 2:9

Will you give His voice the place of highest authority in your mind and heart?

3. What is Jesus a "minister of," according to Hebrews 8:2?

Throughout the book of Hebrews, we have been learning that what we have in Christ is better (He's better than the angels, Moses, and the Old Testament priesthood). Now the author is coming out with another comparison that would have been shocking to the readers at that time. When he says that Jesus is the "minister of the sanctuary" of the *true* tabernacle, he is saying that there is something better than the temple in Jerusalem. Because Jesus is seated at the right hand of the Majesty in heaven, we know that the sanctuary where Jesus serves is there.

4. The readers of Hebrews were being challenged to recognize the difference between the copy (the tabernacle or temple on earth) and the real thing (the tabernacle in heaven). We are challenged to do the same. It's the most natural thing to focus on what we can touch, taste, and see, but God encourages us to lift our eyes to the unseen—to have an eternal focus that is fixed on heaven. What does Saint Paul challenge us to do in 2 Corinthians 4:16–18? Is this your perspective on your circumstances?

Quiet your heart and enjoy His presence. . . . Our true sanctuary is in heaven.

Life is full of "momentary light afflictions" (2 Corinthians 4:17). Some are more painful than others, but all tempt us to fix our eyes on what we feel like in the moment. Shifting our focus to heaven doesn't take away the suffering, but it can completely alter our attitudes. If we know that our suffering has a purpose, we are given strength to endure. When we realize that the way we respond to our circumstances is connected to a heavenly reward, we are less apt to give up. Hebrews 12:2 challenges us to fix our eyes on Jesus. He is ministering in the heavenly sanctuary. Jesus isn't just the King, He is our high priest and intercessor (Hebrews 7:25). He has cleared the way for us to come into God's presence, to stand in the Holy of Holies. He's not just sovereign—He's the Savior.

He doesn't always rescue us from our sufferings; often, He rescues us through them. It's in those times of trial that so much is stripped away—our comfort, our illusions regarding our own abilities, our tendency to be lulled into complacency. Suddenly everything is in Technicolor, and superficial explanations don't suffice. As a result, we are more likely to lift our eyes to heaven and gain a truer, purer perspective.

As we learned in Hebrews 6:19, we have hope as an anchor for the soul. It reaches up into heaven, connecting us on earth with the eternal. May we hold fast to the hope that our high priest is all that has been promised and all that we need. He is enough, and never tires of ministering on our behalf.

Day Two
THE PERFECT OFFERING

Read Hebrews 8:1–4.

1. According to Hebrews 8:3, what is every high priest (including Jesus) appointed to do?

2. A. What did the high priests offer? See Leviticus 16:3, 14–15. (Note: Aaron was Moses' brother and the first high priest.)

   B. What did Jesus offer? See Hebrews 9:12 and 10:10.

3. What do you learn about the burnt offering from the following verses?

   Leviticus 1:3

Leviticus 1:4 (Note: To *atone* means "to cover over, to pacify, to make propitiation."[60] It comes from the root word *kopher*, which is "a price for ransom of a life."[61])

Leviticus 1:5

Leviticus 1:9b

4. What do you learn about how Jesus was the perfect offering from the following verses?

Hebrews 4:15

2 Corinthians 5:17

1 Peter 1:18–19

John 13:1

5. The grain offering (Leviticus 2, 6:7–16) differed from the burnt offering. While the burnt offering made atonement for sins, the grain offering was a way for the Israelites to worship God and acknowledge His provision. The grain offering was likely barley or wheat, and could not contain yeast; it needed to be unleavened. A

---

[60] "Leviticus 1:4," Bible Hub, http://biblehub.com/lexicon/leviticus/1-4.htm.
[61] *The Brown-Driver-Briggs Hebrew and English Lexicon*, s.v. "kopher," Bible Hub, http://biblehub.com/hebrew/3724.htm.

portion of the grain offering was given to the priests to eat. In what sense is Jesus Himself a grain offering? See John 6:32–35 and 12:24.

6. Jesus offered us Himself, holding nothing back. What should be our response? See Hebrews 13:5. What is something specific you can do today out of gratitude for His gift to you?

Quiet your heart and enjoy His presence. . . . Come into His gates with thanksgiving, His courts with praise (Psalm 100:4).

"I glance back in the mirror to the concrete bridge, the one I've boldly driven straight across without second thought, and I see truth reflecting back at me: Every time fear freezes and worry writhes, every time I surrender to stress, aren't I advertising the unreliability of God? That I really don't believe? But if I'm grateful to the Bridge Builder for the crossing of a million strong bridges, thankful for a million faithful moments, my life speaks my beliefs and I trust Him again."[62] —Ann Voskamp

A grateful heart is built one remembrance at a time. It comes through a disciplined determination to be mindful of our thoughts, and to actually thank God for each blessing—the small as well as the great. There is so much that we take for granted. What if tomorrow we only had the things we have thanked God for today?

Just as we take the well-built bridge for granted, we often fail to see the way God is laying the ground beneath our feet, preparing our pathway, providing for us, and removing obstacles. He is the ultimate bridge builder, heart listener, dream maker, wound binder, and conflict resolver.

Surely, it would have been enough to win our hearts for Jesus to have offered Himself in our place on the cross. But He doesn't stop there. He lives to make intercession for us, praying for us continually, and intersects our lives, often in ways we don't realize.

---

[62] Ann Voskamp, *One Thousand Gifts* (Grand Rapids: MI: Zondervan, 2010), 151.

If we want to grow in gratitude toward God, perhaps a good place to start is by confessing the times we forget to notice Him.

See, O merciful God, what return
I, your thankless servant, have made
for the innumerable favors
and the wonderful love you have shown me!
What wrongs I have done, what good left undone!
Wash away, I beg you, these faults and stains
with your precious blood, most kind Redeemer,
and make up for my poverty by applying your merits.
Give me the protection I need to amend my life.
I give and surrender myself wholly to you,
and offer you all I possess,
with the prayer that you bestow your grace on me,
so that I may be able to devote and employ
all the thinking power of my mind
and the strength of my body in your holy service,
who are God blessed for ever and ever. Amen.[63]
Saint Peter Canisius, S.J.

Day Three
THE FLAWLESS MEDIATOR

Read Hebrews 8:4–7.

1. A. According to Hebrews 8:5, where do the Old Testament priests worship and serve?

   B. What did God tell Moses to do according to Hebrews 8:5? How long did Moses spend listening to God when he got those instructions? See Exodus 24:18.

---

[63] Michael Harter, ed., *Hearts on Fire* (St. Louis: Institute of Jesuit Sources, 1993), 24.

Clearly, the pattern mattered, which we see from God's words to Moses to "see that you make everything according to the pattern shown you." God gave a glimpse of the heavenly sanctuary to Moses so he could create an earthly version of it. We'll learn more about what the sanctuary on earth looked like in Hebrews 9. For now, let's just keep in mind that what was on earth was a copy of a heavenly reality.

2. Why was the new covenant considered better than the old covenant? See Hebrews 8:7.

One of those "better" promises is the one made in Psalm 110:4: "You are a priest forever." This refers to Jesus' eternal priesthood, one in which He lives to intercede for us and *mediate* for us. Hebrews 8:6 says that Jesus is "mediator of a better covenant."

A mediator is a go-between, one who attempts to achieve peace between two parties. Moses was the mediator of the old covenant, but he wasn't able to perfectly produce peace between the two parties involved (God and man).

According to *Vine's Expository Dictionary*, "The Mediator should Himself possess the nature and attributes of Him toward who He acts and should likewise participate in the nature of those for who He acts (sin apart); only by being possessed both of deity and humanity could He comprehend the claims of the one and the needs of the other."[64] Only Jesus met both those requirements, which is what qualified Him to be the "mediator of a better covenant."

3. To grapple with the significance of this passage, we need to continue to grow in our understanding of the word *covenant*. That's easier said than done. This meaty subject has been the source of debate among biblical scholars for centuries. Because this is a study on Hebrews and not on the covenants, we'll only be able to scratch the surface of all that can be learned about this topic. We'll use an excerpt from the *Catholic Bible Dictionary* to help us grow in understanding:

> Covenants were ubiquitous in the ancient Near East as well as Greco-Roman culture as a means to forge and maintain relationships between individuals, families, tribes, and even nations. Covenant is also the master-theme of the Bible, which records the various ways throughout history that

---

[64] *Vine's Expository Dictionary of New Testament Words*, s.v. "mediator," https://studybible.info/vines/Mediator.

God has drawn humanity into a familial relationship with himself through divine oaths.

The imperfect rendering of the word "covenant" . . . as "Testament" in the Latin tradition has obscured the fact that the Bible is divided into the Scriptures based on two covenants, the Old and the New . . .

A "covenant" is, in its essence, a legal means to establish kinship between two previously unrelated parties . . . It is incorrect to view a covenant simply as a contract. Generally, a contract involves the exchange of goods, whereas a covenant involves the exchange of persons . . .

In almost every case the central act of covenant-making was the swearing of an oath by one or both of the parties to the covenant . . . The oath generally took the form of a self-curse. The covenant-maker called on God or the gods to inflict death or some other grave penalty upon himself should he fail to keep the obligations of the covenant he was entering.[65]

A. In ancient cultures, covenants were a means to do what?

B. With "covenant" as the master theme of the Bible, what does it record throughout history?

C. The Bible is divided into two parts based on what?

D. While a contract "involves the exchange of goods," what does a covenant involve?

---

[65] Hahn, *Catholic Bible Dictionary*, 168–9.

E. What self-curse did the covenant maker call upon himself should he fail to keep the obligations of the covenant?

4. When the Israelites agreed to uphold their part of the old covenant (Exodus 24:3), they were, in essence, saying that they should be cursed if they failed to keep the law and follow God's rules. The stories of the Old Testament confirm that they were unable to hold to their end of the bargain, although God remained faithful to His. Who should have been cursed as a result of the breaking of the covenant? Who was cursed instead? See Galatians 3:13.

Jesus became a curse for us when He absorbed all our sin on the cross. We are the lawbreakers, yet He took our punishment. This was also the moment that Jesus stepped into the role of priest for us. A priest serves as a mediator between God and man. Jesus' priestly ordination occurred when He grabbed hold of us and allowed our sin to be transferred to Him, paid the price for our sin (death), and then ascended into heaven and grasped hold of the heavenly Father's hand in the heavenly sanctuary, uniting us with His perfect sacrifice. This was no contract involving the exchange of goods. This was a fulfillment of the covenant, involving the exchange of persons.

Quiet your heart and enjoy His presence. . . . Grab hold of His hand of mercy.

We read in the Old Testament the story of Job, a man infamous for his suffering. When wave after wave of affliction washed over him, Job began to explore what it would look like to challenge God in a "lawsuit." But even before he built his argument, he knew the odds were stacked against him. "How can anyone be in the right before God?" he asked. "Should one wish to contend with him, he could not answer him once in a thousand times. . . . For he is not a man like myself, that I should answer him, that we should come together in judgment. Would that there were an arbiter between us, who could lay his hand upon us both" (Job 9:2–3, 32–33).

Job longed for a mediator—someone to grab hold of his hand, one who could make things right between him and God.

This is exactly what Jesus came to do. He knew that we would be unable to keep the old covenant. Mankind deserved the cursing and the consequences, but out of His great love for us, God "made him to be sin who did not know sin, so that we might become the righteousness of God in him" (2 Corinthians 5:21). Jesus was flawless, the spotless lamb, without blemish. Taking on our sin and stain, He gave His life to ransom ours.

Oh, Lamb of God, our flawless mediator, You take away the sins of the world. Have mercy on us and grant us peace.

Day Four
THE NEW HEART

Read Hebrews 8:7–10.

1. We see from Hebrews 8:7 that the old covenant (the first covenant) was not faultless. Summarize the history of the Israelites' relationship to the covenant based on the following verses:

   Exodus 19:5–6 (God is speaking)

   Exodus 19:7–8

   Jeremiah 31:32

   What conclusion does the author of Hebrews draw based on this history? See Hebrews 8:8.

2. A. What was the consequence of the Israelites not standing by the covenant? See Hebrews 8:9.

    B. Was that the end of the story? See Isaiah 54:6–8.

3. Hebrews 8:8–12 quotes an Old Testament prophecy from Jeremiah 31:31–34. This is the longest Old Testament quote in the New Testament, so it's clearly important to the author of Hebrews.

    The prophecy was delivered by Jeremiah after the nation of Babylon had invaded the Israelite nation and destroyed it. The temple (God's dwelling place and where they went to receive forgiveness and mercy) was razed and burned and the people were taken into exile. The promises of God seemed to be null and void. Jeremiah was reflecting on the fact that God's people failed to keep their end of the bargain. Jeremiah realized the people would never be able to keep their part of the covenant—God would have to do more. What was the "more" that Jeremiah prophesied God would do? See Hebrews 8:10.

4. It was not God who had been at fault, nor was it the covenant itself. The problem was the people's inability to keep it. In the words of F. F. Bruce, "What was needed was a new nature, a heart liberated from its bondage to sin, a heart which not only spontaneously knew and loved the will of God but had the power to do it."[66]

    Ezekiel parallels Jeremiah's prophecy in Ezekiel 36:26. What was promised in this passage?

---

[66] Bruce, *The Epistle to the Hebrews*, 190.

So what was the point of the old covenant? If people were going to be unable to hold up their side of the bargain, was it without purpose? Not according to Saint Augustine, who wrote, "The law was given so that grace might be sought; grace was given so the law might be fulfilled."[67]

The law is held up like a mirror, letting us know how much we fall short of what God requires. An honest look into that mirror accompanied by a letting go of self-justification makes it clear that we need a savior. We see our need for grace and as a result are far more likely to receive the life-changing sacraments with open hearts.

Quiet your heart and enjoy His presence. . . . He is waiting to be invited in.

This gift of a new heart—a new nature—is something we all too often take for granted. Many of us are baptized as infants and never fully understand the enormity of what has taken place. In baptism, we are not just given a new heart; we are given a new identity, a new belonging. In Day Three, we learned that a covenant is the way God draws people into a familial relationship. In baptism, we are welcomed into God's family. He becomes our Father, and we are His beloved daughters. But to live out our true identity, we need to have a personal encounter with God. We need to get to know Him in such a way that we can recognize His voice. Author and musician Jonathan David Helser writes, "Identity is discovered through the voice we listen to. We have all been created to be defined by a Father's voice. Every girl is made to hear the words, 'You are beautiful.'"[68] Hearing God's voice above the cacophony of voices that swirl around us requires conversion of heart—a turning toward God. It isn't so much about our feelings as it is about our choices—whom we choose to listen to and follow.

When we choose to offer our hearts to God and follow Him, He infuses us with the divine power to live in the way that He asks us to. It isn't so much about following rules in a methodical way—it's about discovering the best path for flourishing as a chosen, destined child of God. Whatever He requires, He always equips us to accomplish. But He is a gentleman and waits for us to invite Him into the process. Not everyone will experience divine help in the same way—not because extra doses of grace are reserved for a select few, but because so few of us ask for what we need, choosing instead to rely on ourselves. The choice is ours: We can attempt to be our own saviors and do things on our own, or we can "confidently approach the throne of grace to receive mercy and to find grace for timely help" (Hebrews 4:16).

---

[67] Scott W. Hahn, *Romans* (Grand Rapids, MI: Baker Academic, 2017), 130.

[68] Jonathan David Helser, "Your Thoughts Define Me," *Cultivate: The Process of Living From Your Heart*, vol. 1 (Sophia, NC: Cageless Birds Publishing, 2014), 10.

Day Five
THE BETTER COVENANT

Read Hebrews 8:10–13.

1. What do you learn about the new covenant from Hebrews 8:10–12?

   Hebrews 8:10

   Hebrews 8:11

   Hebrews 8:12

2. A. What do we learn about God's character from Micah 7:18–19 that explains how the new covenant will be possible?

   B. The new covenant was made possible by an extravagant act of God's mercy and goodness. The prophet Micah spoke an important truth with his question, "Who is a God like you?" God's mercy may seem too good to be true, especially if we compare Him to people who have disappointed us. The Catechism tells us that parents are "in a way the first representatives of God for man," but that "human parents are fallible and can disfigure the face of fatherhood and motherhood" (CCC 239). What do you learn from the end of CCC 239 that should help us wrestle through disappointment in people without losing our trust in God's goodness?

C. The new covenant says, "They shall be my people" (Hebrews 8:10). This denotes belonging. How is your belonging to God described in Ephesians 1:11?

Being chosen and destined—belonging to God—is not promised to you conditionally. One of the significant differences between the old and the new covenants is the conditional nature of the old one (a promise of protection in return for loyalty and obedience) and the unconditional nature of the new one (a promise of salvation based on God's mercy and Jesus' sacrifice of Himself in our place).

D. Do you feel that you belong to God, that you are chosen and destined? Why or why not? Is it possible that someone has disfigured the face of God in your life, and you need to take time to wrestle with the truth that "no one is father as God is Father"?

3. Hebrews 8:11 promises us that "all shall know me, from the least to greatest."

There is a difference between knowing *about* someone and knowing someone *personally*. Jesus invites us into a personal relationship with Him, in which we grow in intimate knowledge of Him and are utterly known. This is not a conditional relationship in which God says, "I will be faithful to you if you are perfectly faithful to me." The old covenant made it clear that we would never be able to live up to that agreement. Instead, God offers us the new covenant, at great personal cost. This is the offer of an unconditional relationship that is based not on our perfection but on the perfection of God's Son. Jesus kept the old covenant perfectly. He absorbed its curse, not because *He* failed to keep the covenant, but because *we* did. He took the curse so that He could spend eternity with you.

Have you ever experienced God's love as a personal encounter with Him?

Have you ever read the Bible and experienced it coming alive—speaking to your heart personally?

Have you ever been convicted by the Holy Spirit and experienced God, in a sense, holding up a mirror to you so that you can see yourself in a new (likely uncomfortable) way?

Or is God someone you believe in and occasionally say prayers to? Someone you sense is far off, but who needs to be pleased and appeased?

Personal relationships are, by definition, personal. That means my experience of God will no doubt be very different from yours. Because of that, I hesitate to map out exactly what a personal relationship with Him looks like. But one thing I know: It's an encounter that leaves you transformed. He intersects your life and your heart and you are changed.

How has your relationship with Jesus changed you?

4. A.   What did Jesus identify as the new covenant? See Luke 22:20.

B. The personal relationship we are privileged to enjoy with Jesus came about because He shed His blood and gave His body for us. Catholics refer to the Eucharist as "the source and summit of the Christian life" (CCC 1324). It is here that we are invited into the deepest intimacy with Jesus, where He literally comes into our very bodies to bridge any distance between us. Saint John Paul II said, "With the Eucharist, the intimacy becomes total; the embrace between God and man reaches its apex."[69] Is this the way you see and experience the Eucharist?

Quiet your heart and enjoy His presence. . . . He longs for you to draw near.

The offering of such intimacy—an experience of lavish love and unfathomable mercy—deserves a response from us. Ideally, it leads us to press closer to Christ. But at times, according to C. S. Lewis, it can cause the opposite effect:

"An impersonal God"—well and good. A subjective God of beauty, truth and goodness, inside our own heads—better still. A formless light-force surging through us, a vast power which we can tap—best of all. But God himself, alive, pulling at the other end of the cord, perhaps approaching at an intimate speed, the hunter, King, husband . . . that is quite another matter.

There comes a moment when people who have been dabbling in religion suddenly draw back—supposing you really found Him? Or worse still, suppose He found you. If there is a God, you are in a sense alone with him. You cannot put him off with speculations about your neighbors' hypocrisy, or memories of what you have read in books. . . .[70]

In the words of theologian Tim Keller, "If God is this personal—not remote and distant—it's both a wonderful invitation and a frightening responsibility."[71] How will you respond?

---

[69] "Daily Quote: Eucharist," EucharisticVirtue, https://eucharisticvirtue.com/category/daily-eucharistic-quote/.

[70] C. S. Lewis, *Miracles* (New York: HarperOne, 2001), 150.

[71] Tim Keller, "The Lord We Can Know" (sermon, Redeemer Presbyterian Church, New York, March 13, 2005).

Conclusion

The polarization of the right and left in the cultural, political, and theological arenas results in never-ending conversations regarding what is right and what is wrong. Both sides are convinced that they are communicating truth, and all too often, the dialogue between the two results in a predictable impasse.

The need to be right is a steady theme in our culture. It's embedded in our psyche, and we often don't notice how much it can get in the way of a teachable posture and spiritual growth. Yes, there is absolute truth. Truth is not relative, and something is not true simply because it feels like it is. But we would be well served by a willingness to embrace the power of both/and.

Before you panic and think I'm about to delve into heresy (be assured, I am not), I want to draw attention to the way we can tend to allow the call to obedience and the call to intimacy to be polarizing. On the one hand, we can look at our relationship with God as being primarily about obedience. God, out of love for us, tells us how we should live. Our loving, childlike response should be obedience. This focus keeps our eyes on His instructions for morally upright and faithful living and the importance of our adhering to those guidelines.

On the other hand, we can look at a relationship with God as being primarily about intimacy. God, out of love and longing for us, sent His Son to die in our place, so that He could spend eternity with us. He is after our hearts, and longs for us to follow Mary of Bethany's example, sitting at His feet and soaking up His presence.[72] Communion and contemplation become the highest goal.

The desire to be right can cause us to move toward one of these responses to the exclusion of the other, when what is needed is a both/and approach. Our relationship with God should be characterized by both obedience to Him and intimacy with Him. In fact, one should lead to the other.

We want to be women who are led by truth. Endeavoring to walk in this way while navigating the gray that surrounds us can mean we have questions and struggle with doubt. Saint Augustine wrote that doubt is but another element of faith. Wrestling with what we believe and what actions we should take is often evidence of a living faith, of an authentic relationship with Jesus.

---

[72] Luke 10:40–42.

As we walk through life seeking answers and direction, may we never let go of Jesus' hand. May we embrace both obedience and intimacy. May we have the humility to be led by Christ, often on a path that is not clearly illuminated. Even if we feel we cannot see clearly, may we keep listening for His guiding voice. He isn't afraid of our doubts. His love is greater than any uncertainty. He is the constant, the anchor, the truth we can hold on to.

My Resolution

In what specific way will I apply what I have learned in this lesson?

Examples:

1. My current circumstances tempt me to focus on my suffering throughout the day. To counter this and grow gratitude in my heart, I will read the following verses each morning, write them on an index card, and carry it with me: "For this momentary light affliction is producing for us an eternal weight of glory beyond all comparison, as we look not to what is seen but to what is unseen; for what is seen is transitory, but what is unseen is eternal" (2 Corinthians 4:17–18).

2. It is hard for me to believe that as a daughter of God, I am chosen and destined. To counter the doubts with truth, I will read the following verse each morning, write it on an index card, and carry it with me: "In him we were also chosen, destined in accord with the purpose of the One who accomplishes all things according to the intention of His will" (Ephesians 1:11).

3. I recognize that I tend to focus on [obedience or intimacy]. I will choose this week to focus on what comes less naturally, and as a result, grow in a new way. If intimacy comes naturally, I will ask God to reveal a specific area of my life where I need to obey Him. If obedience is my usual focus, I will go to adoration and just sit in the presence of Jesus.

My resolution:

Catechism Clips

CCC 239 By calling God "Father", the language of faith indicates two main things: that God is the first origin of everything and transcendent authority; and that he is at the same time goodness and loving care for all his children. God's parental tenderness can also be expressed by the image of motherhood, which emphasizes God's immanence, the intimacy between Creator and creature. The language of faith thus draws on the human experience of parents, who are in a way the first representatives of God for man. But this experience also tells us that human parents are fallible and can disfigure the face of fatherhood and motherhood. We ought therefore to recall that God transcends the human distinction between the sexes. He is neither man nor woman: he is God. He also transcends human fatherhood and motherhood, although he is their origin and standard: no one is father as God is Father.

CCC 1324 The Eucharist is "the source and summit of the Christian life." "The other sacraments, and indeed all ecclesiastical ministries and works of the apostolate, are bound up with the Eucharist and are oriented toward it. For in the blessed Eucharist is contained the whole spiritual good of the Church, namely Christ himself, our Pasch."

Verse Study

See Appendix 3 for instructions on how to complete a verse study.

Ezekiel 36:26–27

1. Verse:

2. Paraphrase:

3. Questions:

4. Cross-references:

5. Personal Application:

Lesson 12

A PERFECT SACRIFICE

Hebrews 9

Introduction

The roads between my home in Maryland and my parents' house in Virginia were well traveled. I could get there without much thought. Along the route were some of my favorite places to shop, and I knew that territory like the back of my hand. That is, until the powers that be came up with an idea to improve the overall plan of the city in the center of the route. For years everything was under construction, and suddenly it was easy to get lost in familiar territory. This major renovation project meant that alternative routes needed to be provided, and those routes were used for years. I lived through the temporary solution, but never saw the final stage before our move to Florida.

In that same way, God has had a master plan for the best way to reach Him from the very beginning. It's been His plan to make everything right, to deal with evil and wickedness so that ultimately, everything can be put in proper order. But until that plan came into fruition through Jesus, there was another plan in place. It wasn't the final route to Him; in fact, the master plan would render the former obsolete.

Throughout the letter, the author of Hebrews has been begging his readers not to go back to the temporary route when the best one has been provided. It's true that they knew the temporary one like the back of their hands, and the familiarity made it appealing. Because of this, the author needed to convince them that the master plan was far superior. This is what he sets out to do in Hebrews 9.

His writing has relevance for us today, because the comfort of the familiar will often tempt us to go back to past patterns of behavior. Our families of origin have shaped us; unhealthy coping mechanisms can feel like well-worn slippers, and old habits die hard. Jesus offers us a new way to live and encounter God, but if we remain stuck in old patterns, we'll miss out on experiencing it.

For many of us, the road marked by self-reliance and hustling for our worth is the most familiar. It's our default path. Jesus intersects our lives and tells us, "Your new identity as the beloved is given, not found!" But all too often, we go back to the familiar ways of measuring our worth and inadvertently end up trying to earn our salvation, when it has always been purely a gift.

May we learn from the author of Hebrews to keep our eyes on what is best, not settle for what is familiar, and be willing to chart a new course in Christ.

Day One
THE MERCY SEAT

Read Hebrews 9:1–5.

1. According to Hebrews 9:1, what did the first covenant have?

The first covenant's regulations for worship dictated *who* was allowed to approach God, *how* this was to be done, and *when* it was permitted.

The earthly sanctuary was originally called the tabernacle, and later the temple. Hebrews 9 is not a description of the temple in Jerusalem where the Jewish people were currently worshipping. That temple was known as Herod's Temple. It had been rebuilt after the original temple, built by King Solomon (King David's son), was destroyed by the invasion of the Babylonians around 586 BC.

The sanctuary described in Hebrews 9 is the original tabernacle built by Moses in the wilderness. Why was this the author's choice? Likely because the most available recorded details are about that one. Moses was given a vision of exactly how God wanted the tabernacle to be constructed, and that vision was recorded in the book of Exodus. In addition, in Herod's Temple, the Holy of Holies was actually empty. When the Israelites realized that the Babylonians were going to invade, the prophet Jeremiah took the ark of the covenant and hid it. It has never been found. According to 2 Maccabees 2:7–8, "The place is to remain unknown until God gathers his people together again and shows them mercy. Then the Lord will disclose these things, and the glory of the Lord and the cloud will be seen, just as they appeared in the time of Moses and of Solomon."

2. A. The author of Hebrews describes two sections within the tabernacle, referring to them as the "outer one" and the one "behind the second veil." According to Hebrews 9:2, what was found in the outer one, the Holy Place?

B. How is the lampstand described in Leviticus 24:2–4?

The lampstand, also called the menorah, was made of pure beaten gold. Three branches were on either side, and each branch had three cups shaped like almond blossoms with knobs and petals (Exodus 25:31–36).

C. What happened to the bread of offering on every Sabbath? See Leviticus 24:8–9.

D. A literal translation of "bread of offering" is "bread of the face." According to the Talmud (the recorded Jewish oral traditions), there was a beautiful tradition that happened three times a year. During that time, the bread of offering was taken outside, allowing the people to see it. The priests "used to lift it up and exhibit the Bread of the Presence on it to those who came up for the festivals, saying to them, 'Behold, God's love for you!'"[73]

This brings Eucharistic adoration to mind. For Catholics, the Eucharist is the face of Christ. According to 2 Corinthians 3:18, what happens as we gaze on Christ's face in adoration?

---

[73] Babylonian Talmud, Menachot 29A, in Brant Pitre, *Jesus and the Jewish Roots of the Eucharist: Unlocking the Secrets of the Last Supper* (New York: Doubleday, 2010), 130–1.

The Jesuit priest Anthony de Mello said, "Behold God beholding you . . . and smiling."[74] Isn't this a different perspective to bring to adoration? God wants to spend time with you. Longing for an intimate encounter, He hopes you will draw near to be reminded of His love for you. "The bread of the face" patiently waits to bless you.

3. A. What was the area behind the second veil called? What was found there? See Hebrews 9:3.

    B. What was in the ark of the covenant? See Hebrews 9:4.

    C. The ark of the covenant, made of acacia wood and covered in pure gold, housed the tablets of the covenant—the stones etched with the Ten Commandments, carved by God Himself. What significant thing happened at the ark of the covenant? See Exodus 25:21–22.

4. A. What stretched above the ark of the covenant? See Hebrews 9:5.

    The cherubim are a rank of angels, and it was they who were stationed at the entrance of the Garden of Eden in Genesis 3:24 to prevent Adam and Eve from reentering.

    B. What image of the cherubim do we receive from Psalm 80:2 and 99:1?

---

[74] Harter, *Hearts on Fire*, 9.

This imagery depicts the ark of the covenant as God's throne, the place where He rules as our sovereign king.

5. According to Hebrews 9:5, what did the cherubim overshadow?

According to CCC 433, "The mercy seat was the place of God's presence." This was where God's justice and mercy met. In the Old Testament, the high priest would come into the Holy of Holies once a year and sprinkle an animal's blood on the mercy seat. His sole purpose in coming into God's presence was to say, "We are sorry for our sins." God looked on the blood of the animal, and He forgave the people. We will look at the significance of this in greater depth later.

CCC 433 uses the word *expiation*. When we read this word in the New Testament, it is speaking of Jesus. *Expiation* is a big word used to describe the way Christ rescued us from the consequences of our sins. It is the act of His blood being poured out on the cross when He died in our place. In John 13:1, this act was described as Jesus loving His own until the end. There is nothing that Jesus held back. He loved us to the limit, holding nothing back, considering spending eternity with us worth giving His life for.

Quiet your heart and enjoy His presence. . . . Behold God's love for you.

Because of Jesus, "Mercy triumphs over justice" (James 2:13). When suffering tempts us to cry, "It isn't fair," we'd be wise to think about this verse. Why does mercy triumph over justice? Because the sinless Savior received the punishment due us. God's mercy does not flow to us because He has said that sin doesn't matter. The price for sin was paid, but not by the ones who owed the debt (and that would be us). Jesus' death on the cross is the supreme example of life not being fair, and we are the beneficiaries of this unmerited gift of mercy.

What a perspective changer it would be if we truly took that truth deep into our hearts. Wouldn't we look at our circumstances differently? True transformation could take place in our hearts because we'd be far more likely to obey God for the right reasons. We'd obey not because we are afraid of the consequences of disobedience, but because we are so overwhelmingly grateful to Jesus. Our motives would shift and become purified.

Dear Lord,

Forgive me for the times I come into Your presence mindlessly or even arrogantly. When I think of the care that was taken to create just the right environment for man to meet with You in the tabernacle in the temple, it occurs to me that I should take a little more time to prepare my mind and heart to encounter You. You accept me as I am and don't demand that I be perfect to be in Your presence, so it isn't about earning Your love or getting ready to perform for You. But when my mind is not in the right place—when I'm not crystal clear regarding Your greatness, majesty, kindness, and sovereignty—my attitude can head in all sorts of bad directions. I confess the times I accuse You in my heart of holding out on me or not being worthy of my trust. I don't always do this intentionally; it seems to creep into my thinking when life isn't going the way I'd like it to go. When I'm disappointed, I can quickly fall into thinking about how unfair life is, with me as the victim in the story. This thought process always leads to discouragement and disillusionment—never to peace. So please help me in this. May I not lose sight of who You are and what You've done for me.

Day Two
NOT ENOUGH

Read Hebrews 9:6–10.

1. When the Old Testament priests, in "performing their services" (Hebrews 9:6), repeatedly went into the outer tabernacle, what duties were they performing? See the following passages for your answer.

Exodus 27:20–21

Exodus 30:7–8

Leviticus 24:8–9

Note: All these duties were performed in the outer room, the Holy Place.

2. A. On one day each year, the most sacred of rites took place. This was the Day of Atonement, or Yom Kippur. What happened in the Holy of Holies on this festival day? See Hebrews 9:7 and Leviticus 16:1–4, 11–15.

B. Describe the ceremony that followed. See Leviticus 16:20–22.

3. According to Hebrews 9:8, what was the Holy Spirit showing through the layout of the tabernacle and the ceremonies described here?

The Holy Spirit used the architecture of the tabernacle and the ceremonies on the Day of Atonement to teach the important spiritual truth that there was a gulf—a distance—between God and man. Sin created that distance, and a mediator was required to connect them. Throughout the Old Testament, the mediator was the high priest—one man, from one tribe, from one nation. Only he was allowed into God's presence. The only way he could enter was with the blood of a sacrificial victim. His own goodness and best efforts weren't enough to earn him that place, and the other Israelites didn't even get close. They remained many steps removed—away from the Holy of Holies and the Holy Place.

4. According to Hebrews 9:9–10, what are the gifts and sacrifices unable to do?

The conscience is the place with us that acknowledges that we are not enough. God has a standard of holiness that we have failed to keep. The animal sacrifices were never able to cleanse the conscience, and our best efforts, apart from Christ, are just as ineffective. Much can make us look good on the outside, but God has always been most concerned about what is going on deep within us. This is where He most desires transformation. It's in this place that He wants to set us free.

5. Do voices in your head ever whisper to you, "Not enough"? In which areas of your life do you feel that your best efforts fall short of what and who you desire to be?

My friend, this is why Jesus came. We'll read more about this in upcoming verses, but I cannot end today's study without leaving you with hope. Jesus knew that our best efforts would never be enough to erase the stain of sin and the underlying feeling of guilt. Recognizing that the blood of bulls and goats would never perfectly cleanse the conscience, Jesus offered the purest blood, His own. His blood is enough to cleanse and purify us all.

Quiet your heart and enjoy His presence. . . . He offers you covering and cleansing.

The extent of mankind's sin was described by God through the prophet Isaiah: "When you spread out your hands, I will close my eyes to you; though you pray the more, I will not listen. Your hands are full of blood! Wash yourselves clean! Put away your misdeeds from before my eyes; cease doing evil" (Isaiah 1:15–16). But the Israelites were unable to perfectly obey, and we fail in the same way.

But that was not the end of the story. The way out of the mess was promised in Isaiah 1:18: "Come now, let us set things right, says the Lord: Though your sins be like scarlet, they may become white as snow; though they may be red like crimson, they may become white as wool."

But how? One of my favorite old hymns points to the solution:

What can wash away my sin? Nothing but the blood of Jesus. What can make me whole again? Nothing but the blood of Jesus.
Oh, precious is the flow that makes me white as snow. No other fount I know, nothing but the blood of Jesus.

For my cleansing this I see—nothing but the blood of Jesus. For my pardon this my plea—nothing but the blood of Jesus.

Nothing can my sin erase, nothing but the blood of Jesus! Naught of works, 'tis all of grace—nothing but the blood of Jesus!

This is all my hope and peace—nothing but the blood of Jesus! This is my righteousness—nothing but the blood of Jesus![75]

Dear Lord,

Your blood speaks for me when all my self-justification dies down. My heart whispers, "I am not enough." Shame overwhelms me. Guilt holds me in its viselike grip. And this is when Your blood stills and overpowers me. It does for me what I cannot do on my own behalf. It doesn't prove that I am deserving; it proves that Jesus is worthy, selfless, and my substitute. It rises to heaven and satisfies the Father. Justice is served, but not at my expense. I am accepted, but not because of my own merits. It leads me to echo the words of Saint Thérèse of Lisieux: "In the evening of my life I shall appear before You with empty hands, for I do not ask You to count my works. All our justices are stained in Your eyes. I want therefore to clothe myself in Your own justice and receive from Your love the eternal possession of Yourself."[76]

My best efforts aren't enough, but Your blood is more than enough. I need a Savior. I need You. Thank You for rescuing me and for Your promise in John 8:36: "So if the Son makes You free, You will be free indeed." May I be covered by the crimson flow of Your mercy, freedom, and joy.

Day Three
DEEP WITHIN

Read Hebrews 9:11–14.

1. According to Hebrews 9:11, what did Jesus "pass through"?

2. A. In the earthly tabernacle, what prevented people from passing through from the Holy Place to the Holy of Holies? See Exodus 26:33.

---

[75] Robert Lowry, "Nothing but the Blood," 1876.

[76] St. Thérèse of Lisieux, "Act of Oblation to Merciful Love," June 9, 1895.

B. Describe the veil, according to Exodus 26:31.

When Adam and Eve sinned and were expelled from the Garden of Eden, cherubim with a flaming sword were stationed at the east end of the garden, preventing them from coming back in. When the veil in the temple was embroidered with cherubim, it was to remind the people that mankind was separated from God. But a change took place with the creation of the tabernacle. While before this the door to God's presence was closed, it opened a crack with the Holy of Holies. Although only the high priest was allowed to enter once a year, this was still a progression from what had been experienced for generations after original sin entered the world.

3. A. With what did Jesus enter into the sanctuary? What did He obtain through that act? See Hebrews 9:12.

B. For whom did Jesus obtain eternal redemption? See Ephesians 1:7.

C. The *Catholic Bible Dictionary* defines *redemption* as "the payment of a ransom price to liberate someone held in captivity."[77] The opposite of captivity is freedom, which reminds us that Jesus sacrificed His own blood so that we could experience eternal liberation. Is there an area of your life where you would like Jesus to set you free? If so, list it here.

4. According to Hebrews 9:13, what was accomplished by the "blood of goats and bulls and the sprinkling of a heifer's ashes"?

---

[77] Hahn, *Catholic Bible Dictionary*, 758.

According to theologian F. F. Bruce:

> The blood of slaughtered animals under the old order did possess a certain efficacy, but it was an outward efficacy for the removal of ceremonial pollution . . . The sin offerings presented on the Day of Atonement, or at any other time, has no effect on the consciences of those on whose behalf they were brought; they served merely in an external and symbolical manner to counteract the defilement of sin.[78]

Here it is again—the reminder that the conscience wasn't helped by the Old Testament sacrifices.

5. By contrast, what did the blood of Christ accomplish? See Hebrews 9:14.

The blood of Christ is meant to do so much more than just "cleanse the flesh." God isn't satisfied by seeing an external transformation. He wants to see us made clean deep down, within the Holy of Holies in each of us.

It is in this internal place that we find a courtroom, the place where we spend an inordinate amount of time trying to justify our own worth—not to the world, but to ourselves. Would you not agree that the way we speak to ourselves, the way we view ourselves, would often earn us the moniker "our own worst critic"? It is in this deep place that Jesus wants to transform us.

He recognizes that when things quiet down, our minds often start to condemn us. We think of all the things we have failed to do, the things we could have done better. Grappling with the gap between our best intentions and the ultimate reality of who we really are, we say to ourselves, "I'm not enough." We're so aware of the ways we fall short.

When Jesus meets us in this place, He doesn't tell us to pull ourselves up by our bootstraps. Nor does He encourage us to just try harder. Instead, He reminds us that He "offered *himself* unblemished to God" (Hebrews 9:14). The perfect lamb of God laid down His life in our place so that the divine exchange could occur—our sinfulness for His holiness.

---

[78] Bruce, *The Epistle to the Hebrews*, 214.

215

Why was He willing to do this? We find the answer in Ephesians 2:4–5. Jesus offered us this incredible, lopsided, unfair exchange "because of the great love he had for us, even when we were dead in our transgressions." He didn't wait for us to clean up and present the best versions of ourselves. His love for us proved to be boundless even when we were paralyzed and saturated by our sin.

Quiet your heart and enjoy His presence. . . . Come real and let the walls come down.

"See what love the Father has bestowed on us that we may be called the children of God. Yet so we are . . . Beloved, we are God's children now; what we shall be has not yet been revealed. We do know that when it is revealed we shall be like him, for we shall see him as he is." (1 John 3:1–2)

When our voice of self-reproach quiets, we can begin to hear God's voice calling us the beloved. He invites us to walk away from "dead works" in order to "worship the living God." Perhaps the "dead works" referred to in Hebrews 9:14 are those things we do to try to win the love of God, a love that is bestowed and never earned. Maybe this is a reference to the times we behave like performing orphans, thinking that if we can just be perfect, if we can do a little better, maybe then we'll be worthy of becoming a daughter. The opposite of this is a life of worship, with acts of mercy, kindness, and obedience flowing out of the heart of a woman who knows she is accepted and beloved. She knows this acceptance is not based on anything she has done, but is entirely due to the sacrifice of her sinless Savior. We are children of God, a title of privilege and royalty, which is bestowed, not earned.

During those dark times when feelings of inadequacy rush in, when you wonder if you are lovable, when you question your worth, remember this:

> *You are the daughter of the star breather (Psalm 33:6).*
> *You are the apple of His eye (Deuteronomy 32:10).*
> *He calls you His "beautiful one" (Song of Songs 2:10).*
> *Nothing can separate you from His love (Romans 8:38–39).*
> *You are powerful beyond measure (Ephesians 1:19–20).*
> *You have a fresh start, every morning, because of His limitless mercy (Lamentations 3:23–24).*

Straighten your crown, daughter of the King. Go forth in His power, not your own. Rest in your true identity. You are the beloved.

Day Four
THE BLOOD SACRIFICE

Read Hebrews 9:15–22.

Note: This next section contains some of the most challenging verses in the book of Hebrews, so don't get discouraged if it takes a little effort to wrap your mind around the truths contained here. Let's press into the mystery together.

1. A. Jesus is described as "the mediator of a new covenant" in Hebrews 9:15. According to the *Catechism of the Catholic Church*, what is the job of a mediator? (The definition can be found in the Catechism Clips section at the end of this lesson.)

   B. Who are the two "separate or opposing parties" that Jesus, our mediator, reconciled?

   C. What did Jesus' work as our mediator gain for us?

2. Which sins (transgressions) are referred to in Hebrews 9:15?

This verse describes the retroactive power of Christ's death. His death not only obtained mercy and forgiveness for sins that were to be committed from that point going forward (proactive power), it also purchased deliverance for those who had sinned in the past, under the first covenant (retroactive power).

Until Christ's death effected "deliverance from transgressions," the people of God couldn't receive their "eternal inheritance." But His shed blood meant the promise could be fulfilled.

3. To understand the meaning behind the next two verses (Hebrews 9:16–17), it's helpful to know that the Greek word translated "covenant" is *diatheke*, and this word can mean a covenant or a will. While a covenant dealt more with establishing a relationship, a will focused on dispersing property.[79]

Both meanings are relevant to this section of Hebrews. The fractured relationship between God and man needed to be dealt with, and there needed to be a way for the people to receive their inheritance.

A. According to Hebrews 9:16, what must take place for a will to take effect?

B. The same was true for the old covenant. For its promises to take effect, there had to be a death. How was this truth described in Hebrews 9:18?

C. Thinking back on what you have learned about the Old Testament sacrificial system, whose death in the temple was required for the promise of forgiveness to take effect?

An important distinction must be made regarding which sins were forgiven through the sacrificial death of the animals. Only *unintentional* sin was forgiven (Numbers 15:22–31). In addition, the animal sacrifices could not cleanse the conscience (Hebrews 9:9).

A more perfect death was required to repair the relationship between God and man, and there had to be a death for an eternal inheritance to be received.

4. According to Hebrews 9:19–21, what did Moses do after proclaiming the commandments to the people?

---

[79] Healy, *Hebrews*, 180.

5. A. What does Hebrews 9:22 say blood accomplishes?

B. What do we *not* have if no blood is shed?

To repair the enormous breach between God and man that was created by sin, a price would need to be paid. Reconciliation would come at a cost. Blood would need to be shed so that forgiveness could flow.

God doesn't desire the death of His children (2 Peter 3:9, Ezekiel 18:23), so His solution was the ultimate gift of self. An animal, no matter how spotless, could never be a perfect substitute for a person. The perfect substitute—the perfect death, the perfect shed blood—would be offered by Jesus, both God and man.

Quiet your heart and enjoy His presence. . . . He gave His life for yours.

All this talk of blood can be seriously off-putting. Unless we grow in our understanding of why "without the shedding of blood there is no forgiveness," we'll run the risk of considering God bloodthirsty, wrathful, and vindictive.

The last thing we should do in response to these verses in Hebrews is conclude that God is bloodthirsty. Instead, He is sacrificial to the highest degree. In the words of the prophet Isaiah, "But he was pierced for our sins, crushed for our iniquity. He bore the punishment that makes us whole, by his wounds we were healed" (Isaiah 53:5).

We are utterly dependent on the grace of God, and it is the blood of Jesus that gives us access to it. Without His blood, incurable is our wound, and grievous our injury (Jeremiah 30:12). But with it, God will forgive our evildoing and remember our sins no more (Hebrews 8:12). This is the gift of the new covenant, offered to us all, freely. What extravagant, amazing grace.

Day Five
MORE THAN WE DESERVE

Read Hebrews 9:23–28.

1. A. How were the "copies of the heavenly things" (Hebrews 9:23) purified? See Hebrews 9:19–22.

   B. What would be needed for the "heavenly things themselves" to be purified? See Hebrews 9:23.

2. A. According to Hebrews 9:24, what did Jesus enter heaven to do?

   B. What insight do you gain from Romans 8:34 and 1 John 2:1 in terms of what Jesus does in heaven on our behalf?

3. Does Jesus' sacrifice on the cross need to be repeated, as the animal sacrifices were, year after year? See Hebrews 9:25–26.

4. A. What does Hebrews 9:27 say happens after death?

B. What added insight do you gain regarding the finality of death from CCC 1013?

5. What will happen when Jesus appears a second time? See Hebrews 9:28, Acts 1:11, Acts 3:19–21, 1 Thessalonians 4:16, and Matthew 24:30–31.

This life on earth is not all there is. This is the prepping ground, the place where we get ready for heaven. According to 2 Peter 3:9–10, God is patient with us in this process. He doesn't want any of us to spend eternity apart from Him. But there will come a day when we'll be held accountable for the choices we have made and who we have become. This is described in 2 Peter 2:10 as a day when "the earth and everything done on it will be found out."

On that day, religious observances will not be enough. Being a nice person won't be sufficient. Animal sacrifices won't make us acceptable. The only thing that will usher us into the presence of God will be the blood of Jesus covering us. Without blood, there is no forgiveness (Hebrews 9:22). When we think of the cross, we're reminded that real forgiveness always involves suffering. But instead of wanting us to suffer the consequences of our choices, Jesus chose to absorb our pain and sin. This truth should change the way we live. Has it changed you?

Theologian Tim Keller fleshed this out in a sermon called "The Sacrifice." He asked his listeners to imagine walking alongside a railroad track with a friend. Imagine the friend saying, "Let me show you how much I love you," and then throwing himself in front of an oncoming train and getting killed. Would you say, "Oh, how he loved me"? No. You'd say, "What's the matter with him?!" But what if you were walking on the railroad track and suddenly a train came around the corner and at the cost of his life, your friend pushed you out of the way and then was killed, saving your life in the process? That would be different. Then you would be moved by how he loved you. Why? Because there was actual danger.

Keller goes on to make his point that if Jesus died but you didn't really have a problem and you were all right as you were, then His death is not going to change you.

What's the truth? The truth is, we do have a problem, and what we deserve for our sins is death. The blood of Christ has saved us from what we deserve. Jesus isn't just our example; He is our Savior. May we be changed inwardly because gratitude has transformed our perspective.

Quiet your heart and enjoy His presence. . . . Lift your eyes higher.

"But our citizenship is in heaven, and from it we also await a savior, the Lord Jesus Christ. He will change our lowly body to conform with his glorified body by the power that enables him also to bring all things into subjection to himself" (Philippians 3:20).

Life can get so insanely messy. Principles and truths keep us on track and ground our beliefs, but circumstances can crash into our lives that make the most basic truths feel unreal. This becomes especially problematic when we think things on earth should all make sense. If you feel you don't belong, if life is leaving you dissatisfied, if it feels like nothing will ever change, remember that earth is not your home. Your citizenship is in heaven. Saint Paul challenges us to "think of what is above, not of what is on earth . . . your life is hidden with Christ in God" (Colossians 3:2).

The relief is going to come. Clarity will break through the clouds of confusion. The chains will fall off and freedom will be the very air you'll breathe. We live in the in-between, the almost but not yet. During these days, years, and seasons, you need to keep Jesus at the forefront of your mind. Place Him between your heart and your problems. That way when the circumstances press in, it will only bring Jesus closer. True, He doesn't always offer explanation. Instead, He offers His presence, and asks for your trust. Can you believe, despite all evidence making things seem senseless? Can you believe in His goodness, measuring His love not by how many prayers were answered as you'd like but instead by His sacrifice on the cross?

Conclusion

Have you ever felt that you weren't good enough, that you didn't measure up? Perhaps this has translated into a habit of hustling for your worth and doing your best to hide your flaws. Love can feel pretty conditional, and the lengths we go to in order to feel valued and accepted can be exhausting.

The priests and people of the Old Testament had many rituals and rules for entering into God's presence, but no matter how well they followed it all, it was never enough to cleanse the conscience. There was always a place deep within that whispered, "guilty," "not enough," "no access to God." Rituals and rules never cleansed the heart.

Jesus' shed blood changed all that. It was retroactive, cleansing the consciences of all those who loved and followed God before Christ came. And it was proactive, cleansing our consciences, freeing us from death's sting and sin's power and lifting the weight of guilt off our shoulders. The fact that Jesus had to die for us to experience freedom gets rid of any silly notion that our sin doesn't matter. Our forgiveness and acceptance was purchased for us. The ultimate price was paid by Jesus.

You will only frustrate yourself if you spend your life trying to earn God's favor. It is bestowed as a gift of grace and offered to His children. Instead of trying to measure up, confess the times you've tried to be your own savior. He will always meet you in that place with grace upon grace.

The world we live in values personal achievement, autonomy, and self-reliance. God looks at things very differently, and values humility and dependence on Him. Nothing pleases Him more than an attitude like that of Saint Thérèse:

> I have always wanted to be become a saint. Unfortunately, when I have compared myself with the saints, I have always found that there is the same difference between the saints and me as there is between a mountain whose summit is lost in the clouds and a humble grain of sand trodden underfoot by passersby. Instead of being discouraged, I told myself: God would not make me wish for something impossible and so, in spite of my littleness, I can aim at being a saint. It is impossible for me to grow bigger, so I put up with myself as I am, with all my countless faults. But I will look for some means of going to heaven by a little way which is very short and very straight, a little way that is quite new . . . It is your arms, Jesus, which are the lift to carry me to heaven, And so there is no need for me to grow up. In fact, just the opposite: I must stay little and become less and less.[80]

Our heavenly Father stands with arms open wide, welcoming us home. Instead of getting lost in the familiar territory of trying to earn our worth, let's take the new path, the "little way which is very short and very straight." Let's fall into the arms of Jesus, who bring us straight to God and the ocean of His love.

---

[80] St. Thérèse of Lisieux, *Story of a Soul*, trans. John Clarke (New York: Doubleday, 2001), 113.

My Resolution

In what specific way will I apply what I have learned in this lesson?

Examples:

1. I will spend an hour in adoration this week out of gratitude for the fact that I can approach God directly. While there, I will "behold God beholding [me] . . . and smiling" (Fr. Anthony de Mello).

2. I often complain that life is not fair. I will confess this as a lack of gratitude and acknowledge that what would be fair would be me paying the price for my own sin. Instead, Jesus paid it for me. I will thank God that life is not fair—that I have not received what I deserved, but instead have received mercy and grace.

3. I struggle with feelings of inadequacy. To counter the voices of shame and doubt, I will focus on the truths found in Quiet Your Heart, Day Three:

   I am the daughter of the star breather (Psalm 33:6).
   I am the apple of His eye (Deuteronomy 32:10).
   He calls me His "beautiful one" (Song of Songs 2:10).
   Nothing can separate me from His love (Romans 8:38–39).
   I am powerful beyond measure (Ephesians 1:19–20).
   I have a fresh start, every morning, because of His limitless mercy (Lamentations 3:23–24).

My resolution:

Catechism Clips

CCC 433 The name of the Savior God was invoked only once in the year by the high priest in atonement for the sins of Israel, after he had sprinkled the mercy seat in the Holy of holies with the sacrificial blood. The mercy seat was the place of God's presence. When St. Paul speaks of Jesus whom "God put forward as an expiation by his blood," he means that in Christ's humanity "God was in Christ reconciling the world to himself."

CCC 1013 Death is the end of man's earthly pilgrimage, of the time of grace and mercy which God offers him so as to work out his earthly life in keeping with the divine plan, and to decide his ultimate destiny. When "the single course of our earthly life" is completed, we shall not return to other earthly lives: "It is appointed for men to die once." There is no "reincarnation" after death.

MEDIATOR/MEDIATRIX One who links or reconciles separate or opposing parties. Thus Jesus Christ is the "one mediator between God and the human race" (1 Timothy 2:5). Through His sacrificial offering He has become high priest and our unique mediator who has gained for us access to God's saving grace for humanity. Moreover, Mary is sometimes called "mediatrix" in virtue of her cooperation in the saving mission of Christ, who alone is the unique mediator between God and humanity.

Verse Study

See Appendix 3 for instructions on how to complete a verse study.

1 Peter 1:18–19

1. Verse:

2. Paraphrase:

3. Questions:

4. Cross-references:

5. Personal Application:

Lesson 13: Talk

THE SACRED

Hebrews 9

You can view this talk on the accompanying DVD, or please visit our website at walkingwithpurpose.com/videos and select the *Grounded in Hope* Bible Study, then click through to select Videos.

I. No Access

II. The Old Way to Approach God

The temple got more restrictive the closer you got to the Holy of Holies.

Court of the Gentiles: almost anyone
Court of Women: Israelite men and women
Court of Israelites: Israelite men
Holy Place: Israelite priests
Holy of Holies: high priest

Leviticus 17:11

Hebrews 9:22

While the temple provided a means for the Israelites to be forgiven for their sins, it also delivered the steady message: *You are not holy. God is. You have no right to stand in His presence.*

III. The New Way to Approach God

Matthew 27:50

"Through the blood of Jesus, we have confidence of entrance into the sanctuary by the new and living way he opened for us through the veil . . ." (Hebrews 10:19)

The final substitution for sin—the final atonement, the final innocent substitute for man—had to take place in the heavenly tabernacle. What was happening on earth was a copy, a shadow. An innocent substitute, a perfect atonement, a bloody sacrifice would need to be made in the heavenly tabernacle for sin to be permanently dealt with.

Jesus appeared before the Father as the ultimate _____. Remember that atonement is the process of making amends for sin. It's the way of compensating for wrong. Another word for atonement is *satisfaction*. When God the Father looked on the blood of His perfect Son, Jesus, _____ _____ _____. He was satisfied with that sacrifice, and offered forgiveness for anyone covered with Jesus' blood.

Do you want access to the Father? Do you want to enter the Holy of Holies and come into His presence? Do you long to be ushered into His heart?

You need to enter His presence with blood, but not the blood of animals. You enter with the _____.

Romans 5:8–9

Romans 5:1–2

John 1:12

Ephesians 2:13: "But now in Christ Jesus you who once were far away have been brought near through the blood of Jesus."

Discussion Questions

1. Did the statement that we are unable to get rid of our shame—the underlying sense that we are not enough—resonate with you? Why or why not?

2. Did the story of the POW's sacrifice in Thailand impact the way you see Jesus' blood, shed for you?

3. Have you ever encountered God in such a way that you have felt able to be truly yourself? Do you feel safe with Him and free to draw near?

NOTES

Lesson 14

REMAIN CONFIDENT

Hebrews 10

Introduction

I recently had one vacation within another one. Each summer, our brood migrates to Camden, Maine, to unplug and rest. This particular year, my need for respite was a little higher, and I knew that solitude would make all the difference. I was offered a few days alone in an ocean-side house in Port Clyde, Maine, and started packing immediately. That vacation within a vacation provided an extra depth to my summer experience that truly restored my soul.

Putting one vacation inside another may seem complicated, and in that same way, so might putting one teaching inside another. This, incidentally, is what the author of Hebrews has been doing every time he inserts longer passages from the Old Testament into the middle of a chapter. But in the case of both my vacation and his writing, the impact of the whole experience is enhanced by this decision.

In Hebrews 10, the author does this by putting Psalm 40 and Jeremiah 31 into the middle of the chapter. He makes his overall point, but then goes deeper still by delving into these passages.

Once he makes his point, he will reveal to us the purpose and structure of this whole letter—the why behind the writing of Hebrews. We got this intel in an earlier overview, but we'll see it in greater detail in Hebrews 10:32–34. The recipients of the letter are facing persecution and imprisonment, and many of them are walking away from Christ because of it. All along, the author has been encouraging his readers to stay the course by offering rich theological teaching regarding the superiority of Christ, as well as encouragement and exhortation to make sure his words have personal application.

To review, the author has been making the following comparisons:

Hebrews 1–2:   Jesus with the angels and Torah
Hebrews 3-4:   Jesus with Moses and the Promised Land
Hebrews 5-7:   Jesus with priests and Melchizedek
Hebrews 8-10: Jesus with sacrifice and covenant

In all cases, the conclusion is that Jesus is superior.

We will all face circumstances in our lives when evidence would suggest that God isn't coming through for us. This will tempt us to run back to the old coping mechanism of self-reliance (accompanied by the lie that it's all up to us), just giving up, and all sorts of things in between. What they all have in common is a move away from dependence on God.

I know that this study of Hebrews has been heavy on theology, and there have been many moments when you have wondered if what you are reading has anything to do with what you are currently facing. The intent of the writer has always been to lift our eyes to a higher perspective. He hopes that we will stop judging God by our circumstances as we see them and instead take some time to focus on His greatness, His overarching plan throughout all of history, and the truth that He truly is holding it all together.

It makes me think of the words of Saint Peter after watching so many people walk away from Jesus. Jesus asked the disciples, "Do you also want to leave?" Peter answered, "Master, to whom shall we go? You have the words of eternal life" (John 6:67–68).

Peter's question is a good one. Where else do we intend to go, if not to Christ? What or whom do we consider superior to Him? We won't be tempted to run to angels, the Torah, Moses, Melchizedek, or animal sacrifices instead of Jesus, but the modern-day substitutes are no better.

May we choose Christ, not just on the days when He's answering our prayers the way we'd like, but in the midst of trials. May we grasp hold of the lifeline He offers, trusting that it runs all the way into heaven. It is anchored there, and because of this, we will not be shaken. In the darkest of days, we can still find that hope rises with the dawn. His unfailing love meets us with the morning light. The battle may rage on, but we can count on the fact that our God is stronger, and He is *for us*. There is no higher name to call on than the name of Jesus. He can do all things. Remain confident and hold on.

Day One
WHAT GOD REALLY WANTS

Read Hebrews 10:1–10.

1. How is the law described in Hebrews 10:1? What is it unable to do?

While the old sacrifices were able to achieve ceremonial cleanliness, they were never able to cleanse a person deep down, in the place where memories, deep hurts, and hidden sins dwelled.

2. A. How does Hebrews 10:3 describe what happens with the sacrifices?

This verse makes the point that all the law and the sacrifices could do was make a person aware of his or her sin—it never permanently took care of the problem.

B. This "remembrance of sin" isn't just referring to the fact that people remember their sin and then feel guilty. It's referring to God's memory. What does He promise will happen with the new covenant in Jeremiah 31:34?

C. How is this forgiveness described in Isaiah 1:18 and 43:25, and Psalm 103:12?

3. Hebrews 10:4 states clearly and strongly that "it is impossible that the blood of bulls and goats take away sins." Hebrews 10:5–6 then explains what God has always been after. These verses are taken from Psalm 40 and are recorded in

Hebrews as coming from the mouth of Jesus to His Father. What does God *not* desire (Psalm 40:7), and what is He really wanting (Psalm 40:9)?

These verses seem to contradict the Old Testament commandments regarding the importance of sacrifices and offerings. The truth is, God did require sacrifices and offerings, but what He really was after was obedience on the heart level. The same is true today.

What did God really want? What has He always wanted? He wants a human being voluntarily offering to do His will.

4. When you think of your own life, what does it mean for you to seek to do God's will? How do you best listen to His voice? How are you doing on the journey toward discovering His purpose for your life? Is there an area of your life where God's will and your will are disconnected?

5. What happens to us because Jesus came to do God's will? See Hebrews 10:10.

Quiet your heart and enjoy His presence. . . . He will help you do His will.

"Create in me a clean heart, O God; and put a new and right spirit within me." (Psalm 51:10)

God never asks us to do anything that He doesn't equip us to do. In baptism, we have been changed on the inside. What the blood of bulls and goats could never do—transform a person's heart—Christ's blood accomplished. In baptism, we are united to Christ's death and covered with His blood. We're given a new heart, and the Holy Spirit is placed within us. Because we have the Holy Spirit within, we can no longer say, "I can't," when God asks us to follow Him. We may not want to, but that is not the same as being unable to.

The rubber meets the road in those places where our will and God's will diverge. It's human nature to want our own way, and God is a gentleman, so He will never demand that we surrender to Him. Remember, what He most wants is a human being voluntarily *offering to do His will.*

Jesus is our example in this, especially when we remember Him wrestling with God's will in the Garden of Gethsemane. With the words "Father, if you are willing, take this cup away from me; still not my will but yours be done" (Luke 22:42), we are reminded that obedience wasn't easy for Jesus. Why did He obey? Out of love for us. "Christ loved us and handed himself over for us as a sacrificial offering to God for a fragrant aroma" (Ephesians 5:2).

Can we obey out of love for God? If we will, God will lead us "in triumph in Christ and manifest through us the odor of the knowledge of him in every place. For we are the aroma of Christ" (2 Corinthians 2:14–15). In a world that is desperate for God even though so few realize it, our lives can be a perfume that invites people to draw near to Him. As they come close to us, intoxicated by a fragrance that is so unlike what they normally encounter, hearts will soften. Our knowledge put to words often alienates. But a life that voluntarily offers to do God's will is irresistible.

Day Two
BETWEEN THE ALREADY AND THE NOT YET

Read Hebrews 10:11–18.

1. A. According to Hebrews 10:11, what does every priest do?

   B. By contrast, what has Jesus done? See Hebrews 10:12.

2. When God outlined exactly what items would be put in the temple and how they were to be constructed, one piece of furniture was never mentioned: a chair. The priests didn't sit to work; they stood daily at their duties. Their work was never done.

By contrast, Jesus "took his seat forever at the right hand of God." What does this signify according to John 17:4 and 19:30?

The work Jesus came to do is finished, but this doesn't mean He is inactive. He sits on a throne, reigns as king, and intercedes for us.

3. A. According to Hebrews 10:13, what is Jesus waiting for?

   B. Why does God prolong that day of grace when all His enemies will be made His footstool? See 2 Peter 3:9 and Isaiah 30:18.

   C. Is there an area of your life where you are desperate for God to act, to intervene, to make things right? List it here, then meditate on whether it is possible that God's timing, although it feels slow, is perfect because it is actually achieving something greater. Can you open yourself to the possibility that the reason for the delay might be God's desire to show mercy to you or your loved one in a grander way?

4. According to Hebrews 10:14, what did Jesus' one offering accomplish?

This verse refers to Christians as having been made perfect forever (past tense) and becoming consecrated or holy (an ongoing process). Which is it? Has it been accomplished or is it still happening?

We live between the "already" and the "not yet." Jesus is victorious and sits at God's right hand, yet waits for His enemies to be made His footstool. We are cleansed from sin and made pure, yet we have to choose to not let sin "reign in our mortal bodies" (Romans 6:12). Jesus told the people in the synagogue in Luke 4 that a prophecy from Isaiah was fulfilled in their hearing—that liberty was proclaimed to captives and the oppressed could go free—yet there are times when we feel stuck and enslaved.

Living in the midst of this paradox is not tidy. There's a messiness to the process of becoming holy. Appropriating and living out our new freedom is not formulaic. It is a part of being in a living, personal relationship with Jesus, and as with any relationship, there are times when we struggle to understand the other person. Trust isn't dispensed from a spiritual ATM. Doubt, struggles, and confusion are a part of the Christian life.

Living between the already and the not yet with at least an ounce of peace will require a heavenly focus. If we expect it all to come together and make sense here on earth, we will remain perpetually confused and disappointed.

According to 2 Corinthians 5:7, "We walk by faith, not by sight." Even when we can't see more than the next step in front of us, we take the step, and pray that God will help us to trust and believe. We fix our eyes on heaven, knowing it is there, not here, where it all will make sense.

And when we don't understand and our hearts feel shredded, when all we can do is sit in the spot where we pray but the words won't come, when the only things we can cry out to our Father are "Why?" and "When will it get better?" our posture is still open. We are facing Him. We have not turned away. This is still an offering. This is the widow's mite. And while those outside looking in might say it isn't much, Jesus sees it for what it is. It is all we have got. But that also means it is everything.

If this is where you are today, please know that God cares. He is right next to you, holding your hand and weeping with you over the way this world that He loves (and the people in it) are just hemorrhaging pain.

He is at work. Please don't give up, my friend. Now is a moment to just be held. No heroic spiritual disciplines are required. He is wrapping His arms around you. Isaiah 41:13 says, "For I am the Lord, your God, who grasps your right hand." I love that He doesn't say, "Grasp my hand," because sometimes we lack the strength to do that. He says, "I am the one doing the grasping and the holding on." It isn't up to you. When everything falls apart, He carries you and will never let go.

5. Hebrews 10:15–17 contains quotes from Jeremiah 31. The prophet Jeremiah was writing at a time when everything was falling apart around him. There wasn't a person who was exempt from the suffering taking place, and his words became a beacon of hope for the generations that followed. Which of his phrases offer comfort? What do they mean to you today in light of what you are facing?

As he has faithfully done throughout the book of Hebrews, the author invites us to lift our perspective higher. We may be asking God why He doesn't bring relief. These verses remind us that He *has* brought us relief—from the consequences of sin. I know that when we are suffering, our focus doesn't tend to be on what our sins deserve. To mention it at such a time seems callous. But this is where we each have a choice. Will we choose gratitude, even in the face of despair, and appreciate what God has given? This is a counterintuitive response, but it just might be the key to surviving seasons of confusion, enabling us to walk in faith when we don't see clearly.

Quiet your heart and enjoy His presence. . . . Let Him enfold you in His love.

"At present we see indistinctly, as in a mirror, but then face to face. At present I know partially; then I shall know fully, as I am fully known." (1 Corinthians 13:12)

We so badly want to see clearly, to understand, to receive explanations, to avoid confusion. Yet we only see indistinctly. Because we do not have the mind of God, it's impossible for us to make sense of His actions. But what do we know, at least partially? We know that we are known.

We are known intimately by God. He understands our deepest sorrows and fears. He knows our buried dreams and the hopes we hesitate to voice. He sees our best intentions and recognizes who we want to be underneath our failed attempts.

We are not just known; we are loved. God sees our flaws, all the things about us that we would like to change, and He still presses us to His chest and whispers, "You are my beloved." When God created you, He said, "There is nothing I want to change. You are perfect. You are mine."

We don't always understand, but we are always understood. We don't always see clearly, but we are always seen. We don't always like ourselves, but we are always delighted in by our heavenly Father. Take a rest from trying to figure it all out. Just be held by the One who hung the stars and holds back the sea and keeps gravity in place. There is a solid foundation beneath you and you will not be shaken.

Day Three
HUMBLE BOLDNESS

Read Hebrews 10:19–25.

1. A. According to Hebrews 10:19, we have confidence to do what? What is that confidence based on?

   B. The Greek word translated "confidence" is *parresia*. How is this word defined according to CCC 2778?

   C. Reread the Catechism's definition of *confidence*. Does it accurately describe your familial relationship to God? Is there a specific aspect of confidence in your relationship with God in which you would like to grow?

2. A. With what does Hebrews 10:20 equate the veil of the tabernacle?

   B. What occurred in the temple as Jesus gave up His life on the cross? See Matthew 27:51.

   C. What do we learn about the "new and living way" in John 14:6?

In his commentary on Hebrews, Luke Timothy Johnson explains, "The image of passing through the veil of flesh, then, suggests that Jesus himself is the 'way' that gives access to God. His mortal body is the 'veil' that must be passed through in order to find full access to the living God."[81]

3. A. With the words "let us approach," the author of Hebrews encourages us to come near and worship God. Hebrews 10:22 tells us four things that should be true of us as we enter His presence. What are they?

God is always concerned with our hearts. Bringing Him our sincere hearts is the starting point. The Oxford online dictionary defines *sincere* as "free from pretense or deceit; proceeding from genuine feelings . . . saying what [you] genuinely feel or believe; not dishonest or hypocritical."[82] Your heavenly Father wants the *real* you. Don't bring Him your fake fine—He wants to see the mess, the fear, the chaos, the doubt, the joy, the dreams, and the hopes.

The next thing God asks is that we approach Him with a spirit of trust. I know this can be hard, especially when we have been hurt and disappointed. When God does not rescue us from suffering, our trust in Him can take a hit. Trust is not automatic, but it also isn't dependent upon our circumstances. Trust is established when we spend more time learning about God's character and reflecting on all the times He has come through for us, rather than focusing on what we wish was different in our lives. It's like a muscle that needs to be regularly exercised or it will weaken.

B. In the Old Testament, Ezekiel prophesied that God would sprinkle clean water over His people to make them clean. Through the prophet, God said, "I will give you a new heart and a new spirit I will put within you" (Ezekiel 36:26). How did this occur, according to Titus 3:4–5?

It is the sacrifice of Jesus—His blood being sprinkled over us—that washes away every stain on our conscience. Our bodies and souls are washed in baptism, removing

---

81 Johnson, *Hebrews: A Commentary*, 257.
82 *Oxford Living Dictionaries*, s.v. "sincere," https://en.oxforddictionaries.com/definition/sincere.

the stain of original sin, and then cleansed again in the sacrament of reconciliation. We don't approach God in confidence based on the righteous things we have done. According to the prophet Isaiah, "all our just deeds are like polluted rags" (Isaiah 64:5). God doesn't accept us because of what we have done; He accepts us because of what Jesus did. Knowing these two truths helps us to adopt a posture of boldness tempered with humility when we approach God.

4. A. According to Hebrews 10:23, what are we to firmly grasp hold of? Why should we do this?

   B. How do the following verses encourage us to grasp hold of hope? 1 Thessalonians 5:24, 2 Thessalonians 3:3, and Revelation 19:11.

   C. How does the Catechism define hope in CCC 1817?

   D. In whom or what are you tempted to place your hope, instead of in Christ?

If we want to be anchored and steady, we won't base our hope on our circumstances, on others keeping their promises, or on our own strength. We'll ground our hope in the truth that *He who promised is faithful.*

5. A. Even though we base our confidence and hope on God's trustworthiness and faithfulness, that does not mean it doesn't matter how we behave. Hebrews 10:24–25 challenges us to consider growing in a number of ways. What are they?

   B. What is something proactive you can do to be a part of the solution for the problems you see within the family of God?

Quiet your heart and enjoy His presence. . . . God never intended for you to live the Christian life in isolation.

Although our culture encourages individuality at the expense of community, that has never been God's way. When relationships get sticky and community feels complicated, we are all tempted to withdraw. We can do that by escaping behind a screen, by stopping going to church, or by putting a wall around our hearts. God knows that community is messy, but He also knows it's the primary place where we will experience opportunities to grow in holiness. Each of those times of irritation and hurt give us the chance to grow in virtue. They also give us insight into places in our hearts that need healing.

When places in our hearts that are wounded are exposed, our desire for safety goes through the roof. We feel vulnerable and often want to hide. In those times, Jesus asks that we remain in community, and hide in Him. He is our shelter, and He guards us from distress (Psalm 32:7).

If you have been hurt by people who should have welcomed and loved you, perhaps the following prayer based on Psalm 139 will provide comfort.

Loving God,

You see into the depths of my heart and know me completely.
Even when I feel misunderstood, You understand my every thought.
You keep Your eye on me wherever I go; there isn't a step I take that You don't notice.

Even before I speak, You know what I'm about to say.
You also know how people will respond, and that often others' words will cause me to feel judged, embarrassed, or ashamed.
Knowing how words can cut like a knife, You encircle me and rest Your hand upon me.
You remind me, in the face of rejection, of my goodness and dignity.

There is nowhere I can go where Your love has not preceded me.
You are with me in the heights, where others find it hard to be happy for me.
You are with me in the depths, where others don't want to accompany me.
In whatever circumstances I find myself, Your hand guides me and holds me fast.

Anytime I feel "less than" or "too much," may I remember that You created me as I am and declared me good.
Help me to stop basing my sense of worth on what others think of me.
May I stop expecting acceptance when what You experienced was being misunderstood, beaten, spat upon, and rejected by those You came to save.
Why would I expect to be treated better than You?

You formed my inmost being,
Knit me together in my mother's womb,
And call me wonderfully made.
You shaped each one of my days before one of them came to be.
My life is in Your loving, capable hands.
Help me to remember that with You, there is always hope.

Day Four
A STERN WARNING

Read Hebrews 10:26–31.

Gear up for today's passage. It's a grave warning against turning your back on Christ, and it contains some of the strongest wording to be found in the New Testament.

1. A. What can we expect "if we sin deliberately after receiving knowledge of the truth" (Hebrews 10:26)? See Hebrews 10:26–27. (Note: This references the Old Testament system of sacrifice.)

As we saw in an earlier lesson, the Old Testament sin offering covered sins that were committed unintentionally. For sins committed knowingly and willingly, there wasn't a sacrifice prescribed.

The warning that has been threaded throughout Hebrews—to not go back—is based on that truth. The author is telling the reader, "Why go back to that old system? You know how often you sin deliberately. You aren't covered!"

B. You may be wondering what this passage has to do with us. We don't expect animal sacrifices to cover our sins, so does this passage apply to us in any way? Yes, it does. One of the reasons why people walked away from their faith centuries ago remains the same today. Then and now, we don't like it when God puts constraints on our behavior. When He lays out a pattern for the way we should live, and we don't want to change, we are always tempted to turn away. What did 2 Timothy 4:3–4 predict would happen, and what does that prediction have to do with Hebrews 10:26–27? Do you see evidence of this around you today?

2. What happened to a person who rejected the law of Moses? See Hebrews 10:28.

3. A. The author of Hebrews compares rejecting the law of Moses to rejecting the Son of God. How does the author describe that process of rejection? See Hebrews 10:29.

This is a sobering teaching, and we need to pause and let it sink in. Our postmodern culture equates teaching about morality with arrogance. We're told we can define truth for ourselves, and that as long as we aren't hurting anyone, our choices must be OK. Looking to one another for approval instead of to God results in a false sense of security. Just because everyone around you affirms your choices and beliefs does not mean that you have made the right ones from an eternal perspective.

We all are given an inner summons to conversion, but we don't all respond to it with an open heart. You likely have a loved one on your mind when you read these passages. You long to see him or her turn to God, but so far have only witnessed resistance or disinterest. We all know how pride and self-reliance get in the way of surrender to God. We can see it in ourselves and in others. But hurt is also an enormous barrier. In order to open our hearts to God and enter into a relationship with Him, we need to have some degree of trust that He is good. When people have been hurt by others (and this is especially harmful when it's been by someone in the Church), it's natural to wonder why God didn't intervene. Usually healing of the heart needs to take place before conversion can be considered.

B. We don't know what is going on in the hearts of those we love. All too often, our words come off as callous, controlling, and annoying. So, what can we do? Read the following passages, and share the insights received. Then reflect on someone you know whom you desire to experience conversion. What specific action can you take, based on these Scripture passages?

James 5:16

1 Peter 4:8

My specific action:

4. What conclusion is drawn in Hebrews 10:31 based on the observations found in Hebrews 10:26–30?

Theologian Luke Timothy Johnson elaborates on this:

> The worship of the living God is unlike the worship of an idol, whose existence depends on human service. The living God is fearsome precisely because, like his own word, he sees deeply and truly into the heart of his own creatures and demands of them a truth commensurate with his own. It is not a game. It is the most ultimate reality, and therefore, quite properly, "fearful."[83]

5. When you reflect on your own life, do you see areas where you are playing games, making up excuses, or hiding behind a mask with God?

One day we will all "fall into the hands of the living God" (Hebrews 10:31), but those who are covered with the blood of Jesus will find that God's hands are attached to arms that will enfold us in a merciful embrace. For those who choose Christ, the promise is sure:

> "The eternal God is your dwelling place, and underneath are the everlasting arms." (Deuteronomy 33:27)

> "The hand of the Lord is not too short to save." (Isaiah 59:1)

> "While he was still a long way off, his father caught sight of him, and was filled with compassion. He ran to his son, embraced him and kissed him." (Luke 15:20)

It's my prayer that as we reflect on how seriously God takes our posture toward Him (Are we turned away? Are we pursuing Him? Are we humble and obedient?), we would remember why He cares. When God asks that we respond in a certain way, it is always out of love for us and a desire to bring us blessing. He patiently waits for us to turn, and then He runs to us with outstretched arms.

---

[83] Johnson, *Hebrews: A Commentary*, 266.

Quiet your heart and enjoy His presence. . . . Look at His face—He delights in you.

In C. S. Lewis' book The Last Battle, *he paints a picture of what the last judgment might look like. The world is coming to an end, and each creature stands before Aslan (the great lion who symbolizes Jesus):*

> *They all looked straight in his face, I don't think they had any choice about that. And when some looked, the expression of their faces changed terribly—it was fear and hatred . . . And all the creatures who looked at Aslan in that way swerved to their right, his left, and disappeared into his huge black shadow . . . I don't know what became of them. But the others looked in the face of Aslan and loved him, though some of them were very frightened at the same time. And all these came in at the Door, in on Aslan's right.*[84]

Heavenly Father, may we look into Your face and see mercy, invitation, acceptance, and longing. Lord, may we stop second-guessing You and fearing that following Your plan will somehow bring us destruction. Please increase our trust so that we aren't afraid of surrendering to You. May we be confident in Your love and faithfulness.

Day Five
DON'T SHRINK BACK

Read Hebrews 10:32–39.

1. A. What sufferings had the readers of Hebrews experienced? See Hebrews 10:32–34.

   B. Knowing that they "had a better and lasting possession" helped the Hebrews to endure suffering. What additional insight do we gain about this eternal perspective from 2 Corinthians 4:17?

---

[84] C. S. Lewis, *The Last Battle* (New York: HarperCollins, 1982), 751.

C. Where does our focus need to lie if we are going to be able to see our sufferings through this lens? See 2 Corinthians 4:18.

2. It's one thing to grit your teeth through suffering; it's quite another to joyfully accept it. How is this even possible? We can't make ourselves feel an emotion, so how can we experience joy in the midst of hardship? Saint Paul teaches in Galatians 5:22 that joy is a fruit of the Holy Spirit, a grace that comes from Him. It is placed in our hearts as a seed, but we need to cultivate it if it's going to grow. What do the following verses teach us about how to do that?

Philippians 4:6–7

James 1:2–3

Matthew 16:27, Revelation 22:12

It will be very difficult for us to cultivate joy in our hearts if our values are based on what the world says matters most. A shift in perspective is required, one in which eternal things are valued more than temporal ones. What would change if instead of seeking comfort and pleasure, we sought to create a meaningful legacy? How might we look at suffering differently if we saw it as a platform—an opportunity to glorify God—with greater attention being placed on us because of our difficult circumstances? Who is watching you, wondering if your God really does make a difference? What conclusion might he or she draw if there was no explanation for your joy other than that God is real and active in your life?

3. A. What are we told we will need in order to do the will of God? See Hebrews 10:36.

   B. What should motivate us to endure? See Hebrews 10:37.

   C. What causes God to be displeased? See Hebrews 10:38.

These verses promise us that in just a little while, Jesus will return. He will not delay. And His faithful followers will not shrink back when He asks them to step forward. If these were God's words to people who were facing the possibility of being imprisoned or killed—if He told them He would take no pleasure in them if they shrank back—how do you think He responds to us when we sit on our gifts and our callings, when we pull back?

The truth is, you have the spiritual gifts needed to lead people closer to Christ. You have the inner call. Don't doubt this. Don't question whether this is a bunch of fluff and nonsense. The need is enormous. God has gifted *you*. God has called *you*. Ignoring your call means ignoring the life you were meant to live.

What holds you back? What causes you to shrink back from following Christ's lead?

4. When I think of my own life, three things have tempted me to shrink back: limitations, fear, and uncertainty. Perhaps you struggle with them, too. Let's unpack them, one by one.

   A. Limitations

      Along with the spiritual gifts and the call, we also have limitations. We are finite. We aren't God. We have no margin, but boatloads of responsibilities. We are aware of our shortcomings. We may lack support at home. We doubt that God would choose to work through us. How does 2 Corinthians 10:9–10 address the temptation of focusing on our limitations?

We step out with our limitations (we say yes; we obey) and we depend on God every step of the way. God knows that our limitations keep us dependent on Him. He is right there with us, behind us, next to us, in front of us, carrying us forward through the very limitations that we can convince ourselves will guarantee failure.

B. Fear

This is what speaker and author Jennie Allen wrote about the If Gathering (a faith-based event that ultimately hosted twelve hundred women in person and forty-four thousand online) when it was just a vision in her mind and heart: "I am terrified. This could fail. This may not even be from God. And I am going to do it anyway. We have to deal with fear because it is possible that it will make us miss the best parts of life. We all face fear. But we must kill fear like it is the devil, because it usually is."[85]

What does 1 John 4:4 teach us regarding how to fight the fear?

We have to run into the fear and just obey. If we wait for the fear to subside and *then* step out, we'll never move.

C. Uncertainty

Once the idea has been planted in our hearts, we may begin to wonder if this is really God's will for us. If this has happened to you, you are not alone. But the worst thing you can do at this point is quit and just wait for a specific calling to fall from the sky. Why? Because what happens is the time previously spent serving just gets sucked up with distractions. We are the most privileged people on the planet. We must give back. We must do something.

---

[85] Jennie Allen, *Restless* (Nashville, TN: W Publishing, 2013), 181.

What does Proverbs 3:5–6 say we should do when we feel uncertain?

D. Which of these temptations do you struggle with most?

Quiet your heart and enjoy His presence. . . . Listen to His voice.

The point is this:
When our limitations are screaming at us,
when we are so afraid we're going to mess up and get it wrong,
when we aren't even sure this is what God wants us to be doing,
we usually draw the conclusion that it's time to quit.
And sometimes it is.

But I believe that more often than not, this is a time when God is purifying our motives; when He's teaching us to lean into Him; when He's getting ready to show up *in a big way, reminding us that He is the One who is really doing all these things that have eternal value, that He can work through a train wreck. And by that, I mean a person who doesn't have it all together. If we will resist the temptation to quit—if we will* not shrink back—*we will experience grace pouring out of us in ways we never thought possible. Because it's Him, and not us.*

People sometimes ask me how I get it all done. I don't know what they're looking for in my answer—whether they want to hear I have loads of household help or about my "systems" at home. But really, it's what I just said that truly explains how I get it done.

Every day I am reminded of my limitations. They scream at me. They make me feel inadequate. They make me want to quit. They cause me to tell God, "I can't." Every day I fight fear. More often than not, I struggle with uncertainty. And if I had listened to the countless voices telling me that what I was dreaming could not be done, that this vision was too big, asking who was I to attempt something like this with a house full of children . . . Walking with Purpose wouldn't exist.

Don't shrink back—get ready to be amazed at what God can do through a flawed woman who knows that when she is weak, He is strong.

Conclusion

In the spirit of full disclosure, I'll tell you that if you do not shrink back and if you answer God's call, there will be a cost. Callings are costly. And it doesn't just cost us. It costs those closest to us. **So I ask you, can you trust God with the cost?**

Because the alternative—saying no, playing it safe, moving back to what feels comfortable instead of living life on the edge—could very likely be disobedience. Or it might be selfishness packaged as something else. I can't tell you whether this is true for you; only God can. But it's an important thing to figure out.

If you have children, you may be wondering how your radical obedience will affect them. The best way to work through this concern is to think about what your kids truly need. In my opinion, our kids don't need us at every event. They don't need us to be the room mom or the soccer coach, or to give them the most fabulous birthday parties. None of those things are bad, but they can be the wrong choice if they cause us to shrink back and say no to what God is calling us to. Our kids need to see us obeying God, loving Him, knowing Him, and making Him known in the world. That's what we need to model for them. If we place them at the center of our lives, it's quite possible that we will be teaching them that they are at the center of it all, period.

We need to take our place in God's story. We need to do our part. We need to say a lot of nos to say the best yes. Both our nos and our yeses need to be made for the right reasons.

The only way we'll discern the right choice is by pressing into Christ. Our friends can't give us the answer, although they can give us advice. The most logical answer isn't always the right one. It's in quieting our hearts so that we can listen to God's still, small voice. So run to Him. Pursue Him. Lean into the One with all the answers and all the strength you need, because you do not want to be "among those who draw back and perish, but among those who have faith and will possess life" (Hebrews 10:39).

My Resolution

In what specific way will I apply what I have learned in this lesson?

Examples:

1. Hebrews 10:22 challenges me to draw near to God "with a sincere heart and in absolute trust." This is hard for me because I tend to hide my heart from Him. I will go to adoration this week and pour out my feelings honestly in His presence.

2. I recognize that joy is a fruit of the Holy Spirit and that experiencing it in my personal life requires that I choose to cultivate it. I commit to embracing joy this week and will have a zero-tolerance policy in regard to my own complaining. I will ask a friend to hold me accountable.

3. I have felt God calling me to step out, but have allowed my limitations, fear, and sense of uncertainty to hold me back. This week, I will take a concrete step forward in answering His call.

My resolution:

Catechism Clips

CCC 1817 Hope is the theological virtue by which we desire the kingdom of heaven and eternal life as our happiness, placing our trust in Christ's promises and relying not on our own strength, but on the help of the grace of the Holy Spirit. "Let us hold fast the confession of our hope without wavering, for he who promised is faithful." "The Holy Spirit . . . he poured out upon us richly through Jesus Christ our Savior, so that we might be justified by his grace and become heirs in hope of eternal life."

CCC 2778 This power of the Spirit who introduces us to the Lord's Prayer is expressed in the liturgies of East and of West by the beautiful, characteristically Christian expression: *parrhesia*, straightforward simplicity, filial trust, joyous assurance, humble boldness, the certainty of being loved.

Verse Study

See Appendix 3 for instructions on how to complete a verse study.

Proverbs 3:26

1. Verse:

2. Paraphrase:

3. Questions:

4. Cross-references:

5. Personal Application:

Lesson 15

RESILIENT FAITH

Hebrews 11

Introduction

"Faith never knows where it is being led, but it loves and knows the one who is leading." —*Oswald Chambers*

According to CCC 155, faith is an act of the intellect. It's a choice we make to believe—to accept what God has said because He has said it, not because we can prove it. Rather than being a feeling we rustle up, it's something that takes place in our minds. Our emotions can be in a swirl of confusion, unrest, and disquiet, yet the will can move the mind to choose faith.

Faith requires a surrender within the mind—an acceptance that life will not always make sense. What God allows (and at times orchestrates) will often appear to be the opposite of what is good. Faith looks beyond the present evidence to the unchanging character of God. God cannot lie, is good to the core of His being, and has proven His love for us with the sacrifice of His Son. Because of this, we can choose to trust Him.

This surrender of faith is an ongoing process. It's a journey, a process in which we gradually let go and place our lives in His hands. On our trust walk, we spend most of our time blindfolded to the fullness of truth. This can be highly frustrating because when we don't understand, we can easily give in to despair. Letting go of control is essential, and it appears to me that we tend to learn how to do this through *losing* control in areas of life that really matter to us.

To hold on to hope, it's critical that we feed our minds truth about the character of God. The more we know Him as He has revealed Himself in Scripture, the more resilient our faith will be both during the mundane seasons and when storms rage. If we don't love and know the One who is leading, our faith will not withstand the tests that suffering brings.

It's the time we spend in the quiet seasons, getting to know our Savior intimately, that equip us to deal with trials. So let's dive into Hebrews 11, and saturate our minds with truth.

Day One
THE TRUTHFULNESS OF GOD

Read Hebrews 11:1–3.

1. A. How is faith described in Hebrews 11:1?

The Greek word translated "realization" is *hupostasis*. *Hupostasis* can mean "substructure" or "foundation."[86]

This means that faith is the firm foundation we stand on that allows us to hope. Faith allows us to remain steadfast even in the midst of confusion and suffering. It gives us a handle to hold on to, even when the winds of change and uncertainty threaten to blow us off course. We grasp hold of faith and remember that God has not failed us yet. With faith, we stare into the unseen, and trust that He is at work.

B. Have you ever seen God move a mountain in your life? Do you believe you will see Him do it again? Has He ever made a way when there was no way? Do you believe you will see Him do it again? Do not base your answer on your circumstances. Base it on what you know to be true of God. How capable do you think He is?

---

[86] *Thayer's Greek Lexicon*, s.v. "hupostasis," Bible Hub, http://biblehub.com/greek/5287.htm.

2. What are we told we can hope for in the following Scripture passages?

    Titus 2:13

    1 John 3:2–3

    2 Timothy 2:12

    Revelation 22:4–5

It's because of their faith that "the ancients were well attested." It's what distinguished them; it's what all the saints had in common. They were confident in the hope of heaven, and it changed the way they lived on earth.

In the words of Luke Timothy Johnson, "Hope, then, has to do with the future, but it enables people to have boldness and confidence in the present as they move toward that future. What is in the future for the hearers, as for the ancients, is the complete realization of the promises."[87]

3. What important truth do we understand by faith? See Hebrews 11:3.

The point being made here is that the universe was spoken into being by God and depends on Him for its existence.

4. "The ancients" who will be commended throughout Hebrews 11 fixed their eyes on God and His promises even with little evidence of those promises being fulfilled. The promises related to the future, but the ancients acted as if they were

---

[87] Johnson, *Hebrews: A Commentary*, 277.

already true. How did they do this? They were completely convinced that God was truthful, and if He said something would come to pass, then it would.

In what area of your life are you struggling to believe God's promises? Are you fearing the future? Do you have pain from your past? Are you currently suffering? Are you worried about your children or your marriage? Are you doubting the goodness of God?

When you are struggling, the enemy of your soul will attack you by distorting truth. He will do all he can to cause you to doubt the truthfulness and faithfulness of God. The best way to counter a lie is with a declaration of truth. Turn to Appendix 5, "The I Declares." This is an excellent resource for you as you seek to fix your eyes on Jesus and focus on what is true. Read through this appendix, underlining the I Declares that resonate most with you right now.

Quiet your heart and enjoy His presence. . . . He is always true to His word.

"Our soul waits for the Lord, he is our help and shield." (Psalm 33:20)

Faith involves a lot of waiting. During that period between the first spark of hope and the fulfillment of God's promise, we can be assailed by doubt. We aren't alone in this. A reading of the psalms reminds us that doubt, struggles, and questioning have always been a part of the journey of faith.

All too often, when we start to question aspects of our faith, we open our ears wide to all who are ready to plant seeds of doubt, and we close the door on God's voice. How can God keep speaking to us if we stop reading His love letter—the Bible—or we stop going to Mass? As hard as it is, we need to keep listening to Him even during seasons of doubt. Shutting the door to Him and opening another wide to the world will not lead us to peace or fuller understanding.

Staying humble, asking questions, digging for truth, and not being afraid of things that confuse us will help build our trust in God. And when suffering shakes us and doubts dance in our minds, we can call on the Lord to be our anchor and shield. He isn't afraid of our doubts. His love is greater than any uncertainty. He is the constant, the anchor, the truth we can hold on to.

Day Two
THE JOURNEY OF FAITH

Read Hebrews 11:4–12.

What has been called the "Hall of Faith" begins with these verses. The author looks back in history to the people of faith who lived earlier, providing us examples to follow.

1. A. According to Hebrews 11:4, why was Abel considered righteous?

   B. The story of Cain and Abel is found in Genesis 4. In it, the brothers both offer God sacrifices, but Cain's is rejected. The Scripture passage does not explain what was wrong with his offering, but what can we deduce from 1 Samuel 16:7 and Genesis 4:7 as to the reason?

   C. It requires faith to sacrifice something that you value or can't easily replace. What is the costliest thing for you to offer God? Your money? Control? Time? Something else?

2. A. What happened to Enoch? See Hebrews 11:5 and Genesis 5:24.

   B. Enoch was described as a man who "walked with God." A "walking relationship" involves friendship, intimacy, joint decision making, and simply enjoying each other. Bringing Enoch to heaven in such an unusual way allowed

God to make the point that He values this kind of a relationship with us. Is this how you would describe your relationship with God? Is there some aspect of a "walking relationship" that you would like to see more of in your life?

3. A. According to Hebrews 11:6, what do we need in order to please God? What does this verse say we must believe when we approach God?

B. Do you struggle with doubt? If so, when doubts come, how do you typically react?

As much as I know we should always have faith and "just believe," the truth is, many of us struggle with doubt. It comforts me greatly to be able to turn to the rich tradition of the saints and find examples of holy, faith-filled people who struggled to believe. Saint Augustine described doubt as another element of faith. He claimed that doubt and faith do not contradict each other. In fact, doubt can be a part of faith—a step in our journey closer to God in which we lean in and ask questions. When we doubt, we still care. We are seeking to understand better.

When the disciple Thomas doubted and needed proof of Jesus' resurrection, Jesus said, "Have you come to believe because you have seen me? Blessed are those who have not seen and have believed" (John 20:29). And that is certainly true. We are blessed when we can believe without needing to see any evidence. But at the same time, Jesus invited Thomas to lean in, to touch His wounds, to encounter Him personally and confirm that His presence was real.

When the war of doubt versus belief is raging in our heads, we need to guard ourselves against apathy. We should never let go of the fact that if the claims of Christianity are true, then it demands everything, and if they are false, they mean nothing. This means that continuing to seek answers is critical, rather than saying, "Why bother?" when faith falters. This means we keep opening up the Bible and letting God speak to our hearts. Many a skeptic has come to faith during the very research process in which he or she was setting out to disprove it all (Journalist Lee Strobel comes to mind).

Hebrews 11:6 tells us that we should believe not just that God exists, but that He rewards those who seek Him. This means we believe that our God is personal and responds to the cry of our hearts. Far from encouraging a mercenary attitude toward God (one in which we ask in just the right way and then get what we want), this verse challenges us to enter into a personal relationship of trust with our Creator, leaning in when doubts assail.

4. A. How was faith made evident in the life of Noah? See Hebrews 11:7.

    B. Noah was willing to forgo a good reputation in order to do what God asked. What does 1 Corinthians 4:10 suggest might be the cost of doing so?

    C. Are there any situations or relationships in your life in which your reputation as an intelligent, educated, open-minded person is questioned because of your obedience to Christ? If so, is following Him worth the personal cost? Why or why not?

5. A. Why was Abraham able to take the leap of faith and leave what was familiar to follow God? See Hebrews 11:10.

B. Abraham had his eyes fixed on eternity. This is one of the things that allowed him to be fueled by faith instead of fear. Speaker and author Ann Voskamp said, "the way to what we want is often through what we don't want . . . Painfully hard things are part of the price of admission to a purposeful, holy life."[88]

Oh, for the grace and discipline to have this perspective. Is there a circumstance in your life that makes you want to run back to the familiar? Are you tempted to live a life that's more about safety than about self-sacrifice? Which of these heroes of faith (or a personal hero) encourages you to press on, remaining true to the path God has set you on?

Quiet your heart and enjoy His presence. . . . He will lead you by the hand when sight fails.

"By faith, Abraham obeyed when he was called to go out to a place that he was to receive as an inheritance; he went out, not knowing where he was to go." (Hebrews 11:8)

Whither he went, he knew not; it was enough for him to know that he went with God. He leant not so much upon the promises as upon the Promiser . . . O glorious faith! This is thy work, these are thy possibilities . . . It is by no means enough to set out cheerfully with your God on any venture of faith. Tear into smallest pieces any itinerary for the journey which your imagination may have drawn up. Nothing will fall out as you expect. Your guide will keep to no beaten path. He will lead you by a way such as you never dreamed your eyes would look upon. He knows no fear, and He expects you to fear nothing while He is with you.[89]

It's hard to tear up our itineraries or even to loosen our grip on them a little. When we focus on the unknown path, we'll grapple for certainty and control. But if we can shift our eyes and fix them instead on our guide, on His unchanging character, on His perfect record of promise fulfillment, such surrender is possible.

This comes easier for some than for others. For those of us who find this terrifying or impossible sounding, let's echo the prayer of the centurion: "Lord I believe, help my unbelief!" (Mark 9:24)

---

[88] Ann Voskamp, "Second Day, Session 3" (speech, If Gathering, Austin, TX, February 10, 2018).
[89] L. B. Cowman, *Streams in the Desert* (Grand Rapids, MI: Zondervan, 1997), 157–8.

Day Three
TRUSTING GOD'S WORD

Read Hebrews 11:13–22.

1. A. What was true of each of the people mentioned thus far in the Hall of Faith? See Hebrews 11:13.

   B. Write out Saint Paul's words at the end of his life, found in 2 Timothy 4:7–8.

Dying in faith, or finishing well, is the goal. A flashy start may garner attention, but God is looking for disciples who can stay faithful until the end. We'll take a deeper look at what that involves when we study Hebrews 12.

2. A. According to Hebrews 11:14–16, what homeland were the faithful ancients seeking?

   B. Because this is what they sought, what was God's response? See the second part of Hebrews 11:16.

   C. Describe our citizenship, based on Ephesians 2:19 and Philippians 3:10.

It's worth pausing and noting again that the faithful ancients "did not receive what had been promised but saw and greeted it from afar" (Hebrews 11:13). It was their heavenly focus that made this possible, keeping them from the pitfall of expecting all of God's promises to be fulfilled according to their timeline. This pitfall lies before us whenever we or someone we love suffers. All too often, when God doesn't move fast enough for our liking, we question His character.

I say "we" because I am guilty of this, and it isn't because I'm asking for greater wealth or something else that's superficial. When my faith takes the biggest hit, it's usually when I am begging God to bring relief and healing to someone I love. My faith is rocked when I see no evidence of a rescue, do not understand how His will can be achieved in the midst of such personal destruction, and then begin to doubt the promise of Jeremiah 29:11, that His plans are for our welfare and not our woe. My heart becomes confused and train-wrecked.

It's in that moment that I need to remember not just that God's timetable is not my own, but that at the core of His being, He is *good*, and because of that goodness, He is working out His long-range plan in my life and in the lives of my loved ones. I want God to fix what is broken in front of me or within me. He fixes His eyes on what He *most* desires to fix, which is all of our relationships with Him. There are times when God allows unhealed hurts to remain so that we draw closer to Him. Sometimes I am the one being drawn closer; other times He is using my pain to minister to someone else as they observe me on the platform of suffering. This is a lesson I have not wanted to learn, and it's one that I wish were not true, because it involves pain. But it's been said that the hardest suffering to bear is the kind that is senseless, and this perspective gives me something to cling to when God doesn't fix things the way I so deeply desire.

3. A. According to Hebrews 11:11–19, Genesis 15:5–6, and Genesis 22:5; why was Abraham able to offer Isaac as a sacrifice?

B. Pondering this passage, theologian F. F. Bruce writes, "How could the promise of God and the command of God be reconciled? . . . Indeed, the impression which we get from the biblical narrative is that Abraham treated it as God's problem; it was for God, and not for Abraham, to reconcile his promise and his command." This is a mike drop quote for me. I really like to fix things, and there are a host of problems that I am treating as my own, when I am pretty certain they are actually God's. He is the One with the unlimited resources, foreknowledge, and ability to do a miracle. So why would I figuratively take something out of His hands to handle myself? Can you relate? Do you see this tendency in your own life?

4. God allows suffering to intersect our lives because it is precisely in that crucible that we are offered the best opportunity to be transformed into His likeness. In what way did this happen in Abraham's life? See CCC 2572.

CCC 2572 says that "Prayer restores man to God's likeness and enables him to share in the power of God's love that saves the multitude." Exactly how that happens is a mystery. But when we allow suffering to transform us, when we ask not why, but what we can learn from this, when our mind turns to prayer instead of worry or complaining, we become more like God. As we grow more like Him, we are better able to reach into our broken and hurting world with God's love.

If I am honest, if God gave me the choice of healing the person I love or allowing them to continue suffering for the sake of a multitude of people, I would choose the healing of the person I love. No doubt this is why God is in charge and I am not. One day, the curtain dividing earth and heaven will be drawn back, and we'll see that His plan was the best one. In the meantime, our faith requires patience and trust. So I pray that God will fill us with both.

5. What did faith allow Isaac, Jacob, and Joseph to do? See Hebrews 11:20–22.

The four generations of this family (Abraham, Isaac, Jacob, and Joseph) went through all sorts of challenges, including family dysfunction, famine, imprisonment, and slavery. They were led from home to a strange land and finally to the Promised Land, but then had to move to Egypt to avoid death from the famine. Through it all, each one managed to keep his perspective higher than current circumstances, trusting God to fulfill His promises. They were able trust God, despite what the evidence around them suggested. Hebrews commends them for this and includes them in the Hall of Faith, despite their mistakes and inadequacies.

Quiet your heart and enjoy His presence. . . . Place your confidence in Him, not yourself.

In his commentary on Hebrews, F. F. Bruce writes:

> *"Those who honor me I will honor," says God (1 Sam. 2:30). Patriarchs honored God by putting their faith in him; he honored them by calling himself "the God of Abraham, the God of Isaac, and the God of Jacob" (Ex. 3:6). What higher honor than this could be paid to any mortal? These three patriarchs were not faultless, but God is not ashamed to be called their God, because they took him at his word.[90]*

They weren't faultless, so why did God honor the patriarchs? Because they believed that what He said, He would do. They considered His words to be a better measure of what was true than what they were feeling at the time.

What does God say about His Word?

"Heaven and earth will pass away, but my words shall not pass away." (Matthew 24:35)

"The word of the Lord remains forever." (1 Peter 1:25)

"The grass withers, the flower wilts, but the word of our God stands forever." (Isaiah 40:8)

---

[90] Bruce, *The Epistle to the Hebrews*, 300–1.

This is truth we can cling to. As strong as our feelings are, God's Word is truer than our interpretation of our situations, truer than our emotions, truer than our projections and fears.

Day Four
AUDACIOUS FAITH

Read Hebrews 11:23–31.

Much happened between the death of Joseph and the birth of Moses in Egypt. Joseph had held one of the highest positions of power in Egypt, second only to Pharaoh. But a new ruler came to power who knew nothing of Joseph. He saw that "the Israelites were fruitful and prolific. They multiplied and became so very numerous that the land was filled with them" (Exodus 1:7). Out of fear that they might rebel against him, the new king commanded that the midwives kill all the Israelite baby boys. The midwives refused, so the king took his command one step further, telling all Egyptians to throw any Israelite boy they saw into the Nile. It was into these conditions that Moses was born.

1. A. What reasons are given in Hebrews 11:23 to explain why Moses' parents hid him for the three months after his birth?

   B. Once Moses grew too big to hide in the house, what did his mother do, and what was the result? See Exodus 2:1–10.

   C. This story is a type (something in the Old Testament that foreshadows something in the New Testament) of infant baptism. Moses was placed in the water and was saved through this action, and a whole nation as well. Draw parallels from these details of Moses' story to the sacrament of baptism:

   - Moses' mother's faithful act saved him.
   - Moses was under penalty of death but was born again to a new life.

- Moses went into the water as a slave but came out as a free man.

D. When I read that Moses' parents didn't fear the king's edict, I am amazed. It would have terrified me. They had an innate courage that I lack, but I am grateful that I can draw on a divine source of fearlessness when I feel weak. Read the following verses about fear and record your thoughts, applying them to your own life.

Luke 10:19

2 Timothy 1:7

1 John 4:18

2. A. What do you learn from Hebrews 11:24–27 to explain what strengthened Moses' faith when he left Egypt?

B. Walking away from the wealth, power, and status of the Egyptian court required faith, but Moses was able to do it because he had a long-range plan. He knew that what was beneficial in the short term wouldn't be in the long run. Faith helps us to do the same, recognizing that true wealth is that which lasts throughout eternity. In heaven, the scales will be turned, and those who have been humble, gentle, and selfless will receive positions of honor that are now given to many who are self-seeking, proud, and self-reliant. Is there a decision you can make today to invest in eternity?

3. A. Which two major events in Moses' life required personal faith and strong leadership skills? See Hebrews 11:28–29.

B. Moses needed strong faith personally, and the character of a leader so that people would trust him. Read the following verses, noting the qualities required for us not only to step out in faith ourselves, but to lead others to follow:

Psalm 78:72

Philippians 2:3–4

1 Timothy 4:12

We know from Numbers 12:3 that "Moses was very humble, more than anyone else on earth." No doubt his humility helped those following him to believe that he had their best interests at heart.

4. A. Read Joshua 6:12–21 and record why faith was key to the walls of Jericho coming down.

    B. Marching around Jericho definitely required Joshua's faith, but God gave him a special experience to strengthen him just before. Read of it in Joshua 5:13–15. What do you think this event taught Joshua?

5. What heroic act of faith do we see in the life of Rahab? See Hebrews 11:31 and Joshua 2:1–21.

All the people of Jericho were utterly dispirited, full of fear, and trembling because of what they had heard of God's army. But not all made the transition from fear to faith. At first glance, you would think Rahab would have felt disqualified from God's mercy because she was a prostitute. But she had audacious faith—the willingness to reach out and beg God for mercy. And this is what He most wants to see. He doesn't want us to cower in fear, shame, or self-deprecation. He longs for us to lift our eyes to His mercy, provision, and loving character. How many of us have not because we ask not (James 4:2)?

Quiet your heart and enjoy His presence. . . . He will not pull back.

I just love that the author of Hebrews included the prostitute Rahab in this litany of faith. The only other woman mentioned is Sarah, and she was only mentioned in reference to her infertility. Rahab stands alone as a woman honored, serving as a reminder that nothing can disqualify us from being loved and accepted by God, if we will but ask. Too many women "tremble in fear" because they assume what they have done is beyond the reach of God's mercy. The only thing that places us beyond His reach is our unwillingness to ask Him to help us, His daughters. God is a gentleman and won't force Himself on us.

What do you think disqualifies you? Your age? Your past? Your appearance? Your education? None of that matters to God if you come to Him in humility and dependence. Fear, shame, and self-reliance can all tempt us to isolate, but God invites you to draw near. He will not pull back.

Day Five
THE WORLD WAS NOT WORTHY OF THEM

Read Hebrews 11:32–40.

1. A. What did the heroes of Hebrews 11:32 do? See Hebrews 11:33–34.

   B. What do we learn from Hebrews 11:34 about their weakness, and what additional insight do we gain from 2 Corinthians 12:8–9?

   C. Practically speaking, how do you offer your weakness to God in order to receive His strength?

When we are too weak to do the things that we figure will help us out, when we are all out of resources and are utterly depleted, we have a choice between despair and dependence. We all know where despair leads, and it isn't pretty.

But dependence? It's resting in the strength of the Lord, lying in His arms like a little child, and simply trusting. Weakness can be the greatest gift if it causes us to depend on God. Saint Paul tells us that His power works best in weakness. Not in spite of weakness, but *best* in weakness. This is why Paul got to a point where he boasted about his weakness. He used to be ashamed of it, but then everything changed.

It's a paradox, and one that can change your life:

The more weak you are, the more you depend on God.
The more you depend on God, the stronger you get.

2. Hebrews 11:35 describes women who were "tortured but would not accept deliverance, in order to obtain a better resurrection." Read 2 Maccabees 7:1–42 for the story behind this verse. What stands out to you about the faith of the mother?

3. What other things did the faithful ancients endure, according to Hebrews 11:36–37?

I am going to quote this verse the next time one of my kids tells me that life isn't fair. But who am I kidding? *I'm* the one who often looks at my set of circumstances and feels sorry for myself. While I agree that suffering is suffering—having your heart sawed in two is its own kind of misery—I do gain perspective from this list of trials. There is much that God has not asked me to endure. I gain comfort from the truth that He only allows the amount and type of suffering in my life that will ultimately be for my good. It does not *feel* good, but feelings are often an untrustworthy determinant of what is true.

4. A. What was said of the heroes of faith in Hebrews 11:38?

B. What challenge and reward is set before us in Revelation 2:10?

"He is no fool who gives what he cannot keep to gain that which he cannot lose."
—Jim Elliot

5. What had God foreseen that was better for us? See Hebrews 11:40 and CCC 147.

Quiet your heart and enjoy His presence. . . . He is worth any sacrifice.

I cannot explain the reason behind the suffering and injustice I see in the world. Whether it's what I witness up close or on the global stage, evil's victories threaten to beat all the hope out of me. But then I think of what Mister Rogers' mother said in response to scary news: "Look for the helpers." This shift in focus allows hope to reenter the picture. It reminds us that good conquers evil, and "all the darkness in the world cannot extinguish the light of a single candle" (Saint Francis of Assisi).

Whatever God may ask us to endure while remaining faithful, one thing I know for certain: He is worth it. He is worth the sacrifice.

What is He asking of you?

Is it continuing to serve when you are exhausted?
Is it giving even when there is no recognition or acknowledgment of what you've done?
Is it offering forgiveness when you'd rather make the person pay?
Is it continuing to intercede in prayer when you see no evidence that it is making a difference?
Is it talking to your kids about God's love even when it seems they are utterly disinterested?
Is it persevering in a lonely marriage?
Is it choosing to look past what someone is doing to recognize that hurting people hurt people?

I don't know your struggle—suffering is deeply personal. All I know is that if we persevere to the end, there is going to be a glorious reward and all will be worth it. Jesus is preparing a future for us that is beyond our wildest dreams. Relief, joy, reward . . . it is around the corner. Just hold on.

Conclusion

The Hall of Faith brings to my mind my own spiritual heroes, the people who have walked through the darkness while clinging to God's hand. One in particular springs to mind: one of the sweetest, kindest, and gentlest women I know. Countless times she reached out to me when I felt on the outside, inadequate, and judged, and always she met me with grace and a smile. Her comments and interactions weren't earth-shattering, but they made an enormous difference to the state of my heart. When I heard that she had been diagnosed with breast cancer, I was devastated to think of all she'd go through. I know that suffering produces character and depth, but in my opinion, she already had both in spades.

Throughout her cancer treatment, she carried herself with dignity and didn't give in to despair. I asked her what was helping her walk this lonely and difficult path. "Someone spoke into my life quite boldly," she said. "She told me, 'You are not going through this suffering because you need to grow. The person who is going to grow is someone watching you. You are on a platform of suffering, and the way you endure it is making a significant impact on someone near you.'" It was a bold thing to say, and certainly could have been taken the wrong way, but for my friend, it gave her a sense of purpose, bringing meaning to her suffering. Observing her made me long for that depth of faith. And where was it built? Right in the middle of the circumstances we all pray to avoid.

> The staunchest tree is not found in the shelter of the forest, but out in the open where the winds from every quarter beat upon it, and bend and twist it until it becomes a giant in stature . . .

> So in the spiritual world, when you see a giant, remember the road you must travel to come up to his side is not along the sunny lane where wild flowers ever bloom; but a steep, rocky, narrow pathway where the blasts of hell will almost blow you off your feet; where the sharp rocks cut the flesh, where the projecting thorns scratch the brow, and the venomous beasts hiss on every side . . .

> You may shrink back from the ordeal of a fierce storm of trial . . . but go in! God is there to meet you in the center of all your trials, and to whisper His secrets which will make you come forth with a shining face and an indomitable faith that all the demons of hell shall never afterwards cause to waver.[91]

---

[91] Cowman, *Streams in the Desert*, 270.

My Resolution

In what specific way will I apply what I have learned in this lesson?

Examples:

1. To build my faith daily, I will print out "The I Declares" (found in Appendix 5 and also as a download on the Walking with Purpose website) and keep it in a prominent place in my home.

2. I struggle with doubt, and when the questions and feelings of unsettledness take over, I tend to spiritually check out or distract myself. This week, I will do the opposite, and will read articles or a book written by skeptics who have come to faith. (*The Case for Christ* by Lee Strobel is a recommendation.)

3. I will make a list of my own spiritual heroes and take the time to write to them to let them know how their faith has impacted mine.

My resolution:

Catechism Clips

CCC 147 The Old Testament is rich in witnesses to this faith. The Letter to the Hebrews proclaims its eulogy of the exemplary faith of the ancestors who "received divine approval". Yet "God had foreseen something better for us": the grace of believing in his Son Jesus, "the pioneer and perfecter of our faith".

CCC 2572 As a final stage in the purification of his faith, Abraham, "who had received the promises," is asked to sacrifice the son God had given him. Abraham's faith does not weaken ("God himself will provide the lamb for a burnt offering."), for he "considered that God was able to raise men even from the dead." And so the father of believers is conformed to the likeness of the Father who will not spare his own Son but will deliver him up for us all. Prayer restores man to God's likeness and enables him to share in the power of God's love that saves the multitude.

Verse Study

See Appendix 3 for instructions on how to complete a verse study.

Romans 5:3–4

1. Verse:

2. Paraphrase:

3. Questions:

4. Cross-references:

5. Personal Application:

Lesson 16

FIX YOUR EYES ON JESUS

Hebrews 12 and 13

Introduction

The core question of Hebrews that we have been exploring is: "If God loves me, if He wants me to have joy and peace, then why is this so hard, and how can I remain faithful?" The author of Hebrews didn't give us a quick answer; instead he has taught us, lesson by lesson, that the grand narrative of our life is a journey. It's not a sprint; it's a marathon, and the only way we'll make it to the finish line is if we fix our eyes on Jesus.

We have two chapters left, one of which contains some of my favorite verses (Hebrews 12), and the other of which can seem a bit anticlimactic at first glance (Hebrews 13). Hebrews 13 reads like an ad hoc collection of final instructions, which are good in themselves, but rather unrelated to our overall theme. But if we look at it in this way, we'll miss the author's incredibly important concluding point. What he is sharing with us in Hebrews 13 is that if we want to make it on this journey—if we are going to survive the inevitable difficulties and sufferings of the Christian life—we must be deeply engaged in a community of faithful followers of Jesus. This collection of final instructions is not a miscellaneous to-do list. They are descriptions of what this radical community is supposed to look like.

When we read the Bible, we need to remember that chapter and verse divisions weren't a part of the original writing. They were added later for reference. Sometimes this impacts the overall reading and meaning, and this is the case with Hebrews 12 and 13. Hebrews 12 talks about Mount Sinai, the place where God's presence came down to earth. His presence—His glory—was terrifying to the people, and all knew that if they touched the mountain, they would die. Needless to say, they wanted to know how they were supposed to approach God, how He wanted to be worshipped. These instructions were given in the book of Leviticus, and the list of rules and regulations is lengthy.

But when Jesus came, everything changed. He opened a new way to the Father, and as a result, we can draw near to the throne of grace with confidence. That being said, it doesn't mean that how we approach God no longer matters.

Remembering that Hebrews 12 and 13 didn't originally show a division, we can see that chapter 13 answers the question of how we should approach God now. The way our worship of Him is described in Hebrews 13 does not have to do with regulations about our food, clothing, or cleanliness as was true of the instructions in Leviticus, but it has everything to do with how we love.

How are we to worship God? We worship Him by loving one another radically as brothers and sisters (Hebrews 13:1). We entertain strangers (Hebrews 13:2). We remember the prisoners (Hebrews 13:3). This is a description of a community of believers who are shaped by one another as they meet one another's needs, remain open and vulnerable, hold each other accountable, and welcome all.

Matthew 25 is a radical living out of Jesus' words: "I was hungry and you gave me food, I was thirsty and you gave me drink, a stranger and you welcomed me, naked and you clothed me, in prison and you visited me . . . Amen, I say to you, whatever you did for one of these least brothers of mine, you did for me."[92]

How do we fix our eyes on Jesus? We follow the example of Saint Teresa of Calcutta, who said, "I see Jesus in every human being. I say to myself, this is hungry Jesus, I must feed him. This is sick Jesus. This one has leprosy or gangrene; I must wash him and tend to him. I serve because I love Jesus."

Day One
FORGET YOUR WEARINESS

Read Hebrews 12:1–4.

1. A. According to Hebrews 12:1, what surrounds us as we persevere in running the race of faith?

---

[92] Matthew 25:35–36, 40.

B. How is "the cloud of witnesses" described in CCC 2683? What do they do? What do they offer to Christians as we run the race of faith?

C. Is there a particular saint whom you most naturally turn to for intercession? If so, why?

2. A. What do we need to get rid of if we are going to "persevere in running the race that lies before us"? See Hebrews 12:1, Romans 13:12, Ephesians 4:22, Ephesians 4:25, Colossians 3:8, James 1:21, and 1 Peter 2:1.

B. Take a moment and reflect on the things that are impeding or slowing you down in your spiritual race. It's possible that something innocent or harmless for others is holding you back in your pursuit of holiness. List here the burdens or sins that you long to be rid of. Then write a short prayer asking the Holy Spirit to give you the self-discipline to make a change. Conclude with a specific action you can take.

The sin or burden I want to throw off:

The reason it holds me back from my pursuit of holiness:

Holy Spirit, please . . .

My specific action is:

3. A. Where should our eyes be fixed as we run the race of faith? See Hebrews 12:2.

   B. Why was Jesus able to endure the cross? See Hebrews 12:2.

   C. The author of Hebrews challenges us to be so focused on Jesus that we have a singleness of purpose and an ability to ignore distractions, recognizing that Jesus is the ultimate prize. How did Saint Paul describe this perspective in Philippians 3:8?

4. What does Hebrews 12:3 say we should consider so that we do not grow weary and lose heart?

It's so easy to write the correct answer to that question, and yet still feel weary and fainthearted. The thought of "Jesus enduring opposition from sinners" can seem far removed from our current trials. That's why it's important that we pause here and lean in closer for understanding. Perhaps what the writer of Hebrews wants us to remember is that we are never alone in our suffering. Feeling that no one understands what we are going through makes the trials even harder to bear. We are being reminded that there is no emotion or pain that Jesus has not Himself endured. Our circumstances might be quite different from His, but He understands the way it *feels*.

Archbishop Fulton Sheen describes what Jesus endured on the cross:

> For example, did God ever have a migraine headache as if His head were crowned with thorns? Does God know anything about the torn flesh of those that are brought into the accident wards of hospitals? Does God know anything about loneliness as if He were abandoned by His most trusted friends? Does God know anything about hunger? Did He ever go without food for three days? Or five days? Does God know anything about thirst? Yes. God went through all these things in the person of Christ, and all we have to do is walk in His footsteps. But the important point is that He transferred to Himself all our sicknesses and our illnesses. . . . He was at the very brink of hell, and from that time on no one could ever say God does not know anything about despair, about anxiety. Yes, He felt it all. He transferred it upon Himself.[93]

He knows. He understands. We are never alone in our suffering.

5. A. What point does the author of Hebrews make in verse 5?

B. Hebrews 12:5 seems to me to be the biblical way of saying, "Things could be worse." I'm sure there's a far deeper theological meaning that could be gleaned from this verse, but that's the application I grab hold of. Regaining perspective can be a total game changer. When our eyes are fixed on our circumstances, not on our Savior, we can be quick to think that we are in the deepest pit of misery. Yet the truth is, there is always something we can be grateful for. Being *told* to count your blessings in the midst of difficulty is incredibly irritating and usually insensitive, but what might change if *we reminded ourselves* to do this?

After spending years inwardly rolling my eyes at people who told me to practice gratitude, I was given a little treasure of a book called *The Five-Minute Journal.* Created by Alex Ikonn and UJ Ramdas, this little tool has changed my mind-set quite remarkably, and it bears a striking similarity to the gratitude advice I've been given countless times before. This book has helped me develop a pattern in which I begin the day by listing three things I am grateful

---

[93] Archbishop Fulton Sheen, *St. Thérèse: A Treasured Love Story* (Irving, TX: Basilica Press, 2007), 140–1.

for, three things that would make today great, and a daily affirmation. Then just before bed, I'm prompted to record three amazing things that happened today and how I could have made the day even better.

The truth is, there is much to be thankful for. Most of us haven't gotten to the point of shedding blood because of our faithfulness to Christ. So, despite the current suffering you may be facing, which I acknowledge most certainly can lead to weariness and discouragement, what are three amazing things that have happened today?

Quiet your heart and enjoy His presence. . . . Lift your eyes to Jesus.

Two runners who raced to break the four-minute mile record give us an excellent illustration of the importance of where we place our focus. These men, Roger Bannister (a Brit) and John Landy (an Australian), met at the British Empire and Commonwealth Games in Vancouver, BC, in 1954. They had both recently done the impossible, breaking the four-minute barrier and enjoying the fame this accomplishment brought. Because they had each achieved this milestone in separate countries, all eyes were on them to see who would win when the two competed together in Canada.

The Guardian *newspaper describes what happened:*

> *The race became known as the Miracle Mile, and more than 60 years later is still among the most famous in the history of modern athletics. Landy led for much of the race, with Bannister close behind, then, at the final turn, Landy looked over his left shoulder to check where Bannister was and the British runner overtook the Australian on the right. Both men finished in under four minutes but Bannister was the winner. A bronze statue of the moment Landy glanced around now stands outside the Pacific National Exhibition in Vancouver, and Landy once joked that while Lot's wife was turned into a pillar of salt for looking back: "I am probably the only one ever turned into bronze for looking back."[94]*

---

[94] Michael McGowan, "How Roger Bannister and Australian John Landy Raced to Break the Four-Minute Mile," *Guardian*, March 5, 2018, https://www.theguardian.com/sport/2018/mar/05/how-roger-bannister-and-australian-john-landy-raced-to-break-the-four-minute-mile.

All was lost for Landy in that moment when he looked over his left shoulder. The tape of the race has been played and replayed, driving home the point that this tiny lapse in focus proved very costly in the end.

When our eyes come off of Jesus and are fixed instead on our hardships and challenges, we are likely to falter. But if we can shift our focus to our Savior, our heart can become steadfast, regardless of what is swirling around us.

Dear God,

You are our refuge and our strength, an ever-present help in times of distress. Therefore, we will not fear, even though the earth is shaken and mountains quake to the depths of the sea, though its water rage and foam and mountains totter at its surging.

You are in our midst; we shall not be shaken; God will help us at break of day. Though nations rage and kingdoms totter, You utter Your voice and the earth melts.

You, the Lord of hosts, are with us; our stronghold is the God of Jacob (adapted from Psalm 46).

Day Two
THE BURNING LOVE OF GOD

Read Hebrews 12:5–13.

1. What are we not to forget, according to Hebrews 12:5–6?

The truths contained in these verses are some of the hardest to swallow when your life is consumed by pain. When exhaustion, weariness, and hopelessness feel like the norm, the thought of God being behind the pain can lead us to a very dark place or shut us down emotionally. I tend toward the latter. Because I don't want to accuse God of wrongdoing yet cannot reconcile my current circumstances with my opinion of how a loving father should behave, I tend to turn off my brain and my heart. This is not a good response, and it does not lead me to peace, strength, or growth.

Laura Story's autobiography, *When God Doesn't Fix It*, tells of her own struggle in this regard. Laura is a Christian worship leader and recording artist whose life was turned upside down when her husband was diagnosed with a brain tumor early in their marriage. It affected his personality, memory, and everything about their life. She writes about a time when she began to question everything she thought she believed:

> I decided I needed more proof about God's promises. So, every time I felt God had betrayed me, I would go back to the Bible to search for the promise or commitment that God had broken. The problem was, I couldn't find any verse that said he owed me anything. Or a verse that said if I was good enough, I deserved something. I began to realize that my disappointment with God wasn't something he'd done to me; it was something I'd done to him. I had put conditions on our relationship that were never meant to exist.[95]

I, too, have gone to the Bible in search of what I feel I deserve. When this has been my perspective, I've looked at God as the powerful holder of all good gifts who is holding out on me. I can sit in this pit of self-pity endlessly, or I can ask God to lift me out, and begin the hard soul work of transforming my mind-set. God will help me with this, but I need to make the decision to change and do whatever it takes to think differently.

2. The enemy of our soul will tempt us to forget God's faithfulness and goodness; it is our job to remember. This act of remembering is the part we play in the decision to change our perspective from one of entitlement to one of gratitude and surrender. These are the steps I go through mentally that have helped me to make this shift. Read the step, then summarize the corresponding Bible verse.

Remember the greatness of God. *Job 38:1–13*

---

[95] Laura Story, *When God Doesn't Fix It* (Nashville, TN: W Publishing Group, 2015), 45.

Submit to His sovereignty. *James 4:7* and *Luke 22:42*

Recognize His love for us. *Romans 5:8*

Identify what matters most to Him. *Luke 10:25–28*

Fix your eyes on heaven. *Revelation 21:3–5*

Our salvation and spiritual healing are of paramount importance to God. This priority surpasses that of our comfort; as a result, discomfort and pain will often be put in the service of our spiritual growth.

3. How are we to view our trials, and for what reason? See Hebrews 12:7–10.

4. A. In the midst of it, discipline is painful. But what does it bring later? Does this happen automatically, or only for certain people? See Hebrews 12:11.

I would propose that we will be trained by discipline only if we are able to make the shift in mind-set described in question 2. Without this perspective, we are far more likely to become bitter rather than better. What are we doing when we make this mental shift? We are moving from delusion to truth. We are then able to be led by truth and trained by discipline.

This process requires a teachable spirit. This is the opposite of being defensive, preferring comfort to holiness, and pridefully thinking we know better than God. It requires a spirit of humility. Father John Bartunek describes this virtue well in his devotional, *The Better Part*:

> Being led by truth requires humility. It requires recognizing a higher authority than oneself: if I am obliged to discover, accept, and conform to what is objectively true (morally, physically, historically), then I am not autonomous; I am not the master of my universe; I am not God. That act of humility, which frees us from the enervating bonds of selfishness, is hard to make. Our fallen human nature tends toward pride, self-sufficiency, control and dominance. To resist that tendency requires courage. It takes courage to obey the truth and expose oneself to the burning love of God.[96]

B. What might change for you if you looked at suffering and the Lord's discipline as "the burning love of God"?

5. A. What are we encouraged to do in the face of trials? See Hebrews 12:12–13.

To strengthen our drooping hands and weak knees and make straight paths for our feet, we have got to grab hold of the spiritual tools God provides for us. Scripture provides comfort, strength, and direction. Prayer fortifies us and draws us into the embrace of God. The Eucharist nourishes, transforms, and satisfies us. Reconciliation burns away our sin and fortifies us for the spiritual battle. Adoration helps us become more like Jesus as we contemplate Him.

---

[96] John Bartunek, L.C., *The Better Part: A Christ-Centered Resource for Personal Prayer* (Hamden, CT: Circle Press, 2007), 977.

B. All these spiritual riches are provided for us, but it is up to us to use them. All too often, when we are weak and drooping, we seek to escape and numb out. We seek comfort instead of things that spiritually strengthen us. Which cheap substitutes do you find you turn to, and which spiritual disciplines could you turn to instead?

Quiet your heart and enjoy His presence. . . . He will always come.

"Strengthen hands that are feeble,
Make firm knees that are weak,
Say to the fearful of heart:
Be strong, do not fear!
Here is your God, he comes with vindication;
With divine recompense
He comes to save you." (Isaiah 45:3–4)

We long to be saved from, *but God often saves us* through. *We can be made more like Jesus through the very things that we think will destroy us. It all depends on our perspective and our response.*

Oh, for the courage to step into trials with a teachable heart, one purified by the desire to be conformed to the image of Christ more than anything else.

"Hold the cross high so I can see it through the flames!" —Saint Joan of Arc

Day Three
PEACE AND HOLINESS

Read Hebrews 12:14–29.

Moving away from his writing about trials and suffering, the author of Hebrews now challenges us to be proactive in our pursuit of godliness as we journey toward heaven.

1. A. Which exhortations are given in Hebrews 12:14–16?

B. What is at stake when we decide whether or not to strive for holiness?

C. Making sure that no one misses the grace of God is intricately tied to our holiness. Sharing our faith is less about having the perfectly crafted argument or explanation and more about imagining the love of God in our fractured and hurt world. One of the most important yet most difficult ways we can do this is by getting rid of any bitterness in our hearts. It's interesting that bitterness is described in Hebrews 12:15 as a root. It is below the surface, often unseen, and easy to deny or hide. Nevertheless, we see evidence of inner bitterness whenever we find hypersensitivity, a lack of gratitude, grudges, mood swings, and a lack of forgiveness. Blogger Erin Davis describes four questions to help us spot a bitter root:

1) Am I replaying the tapes?
   Do you find yourself constantly replaying the tapes of a conversation with someone? . . . Bitterness flourishes in the soil of justification. I've found that when I fixate on my interactions with a specific individual, I am looking for justification for the anger or frustration I am feeling in a relationship. I've learned that if I find myself replaying the tapes often, I should see it as [a] red flag that something is off in my own heart.

2) Is my mouth out of control?
   Romans 3:14 says, "Their mouth is full of curses and bitterness." There is a connection between the junk that comes out of our mouths and the bitterness that tends to take root in our hearts. . . . If you are trying to deal with the way you speak and gaining no ground, it's possible that you need to dig deeper and yank out the root of the problem.

3) Am I sick?
   Psychologist Dr. Carsten Wrosch has studied bitterness for fifteen years. He says: "When harbored for a long time, bitterness may forecast patterns of biological dysregulation (a physiological impairment that can affect metabolism, immune response or organ function) and physical disease."

Scientists have concluded that bitterness, if left unchecked, interferes with the body's hormonal and immune systems. Bitter people tend to have higher blood pressure and heart rate and are much more likely to die of heart disease and other illnesses.

4) Is my clan bitter?
   Like all weeds, bitterness has a way of spreading. Is your marriage marked by bitterness? Are your children bitter? Does your group of friends tend to sit around and gripe? . . . Is it possible that your own bitterness has had a ripple effect?[97]

Do you see evidence of a root of bitterness in your heart?

So how do we rid ourselves of bitterness? In his excellent article on breaking free from bitterness, author and speaker Jim Wilson shares that when we sin, we feel guilt, but when we feel that others have sinned against us, we feel bitterness. He also points out that it's not as important that the evil be great; far more significant is how close we are to the person. Something happens, we feel hurt, and bitterness takes root. What does the world around us suggest that we do to deal with it? Wilson proposes that we are directed to one of two responses: either keep the bitterness in and make yourself sick, or let it out and spread the sickness around. But Christians are called to respond differently. We are to get rid of the bitter root. To do this, however, we need God's help. Wilson illustrates what this looks like with a personal story:

How can we tell if we are bitter? One good rule of thumb is this: Bitterness remembers details.

Many years ago, I was working in our bedroom at my desk. My wife, Bessie, was reading in bed. Whatever I was doing wasn't going well. Bessie said something to me and I turned around and let her have it. It was something unChristian. She looked at me in amazement and got up and left the room. I sat there thinking, "She should not have said it. Look what she said. Look, look, look." I did that for around 10 minutes, maybe longer . . .

---

97 Erin Davis, "4 Ways to Stop a Bitter Root," *True Woman*, September 18, 2018, https://www.reviveourhearts.com/true-woman/blog/four-ways-to-spot-a-bitter-root/.

I . . . got up and went over to my side of the bed, got on my knees and said, "Lord, I was the only one at fault. It was my bitterness and my sin. I am confessing it, forsaking it, and please forgive me."

I got up off my knees and said, "But look what she said." I got back on my knees. "God, I'm sorry for what I did. I accept the responsibility. It was my sin and mine only."

I got up off my knees and said, "God, you and I know who is really at fault." I knelt back down. I stayed on my knees for 45 minutes until I could get up and not say, "Look what she said."

I do not remember now what she said, and I do not remember what I was doing at the desk. I do not remember the details. The only thing I remember now is getting up. But I also know that if I had not taken care of the bitterness I would know to this day exactly what she had said. That is the nature of bitterness.[98]

D. If you have a root of bitterness in your heart, are you willing to get on your knees right now and confess it?

2. Hebrews 12:18–21 recounts the Israelites' reaction to God's presence on Mount Sinai when the old covenant was sealed. Describe the atmosphere and the overriding emotion of the people.

3. The account of Mount Zion (also described as "the city of the living God" and "the heavenly Jerusalem") recorded in Hebrews 12:22–24 speaks of God's dwelling place in heaven. Who is there?

---

[98] Jim Wilson, "How to Be Free from Bitterness," http://storage.cloversites.com/gracecovenantpresbyterianchurch2/documents/Bitterness%20Article.pdf.

In the city of God, we will approach Him in gratitude and awe rather than fear. We are invited to "confidently approach the throne of grace" (Hebrews 4:16) "not because of any righteous deeds we had done but because of his mercy" (Titus 3:5). When we get there, we will be greeted by an assembly of angels, fellow Christians, God, and Jesus.

Why is this possible? We can approach because of "the sprinkled blood that speaks more eloquently than that of Abel" (Hebrews 12:24).

4. What was the lesser case and what was the greater case in this passage? (Note: It references Hebrews 12:18–24.)

The greater case is the warning we are now receiving from God through Jesus. The writer of Hebrews is begging his readers not to turn a deaf ear to these warnings. God's voice shook the earth when He spoke at Mount Sinai, but one day He will rock the heavens. His grace is on offer now, but God is a gentleman and will not force Himself on us. He waits, today, to see what (or whom) we will choose.

5. A. According to Hebrews 12:28, what are we receiving, and what should be our response?

   B. Why are we to respond in this way? See Hebrews 12:29.

Quiet your heart and enjoy His presence. . . . "Offer to him, on the altar of the heart, the sacrifice of humility and praise."[99]

God is not an indifferent bystander waiting to see who joins Him in eternity. He is passionate about our holiness and desperately wants each of us to spend eternity in heaven. But neither is God our

---

[99] Saint Augustine, *The City of God* (London, UK: Penguin Books, 2003), 375.

cosmic good buddy. He is "a consuming fire" (Hebrews 12:29), burning away the dross and shaking the heavens to rid us of the things that hold us back from Him.

Our response to this reality should not be fear; it should be gratitude. He never asks anything of us that He doesn't equip us to carry out. He never asks us to put anything down that would ultimately have been for our good. God is utterly for us, and also beyond us, able to see better than we what is truly needed and beneficial.

What needs to be shaken loose in your life?

Which "burden and sin that clings to [you]" needs to be flung aside so that you can run your race to heaven?

Take some time to ask God to help you get rid of whatever is holding you back or slowing you down. Then commit to a specific action that shows Him that you are cooperating with His grace—relying on Him, but obediently doing your part.

Day Four
LAST WORDS

Read Hebrews 13:1–8.

Now we come to the description of true Christian community. It's a description of how we are to love and worship. There is an intensity and an openness to it. It was radical love then and now. Immersing ourselves in it is critical if we are going to persevere in the Christian life.

1. A. According to Hebrews 13:1–2, what behavior are we encouraged to continue, and what should we be mindful not to neglect? Why?

   B. I believe we typically confuse hospitality with entertaining. Sadly, this means we often spend more time on our Pinterest boards than welcoming people into our homes. Far from needing the "perfect aesthetic environment," people want to relax and feel accepted. Our imperfection actually cultivates a sense of belonging and safety for others. Why? Because people feel more able to be real when they see we aren't living a flawless life.

We create powerful opportunities for meaningful connection when we open our homes and hearts to others. In the comfort and intimacy of that space, it's possible to let down one's guard and explore what we believe about the more meaningful things in life. With no agenda and no rush, hearts are offered the opportunity to open and sometimes mend. Henri Nouwen wrote, "Hospitality means primarily the creation of free space where the stranger can enter and become a friend instead of an enemy. Hospitality is not to change people, but to offer them space where change can take place."[100]

Is your home a free space where people feel welcomed, loved, and able to be themselves? If so, why? If not, what do you think is standing in the way?

2. According to Hebrews 13:3, of whom should we be mindful, and why?

In his article on Catholic prison ministry, Father John Coleman shared the following statistics, taken from research done by the USCCB:

- In 2000, 30 percent of prisoners in state prisons were baptized Catholics.
- More than half a million children have a parent in jail.
- America's prison population is six to twelve times higher per capita than that of other Western countries.[101]

Hopelessness abounds, and faith in rehabilitation has diminished. How should we respond? Religious and laypeople in Arlington, Virginia, give some ideas through their example: They visit the prisoners one-on-one, organize Mass and reconciliation, conduct Bible studies and faith-sharing groups, and provide pre-GED tutoring, ESL programs, and training in basic computer skills.[102] If we aren't able to physically go to prisons, we can pray daily for inmates, prison ministries, chaplains, and the correctional officers. If families of victims or offenders are known in the parish, support can be offered to them as well.

---

[100] Henri J. M. Nouwen, *Reaching Out: The Three Movements of the Spiritual Life* (New York: Doubleday, 1975), 71.

[101] John A. Coleman, "Catholic Prison Ministry," *America: The Jesuit Review*, February 4, 2014, https://www.americamagazine.org/ content/all-things/catholic-prison-ministry.

[102] Ibid.

3. A. Hebrews 13:4–6 addresses areas we often struggle with—marriage and money. What exhortation are we given about marriage and sex in Hebrews 13:4? What warning is given?

There is no doubt that marriage is under attack today. Its very definition has been changed in mainstream culture. Those who believe that marriage can only be between a man and woman and that sexual union is holy and should be reserved for marriage are considered narrow-minded, out of touch, and judgmental. As we listen to opinions on our left and our right, let's not fail to look up and listen to God. As He said in Sirach 23:18–19, "The man who dishonors his marriage bed says to himself, 'Who can see me? . . . Who can stop me from sinning?' He is not mindful of the Most High, fearing only human eyes. He does not realize that the eyes of the Lord, ten thousand times brighter than the sun, observe every step taken and peer into hidden corners."

B. According to Hebrews 13:5, what should our lives be free from? Why?

Some of our trouble lies in our confusion between our wants and needs. I'm convicted by the words of Saint Basil the Great: "The bread you store up belongs to the hungry; the cloak that lies in your chest belongs to the naked; the gold you have hidden in the ground belongs to the poor."

4. A. What are we told to do in Hebrews 13:7?

B. Which Christian leaders have had a significant impact on your life? Do you see "the outcome of their way of life"? In what sense? How can you imitate them? Try to come up with a specific and measurable goal.

5. What assurance are we given in Hebrews 13:8? What difference does that make to you, personally?

Quiet your heart and enjoy His presence. . . . Lean on Him.

When all around us shifts and changes, it's a tremendous comfort to know that Jesus never does. He is the same yesterday, today, and forever. We can count on Him. Turn the words of the hymn "My Hope Is Built on Nothing Less" into a prayer of gratitude for the solid foundation and help He never fails to provide. And take note of all the things you have learned about in your study of Hebrews that are featured in this hymn. You are reading these lyrics today with far greater insight than you would have months ago.

My Hope Is Built on Nothing Less
My hope is built on nothing less
Than Jesus Christ, my righteousness;
I dare not trust the sweetest frame,
But wholly lean on Jesus' name.

On Christ the solid Rock, I stand;
All other ground is sinking sand,
All other ground is sinking sand.

When darkness veils His lovely face,
I rest on His unchanging grace;
In every high and stormy gale,
My anchor holds within the veil.

His oath, His covenant, His blood,
Support me in in the whelming flood;
When all around my soul gives way,
He then is all my hope and stay.[103]

---

[103] Edward Mote and William Batchelder Bradbury, "My Hope Is Built on Nothing Less" (1834).

Day Five
FINAL TEACHING AND BLESSING

Read Hebrews 13:9–25.

1. A. As we saw in Hebrews 13:8, Jesus is unchanging. These next verses remind us that truth is unchanging as well. What are readers warned about in Hebrews 13:9?

    B. What does Saint Paul have to say about this subject in Ephesians 4:14?

    C. Which strange teachings was the author of Hebrews talking about?

Old Testament dietary laws were strictly observed by many and considered a critical way to attain holiness. But as Jesus said in Mark 7:15, "Nothing that enters one from outside can defile that person; but the things that come out from within are what defile."

While we are unlikely to believe that we'll attain spiritual perfection through what we do or don't eat, we can fall into the trap of thinking we can *earn* God's grace through our behavior. The truth is, at no point do we deserve God's grace, no matter how much we follow His guidelines. What is the balance seen in the spiritually mature? They strive for spiritual perfection through the help of the Holy Spirit, all the while knowing that salvation is an unearned gift from Him.

2. According to CCC 1182, what altar is the author referring to in Hebrews 13:10?

3. A. Where were the bodies of the animal sacrifices burned and where did Jesus suffer? See Hebrews 13:11–12.

    B. Where are we to go? Why? See Hebrews 13:13–14.

The author of Hebrews is encouraging his readers to bypass the temple sacrifices and go straight to the cross for forgiveness. In the Old Testament, whatever was "outside the camp" was considered unclean. It meant you were outside the community. This certainly wasn't a comfortable place to be, and feelings of rejection were the norm there. Being outside the camp required a willingness to suffer out of loyalty to Christ.

4. A. What actions are we encouraged to take in Hebrews 13:15–16?

    B. We are to be both contemplative and conquering. This means we devote ourselves to concrete acts of service and remain in a spirit of prayer while we are doing them. In the words of Pope Francis, "We are called to be contemplatives even in the midst of action." Anytime we ask the Holy Spirit to do the work through us, we are both contemplative and conquering as we serve. Most of us tend toward one side or the other, preferring to serve God either through our prayer life or through apostolic activity. But both are needed. As you look at your own life, which do you find easier—cultivating a life of prayer or of service?

5. A. Which instructions are given in Hebrews 13:17–19 regarding the way we should relate to our leaders?

B. Why do leaders desperately need our prayers? Christian leaders are especially targeted for attack by the enemy of our souls, and our prayers can serve as a hedge of protection around them. There is much at stake in terms of the morality of a Christian leader; his or her fall from grace has ripple effects that are widely felt. In addition, leaders and teachers in the Church "will be judged more strictly" (James 3:1). God will hold leaders accountable for the way they have cared for the souls entrusted to them.

Which leaders do you feel called to pray for? List them here. Will you commit to regularly praying for them? Just think of the difference we would see if we stopped complaining about our priests and leaders and instead devoted that time to praying for them.

Quiet your heart and enjoy His presence. . . . Bow your head for the blessing.

"May the God of peace, who brought up from the dead the great shepherd of the sheep by the blood of the eternal covenant, Jesus our Lord, furnish you with all that is good, that you may do his will. May he carry out in you what is pleasing to him through Jesus Christ, to whom be glory forever and ever. Amen." (Hebrews 13:20–21)

These verses promise us that God will furnish us with everything we need to do His will. The original Hebrew word for furnish can also mean "to mend" and "to complete what is lacking." The same word is used in Matthew 4:21 to describe the disciples James and John mending their fishing nets. Saint Paul uses it in Galatians 6:1 to describe restoring a brother or sister in Christ who has been caught in sin. The prayer in Hebrews 13:20 asks God to furnish us with all we need to mend and restore what is broken around us. For many of us, this starts not just within our families, but within our own hearts.

When we feel disqualified from or not good enough for the spiritual pilgrimage, God can pick us up and untangle the mess of our lives. He leans in close and assures us that there is purpose for our lives. No matter what dilemma we may find ourselves in, He can always put us back together so that we can not only do His will but also leave a lasting impact. He gives us all we need for this to happen through the gift of the indwelling Holy Spirit.

Take some time to talk to the Lord about an area of your life where you need mending, equipping, or restoration. Ask Him to come into your life and create beauty from the ashes. This is a prayer He faithfully answers, each and every time.

Conclusion

The letter had arrived, the people had gathered, a hush filled the room, and the anointed words were read. It had begun with the words, "In many and various ways, God spoke of old to our fathers by the prophets; but in these last days he has spoken to us by a Son" (Hebrews 1:1). Now the letter was rolled back up, and discussion of it began.

Much had been contained in those pages—words of encouragement, exhortation, challenge, instruction. Now the real work needed to happen: applying what they had heard to their daily lives.

They looked around the room at one another. No one was naturally drawn to every person in the room—of course some people were closer to each other than others. Preferences and different levels of intimacy were as true there as in any other community. But they knew they were being challenged to love one another as *family*, regardless of differences. They were to allow all points of their lives to connect with one another, sharing their hearts and possessions with abandon.

But these words weren't just for them. Jesus asks us to do the same—to worship Him in the context of messy community. We are called not just to attend Mass, but to relate to one another as sisters and brothers. We aren't just supposed to show up; we're to make the effort to belong. This is a critical part of worshipping God because one of the key ways He shapes us is in the crucible of relationships. This means we enter into relationships not with a closed heart, but with openness and willingness to be vulnerable and to sacrifice.

Thinking about this makes me so aware of how much I want to be in control of how I worship. I want safety, privacy, and to be sure my needs are going to be met. God asks me to trust Him and lean into others. I find that a little bit scary because I have been hurt in community. Maybe you have, too.

The gospel of grace calls us to this radical level of self-giving, but we are steeped in a culture that encourages us to live selfishly. On either end of the conservative–liberal spectrum, we find intense individualism. The liberal end will struggle with Hebrews 13:4, which says that the marriage bed is to be pure—that any sex outside of marriage is a sin. The argument will be made that it's my body and I can do with it as I like. The conservative end will struggle with Hebrews 13:5, which challenges us to see our money as belonging to God, to be used to build up the kingdom. The argument will be made that it's my money, I made it, and I can do with it as I wish. In both cases, the focus is on the individual, not the community.

Why is the Church exploding in Africa and Latin America? Could it be that those areas of the world have retained a focus on community that we have lost? Is our individualism hampering the spread of the gospel? I believe it is.

What are we to do? How can we find the strength and desire to live counterculturally—which in this case means choosing community over self-indulgent isolation? What is underneath our tendency to self-protect and look out for ourselves first?

I believe fear is the culprit. And if we were to follow the thread of fear to its root, I believe we would find that we are ultimately afraid of being alone. We fear that if we love radically, we'll be stripped and left naked. We fear that if we reveal ourselves vulnerably, we'll be rejected and abandoned. We fear that if we let go of control of our money, we'll lose it all and be left with nothing.

God responds to our fear in Hebrews 13:5 with the words, "Be content with what you have, because [God] has said, 'I will never forsake you or abandon you.'" That is the guarantee He gives us. He knows the risk found in community; Jesus Himself experienced betrayal and abandonment by the people who were supposed to stay closest. Yet He asks us to venture out into the deep, trusting that no matter how many times we are disappointed, burned, betrayed, or hurt, He will never leave us. He will always be the balm that not only brings comfort but also heals.

We cannot run this race alone. As tempting as it is to just rely on ourselves, we need one another. May God give us just a little more courage than fear to open wide and embrace our brothers and sisters. May this be our spiritual act of worship.

My Resolution

In what specific way will I apply what I have learned in this lesson?

Examples:

1. I feel challenged to open my heart and home in the spirit of Christian hospitality. I will get something on the calendar and choose to ignore my desire to create perfection, striving instead to create a welcoming atmosphere.

2. I feel especially convicted by the exhortation in Hebrews 13:3 to care for prisoners. I will follow the examples given of the religious and laypeople and offer my support in a specific way (record it here and commit to an action step to make it happen).

3. I've identified a Christian leader whose life has made an impact on me. I will choose to imitate him or her in a specific way (record it here and commit to an action step to make it happen).

My resolution:

Catechism Clips

CCC 1182 The *altar* of the New Covenant is the Lord's Cross, from which the sacraments of the paschal mystery flow. On the altar, which is the center of the church, the sacrifice of the Cross is made present under sacramental signs. The altar is also the table of the Lord, to which the People of God are invited. In certain Eastern liturgies, the altar is also the symbol of the tomb (Christ truly died and is truly risen).

CCC 2683 The witnesses who have preceded us into the kingdom, especially those whom the Church recognizes as saints, share in the living tradition of prayer by the example of their lives, the transmission of their writings, and their prayer today. They contemplate God, praise him and constantly care for those whom they have left on earth. When they entered into the joy of their Master, they were "put in charge of many things." Their intercession is their most exalted service to God's plan. We can and should ask them to intercede for us and for the whole world.

Verse Study

See Appendix 3 for instructions on how to complete a verse study.

1 Peter 1:22

1. Verse:

2. Paraphrase:

3. Questions:

4. Cross-references:

5. Personal Application:

Lesson 17: Talk

THE RACE

Hebrews 12:1–8

You can view this talk on the accompanying DVD, or please visit our website at walkingwithpurpose.com/videos and select the *Grounded in Hope* Bible Study, then click through to select Videos.

I. The Race

"Therefore, since we are surrounded by such a great cloud of witnesses, let us throw off everything that hinders and the sin that so easily entangles. And let us run with perseverance the race marked out for us . . . fixing our eyes on Jesus." (Hebrews 12:1–2)

The word *race* comes from the Greek word *agon* (ag-one'). We get the word *agony* from this root word, and the word *race* could also be translated "conflict," "struggle," or "fight." What the author of Hebrews wants us to understand is that life is a race, and the race is one of agonizing struggle. It isn't a short sprint—it's a marathon.

To get to the finish line, you have to remain faithful even when it stops being fun.

The race goes to those who _____.

The race also goes to those who are willing to _____.

II. The Arena

What are these things that we crave but can survive without?

We crave _____.
We crave _____.

We crave _____.

Who is with us in the arena?

The _____.
The cloud of _____.
Your home _____.

Who should have the best seat in the arena?

We are to give *Him* the best seat in the arena, and never, ever take our eyes off of Him.

III. The Runner

IV. The Cost

"My son, do not make light of the Lord's discipline, and do not lose heart when he rebukes you, because the Lord disciplines the one he loves, and he chastens everyone he accepts as his son." (Hebrews 12:5–8)

"Everything difficult points to something more than our theory of life yet embraces." —George MacDonald

Discussion Questions

1. Which of the three things we crave but can survive without are the hardest for you to give up? Approval? Control? Comfort?

2. Can you think of a time in your life when you grew weary and lost heart, and your expectations were a big part of the problem? To help you identify this, look at the source of the suffering—was it the shock, the confusion, the self-pity, or the disbelief that was the source of the difficulty?

3. Do you agree with the quote from author George MacDonald, "Everything difficult points to something more than our theory of life yet embraces"? Why or why not?

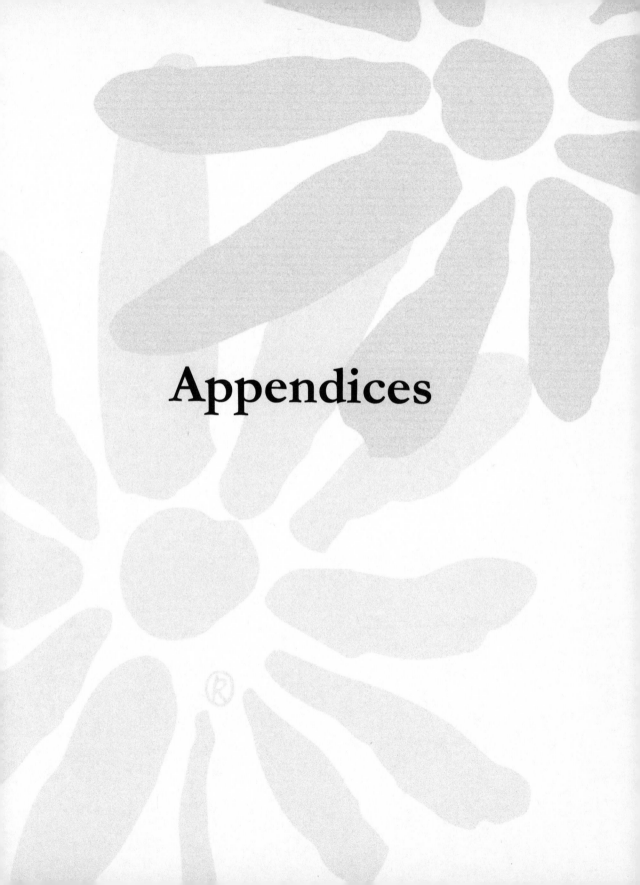

Appendices

NOTES

Appendix 1
SAINT THÉRÈSE OF LISIEUX

Patron Saint of Walking with Purpose

Saint Thérèse of Lisieux was gifted with the ability to take the riches of our Catholic faith and explain them in a way that a child could imitate. The wisdom she gleaned from Scripture ignited a love in her heart for her Lord that was personal and transforming. The simplicity of the faith that she laid out in her writings is so completely Catholic that Pope Pius XII said, "She rediscovered the Gospel itself, the very heart of the Gospel."

Walking with Purpose is intended to be a means by which women can honestly share their spiritual struggles and embark on a journey that is refreshing to the soul. It was never intended to facilitate the deepest of intellectual study of Scripture. Instead, the focus has been to help women know Christ: to know His heart, to know His tenderness, to know His mercy, and to know His love. Our logo is a little flower, and that has meaning. When a woman begins to open her heart to God, it's like the opening of a little flower. It can easily be bruised or crushed, and it must be treated with the greatest of care. Our desire is to speak to women's hearts no matter where they are in life, baggage and all, and gently introduce truths that can change their lives.

Saint Thérèse of Lisieux, the little flower, called her doctrine "the little way of spiritual childhood," and it is based on complete and unshakable confidence in God's love for us. She was not introducing new truths. She spent countless hours reading Scripture and she shared what she found, emphasizing the importance of truths that had already been divinely revealed. We can learn so much from her:

> The good God would not inspire unattainable desires; I can, then, in spite of my littleness, aspire to sanctity. For me to become greater is impossible; I must put up with myself just as I am with all my imperfections. But I wish to find the way to go to Heaven by a very straight, short, completely new little way. We are in a century of inventions: now one does not even have to take the trouble to climb the steps of a stairway; in the homes of the rich, an elevator replaces them nicely. I, too, would like to find an elevator to lift me up to Jesus, for I am too little to climb the rough stairway of perfection. So I have looked in the

books of the saints for a sign of the elevator I long for, and I have read these words proceeding from the mouth of eternal Wisdom: "He that is a little one, let him turn to me" (Proverbs 9:16). So I came, knowing that I had found what I was seeking, and wanting to know, O my God, what You would do with the little one who would answer Your call, and this is what I found:

"As one whom the mother caresses, so will I comfort you. You shall be carried at the breasts and upon the knees they shall caress you" (Isaiah 66:12–13). Never have more tender words come to make my soul rejoice. The elevator which must raise me to the heavens is Your arms, O Jesus! For that I do not need to grow; on the contrary, I must necessarily remain small, become smaller and smaller. O my God, You have surpassed what I expected, and I want to sing Your mercies. (Saint Thérèse of the Infant Jesus, *Histoire d'une Ame: Manuscrits Autobiographiques* [Paris: Éditions du Seuil, 1998], 244.)

Appendix 2
SCRIPTURE MEMORY

"The tempter approached and said to him, 'If you are the Son of God, command that these stones become loaves of bread.' He said in reply, 'It is written: One does not live by bread alone, but by every word that comes forth from the mouth of God" (Matthew 4:3–4).

Jesus was able to respond to Satan's temptations because He knew God's truth. When He was under fire, He didn't have time to go find wisdom for the moment. It had to already be in His head. He had memorized Scripture, and found those words to be His most effective weapon in warding off temptation.

Do you ever feel tempted to just give in? To take the easy way when you know the hard way is right? Does discouragement ever nip at your heels and take you to a place of darkness? If you memorize Scripture, the Holy Spirit will be able to bring God's truth to your mind just when you need to fight back.

Ephesians 6:17 describes Scripture as an offensive weapon ("the sword of the Spirit"). How does this work? When negative thoughts and lies run through our minds, we can take a Bible verse and use it as a weapon to kick out the lie and embrace the truth. Verses that speak of God's unconditional love and forgiveness and our new identity in Christ are especially powerful for this kind of battle. When we feel defeated and like we'll never change, when we falsely assume that God must be ready to give up on us, the Holy Spirit can remind us of 2 Corinthians 5:17: "If anyone is in Christ, [she] is a new creation. The old has gone. The new has come!"

That's not the only way memorized Scripture helps us. The Holy Spirit can bring one of the truths of the Bible to our mind just before we might make a wrong choice. It's like a little whisper reminding us of what we know is true, but there's power in it, because we know they are God's words. For example, in the midst of a conversation in which we aren't listening well, the Holy Spirit can bring to mind Proverbs 18:2: "Fools take no delight in understanding, but only in displaying what they think." This enables us to make a course correction immediately instead of looking back later with regret. As it says in Psalm 119:11, "I have hidden your word in my heart *that I might not sin against you*" (emphasis added).

You may think of memorizing Scripture as an activity for the über-religious, not for the average Christian. A blogger at She Reads Truth (shereadstruth.com) describes it this way: "Recalling Scripture isn't for the overachievers; it's for the homesick." It's for those of us who know that earth isn't our home—heaven is. It's for those of us who don't want to be tossed all over the place by our emotions and instead long to be grounded in truth.

But how do we do it? Kids memorize things so easily, but our brains are full of so many other bits of information that we wonder if we're capable of doing it. Never fear. There are easy techniques that can help us to store away God's words in our minds and hearts. Pick a few that work for you! *You can do it!*

1. Learning Through Repetition
Every time you sit down to do your Bible study, begin by reading the memory verses. The more you read them, the sooner it will be lodged in your memory. Be sure to read the reference as well. Don't skip that part—it comes in handy when you want to know where to find the verse in the Bible.

2. Learning Visually
Write the memory verse *in pencil* on a piece of paper. Read the entire verse, including the reference. Choose one word and erase it well. Reread the entire verse, including the reference. Choose another word and erase it well. Reread the entire verse, including the reference. Repeat this process until the whole verse has been erased and you are reciting it from memory.

3. Learning Electronically
Go to our website under Courses and save the *Grounded in Hope* Memory Verse Image to your phone's lock screen. Practice the verse every time you grab your phone.

4. Learning by Writing It Down
Grab a piece of paper and write your verse down twenty times.

5. Learning by Seeing It Everywhere
Display the gorgeous WWP memory verse card somewhere in your house. Recite the verse each time you pass by it. But don't stop there: Write your verse down on index cards and leave them in places you often linger—the bathroom mirror, the car dashboard, whatever works for you.

6. Learning Together
If you are doing this Walking with Purpose study in a small group, hold each other accountable and recite the memory verse together at the start and end of each lesson. If you are doing this study on your own, consider asking someone to hold you accountable by listening to you say your verse from memory each week.

WE HAVE HOPE as an ANCHOR for our SOUL FIRM and SECURE

Hebrews 6:19

walking with purpose

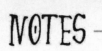 NOTES

LET US RID ourselves of every burden & SIN that clings to us and persevere in running the grace... keeping our eyes fixed on JESUS.

HEBREWS 12:1-2

walking with purpose

Full-color free printables available at walkingwithpurpose.com/free-printables.

313

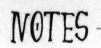

NOTES

Appendix 3
HOW TO DO A VERSE STUDY

A verse study is an exciting Bible study tool that can help to bring the Scriptures to life! By reading, reflecting on, and committing a verse to memory, we open ourselves to the Holy Spirit, who reveals very personal applications of our Lord's words and actions to our daily lives.

Learning to do a verse study is not difficult, but it can be demanding. In this Walking with Purpose™ study, a Bible verse has been selected to reinforce a theme of each lesson. To do the verse study, read the verse and then follow these simple instructions. You'll be on your way to a deeper and more personal understanding of Scripture.

- **Read the verse and the paragraph before and after the verse.**

- **Write out the selected verse.**

- **Paraphrase.**
  Write the verse using your own words. What does the verse say?

- **Ask questions.**
  Write down any questions you have about the verse. What does it say that you don't understand?

- **Use cross-references.**
  Look up other Bible verses that help to shed light on what the selected verse means. A study Bible will often list cross-references in the margin or in the study notes. Another excellent resource is Biblehub.com. This website allows you to enter a specific Bible verse and it will provide many cross-references and additional insights into the passage of Scripture you selected. Record any insights you gain from the additional verses you are able to find.

- **Make a personal application.**
  What does the verse say to you personally? Is there a promise to make? A warning to heed? An example to follow? Ask God to help you find something from the verse that you can apply to your life.

The recommended Bible translations for use in Walking with Purpose™ studies are: The New American Bible, which is the translation used in the United States for the readings at Mass; The Revised Standard Version, Catholic Edition; and The Jerusalem Bible.

A SAMPLE VERSE STUDY

1. **Verse:**
   John 15:5   "I am the vine, you are the branches. Those who abide in me and I in them bear much fruit, because apart from me you can do nothing."

2. **Paraphrase:**
   Jesus is the vine, I am the branch. If I abide in Him, then I'll be fruitful, but if I try to do everything on my own, I'll fail at what matters most. I need Him.

3. **Questions:**
   What does it mean to abide? How does Jesus abide in me? What kind of fruit is Jesus talking about?

4. **Cross-references:**
   John 6:56   "He that eats my flesh, and drinks my blood, abides in me, and I in him." This verse brings to mind the Eucharist, and the importance of receiving Christ in the Eucharist as often as possible. This is a very important way to abide in Jesus.

   John 15:7   "If you abide in me, and my words abide in you, ask for whatever you wish, and it will be done for you." How can Jesus' words abide in me if I never read them? I need to read the Bible if I want to abide in Christ.

   John 15:16   "It was not you who chose me, but I who chose you and appointed you to go and bear fruit that will remain, so that whatever you ask the Father in my name he may give you." Not all fruit remains. Some is good only temporarily—on earth. I want my fruit to remain in eternity—to count in the long run.

   Galatians 5:22–23   "The fruit of the Spirit is love, joy, peace, patience, kindness, generosity, faithfulness, gentleness, self-control." These are some of the fruits that will be seen if I abide in Christ.

5. Personal Application:

I will study my calendar this week, making note of where I spend my time. Is most of my time spent on things that will last for eternity (fruit that remains)? I'll reassess my priorities in light of what I find.

 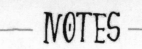

Appendix 4
CONVERSION OF HEART

The Catholic faith is full of beautiful traditions, rituals, and sacraments. As powerful as they are, it is possible for them to become mere habits in our lives, instead of experiences that draw us close to the heart of Christ. In the words of John Paul II, they can become acts of "hollow ritualism." We might receive our first Communion and the sacraments of confession and confirmation, yet never experience the interior conversion that opens the heart to a personal relationship with God.

Pope Benedict XVI has explained that the "door of faith" is opened at one's baptism, but we are called to open it again, walk through it, and rediscover and renew our relationship with Christ and His Church.[106]

So how do we do this? How do we walk through that door of faith so we can begin to experience the abundant life that God has planned for us?

GETTING PERSONAL

The word *conversion* means "the act of turning." This means that conversion involves a turning away from one thing and a turning toward another. When you haven't experienced conversion of heart, you are turned *toward* your own desires. You are the one in charge, and you do what you feel is right and best at any given moment. You may choose to do things that are very good for other people, but the distinction is that *you are choosing.* You are deciding. You are the one in control.

Imagine driving a car. You are sitting in the driver's seat, and your hands are on the steering wheel. You've welcomed Jesus into the passenger's seat, and have listened to His comments. But whether or not you follow His directions is really up to you. You may follow them or you may not, depending on what seems right to you.

When you experience interior conversion, you decide to turn, to get out of the driver's seat, move into the passenger's seat, and invite God to be the driver. Instead of seeing Him as an advice giver or someone nice to have around for the holidays, you give Him control of every aspect of your life.

More than likely, you don't find this easy to do. This is because of the universal struggle with pride. We want to be the ones in charge. We don't like to be in

---

[106] Pope Benedict XVI, *Apostolic Letter: Porta Fidei*, for the Indiction of the Year of Faith, October 11, 2011.

desperate need. We like to be the captains of our ships, charting our own courses. As William Ernest Henley wrote, "I am the master of my fate: I am the captain of my soul."

Conversion of heart isn't possible without humility. The first step is to recognize your desperate need of a savior. Romans 6:23 states that the "wages of sin is death." When you hear this, you might be tempted to justify your behavior, or compare yourself with others. You might think to yourself, "I'm not a murderer. I'm not as bad as this or that person. If someone were to put my good deeds and bad deeds on a scale, my good ones would outweigh the bad. So surely I am good enough? Surely I don't deserve death!" When this is your line of thought, you are missing a very important truth: Just one mortal sin is enough to separate you from a holy God. Just one mortal sin is enough for you to deserve death.[107] Even your best efforts to do good fall short of what God has required in order for you to spend eternity with Him. Isaiah 64:6 says, "All our righteous acts are like filthy rags." If you come to God thinking that you are going to be accepted by Him based on your "good conduct," He will point out that your righteousness is nothing compared to His infinite holiness.

Saint Thérèse of Lisieux understood this well, and wrote, "In the evening of my life I shall appear before You with empty hands, for I do not ask You to count my works. All our justices are stained in Your eyes. I want therefore to clothe myself in Your own justice and receive from Your love the eternal possession of Yourself."[108]

She recognized that her works, her best efforts, wouldn't be enough to earn salvation. Salvation cannot be earned. It's a free gift. Saint Thérèse accepted this gift, and said that if her justices or righteous deeds were stained, then she wanted to clothe herself in Christ's own justice. We see this described in 2 Corinthians 5:21: "God made him who had no sin to be sin for us, so that in him we might become the righteousness of God."

How did God make Him who had no sin to be sin for you? This was foretold by the prophet Isaiah: "But he was pierced for our transgressions, he was crushed for our iniquities; the punishment that brought us peace was upon him, and by his wounds we are healed" (Isaiah 53:5).

---

[107] One sin was enough to merit death for the first human beings, who were in the state of preternatural perfection. For us, joined to Christ in His Body, one mortal sin merits death. Venial sin does not, although venial sin makes it easier to commit mortal sin. See CCC 1854–1864.

[108] Saint Thérèse, "Act of Oblation to Merciful Love."

Jesus accomplished this on the cross. Every sin committed, past, present, and future, was placed on Him. Now, *all the merits of Jesus can be yours*. He wants to fill your empty hands with His own virtues.

But first, you need to recognize, just as Saint Thérèse did, that you are little. You are weak. You fail. You need forgiveness. You need a savior.

When you come before God in prayer and acknowledge these truths, He looks at your heart. He sees your desire to trust Him, to please Him, to obey Him. He says to you, "My precious child, you don't have to pay for your sins. My Son, Jesus, has already done that for you. He suffered so that you wouldn't have to. I want to experience a relationship of intimacy with you. I forgive you.[109] Jesus came to set you free.[110] When you open your heart to me, you become a new creation![111] The old you has gone. The new you is here. If you will stay close to me, and journey by my side, you will begin to experience a transformation that brings joy and freedom.[112] I've been waiting to pour my gifts into your soul. Beloved daughter of mine, remain confident in me. I am your loving Father. Crawl into my lap. Trust me. Love me. I will take care of everything."

This is conversion of heart. This act of faith lifts the veil from your eyes and launches you into the richest and most satisfying life. You don't have to be sitting in church to do this. Don't let a minute pass before opening your heart to God and inviting Him to come dwell within you. Let Him sit in the driver's seat. Give Him the keys to your heart. Your life will never be the same again.

---

[109] "If we acknowledge our sins, he is faithful and just and will forgive our sins and cleanse us from every wrongdoing." 1 John 1:9

[110] "So if the Son makes you free, you will be free indeed." John 8:36

[111] "So whoever is in Christ is a new creation: the old things have passed away; behold, new things have come." 2 Corinthians 5:18

[112] "I will sprinkle clean water over you to make you clean; from all your impurities and from all your idols I will cleanse you. I will give you a new heart, and a new spirit I will put within you. I will remove the heart of stone from your flesh and give you a heart of flesh." Ezekiel 36:25–26

NOTES

Appendix 5
THE I DECLARES

~I declare that I am a beloved daughter of the King.

~I declare that being a beloved daughter of the King gives me authority over the enemy.

~I declare that God has a plan for my life.

~I declare that His plan is for my good.

~I declare that God will not abandon me in this moment.

FEAR OF THE FUTURE
Counter your what-ifs with the truth.

~I declare that God has not given me a spirit of fear, but a spirit of power, love, and a sound mind (2 Timothy 1:7).

~I declare that *you* are my peace, not perfect circumstances (Ephesians 2:14).

~I declare if I present my requests to you with a spirit of gratitude, your peace will guard my heart and mind (Philippians 4:6–7).

~I declare that if I seek first your kingdom and righteousness, then all the things I need will be given to me as well (Luke 12:31).

~I declare that if I trust in you with all my heart and don't lean on my own understanding, you will make my path straight (Proverbs 3:5–6).

~I declare that God's plans for me are to prosper me and not harm me, to give me a hope and a future (Jeremiah 29:11).

PAIN FROM THE PAST
Counter your if-onlys with the truth.

~I declare God has thrown my sin as far as the east is from the west (Psalm 103:12).

~I declare God will restore the years the locusts have eaten (Joel 2:25).

~I declare that if I confess my sin, God is faithful and just and will forgive it (1 John 1:9).

~I declare that when you forgive, my sins that were like scarlet become as white as snow (Isaiah 1:18).

~I declare that you are doing a new thing in my life: You are making a way in the wilderness and streams in the wasteland (Isaiah 43:19).

~I declare that I am a new creation in Christ. The old is gone. The new is come (2 Corinthians 5:17)!

CURRENT SUFFERING
Counter the discouragement and hopelessness with the truth.

~I declare that when I am weak, you are strong within me (2 Corinthians 12:10).

~I declare that no temptation has seized me except that which is common to man. And you will always provide a way out so that I can stand up under it (1 Corinthians 10:13).

~I declare that God will restore, support, strengthen, and establish me (1 Peter 5:10).

~I declare that no amount of suffering can separate me from the love of God (Romans 8:35).

~I declare that I am uniquely equipped to provide comfort to others because I truly understand. The comfort you've given me can be poured out to others who are suffering in the same way I am (2 Corinthians 1:3–4).

~I declare that my light and momentary troubles are achieving for me an eternal glory that far outweighs them all (2 Corinthians 4:17).

STRUGGLE IN MARRIAGE
Counter the heaviness with the truth.

~I declare God's arm is not too short to save us. He can reach into my heart and into my husband's heart and draw the two of us together (Isaiah 59:1).

~I declare that if you are for us, who can be against us (Romans 8:31)?

~I declare that I can hold firmly to hope, because you, the One who promised, are faithful (Hebrews 10:23).

~I declare that when we lack love, you can give us divine love for each other (Romans 5:5).

~I declare that what God has joined together, no one should separate (Mark 10:9).

~I declare that you are our lamp, and you can turn our darkness into light (2 Samuel 22:29).

WORRY ABOUT YOUR CHILDREN
Counter the feelings of powerlessness with the truth.

~I declare that you who began a good work in my child will bring it to completion (Philippians 1:6).

~I declare that you can reach down from on high and take hold of my child, drawing him out of deep waters (2 Samuel 22:17).

~I declare that my work as a mother will be rewarded and that my child will come back from the land of the enemy (Jeremiah 31:16).

~I declare that there is hope in my future and in my child's future, and that my child will come back to her own border (Jeremiah 31:17).

~I declare that all your promises are *yes* in Jesus, and that not one word of your promises has ever failed (2 Corinthians 1:20; 1 Kings 8:56).

~I declare that you are able to accomplish abundantly more than all I could ask or imagine (Ephesians 3:20).

DOUBTING THE GOODNESS OF GOD
Counter the loss of trust with the truth.

~I declare that just because I don't understand what you are allowing does not mean you are not good. I declare that your thoughts are not my thoughts, and your ways are not my ways. For as the heavens are higher than the earth, so are your ways higher than my ways, and your thoughts than my thoughts (Isaiah 55:8–9).

~I declare that your grace and goodness sometimes visit in uncomfortable forms. "You wound and you heal" (Deuteronomy 32:39). But you allow the wound so that we heal more deeply.

~I declare that you are gracious, slow to anger, and abounding in steadfast love and faithfulness, keeping steadfast love for the thousandth generation, forgiving iniquity, transgression, and sin (Exodus 34:6–7).

~I declare that you are a sun and shield, that you give grace and glory. I declare that you don't withhold any good thing from those who walk uprightly (Psalm 84:11).

~I declare that your steadfast love never ceases; your mercies never come to an end. They are new every morning. I declare that great is your faithfulness (Lamentations 3:22–23).

~I declare that you are good—a stronghold in the day of trouble. I declare that you know those who take refuge in you (Nahum 1:7).

STRUGGLE WITH BEING SINGLE
Counter the discontent with the truth.

~I declare that I do not need to be afraid, that I will not be put to shame. I do not need to fear disgrace because I will not be humiliated (Isaiah 54:4).

~I declare that my maker is my husband—the Lord Almighty is His name. The Holy One of Israel is my redeemer (Isaiah 54:5).

~I declare that You will have compassion on me with everlasting kindness (Isaiah 54:8).

~I declare that there is a time for everything, and a season for every activity under the heavens (Ecclesiastes 3:1).

~I declare that if I seek first Your kingdom and Your righteousness, all these things will be given to me as well (Matthew 6:33).

~I declare that I do not need to worry about tomorrow (Matthew 6:34).

~I declare that if I trust in You with all my heart and don't lean on my own understanding, You will make my path straight (Proverbs 3:5–6).

~I declare that charm is deceptive and beauty is fleeting, but a woman who fears the Lord is to be praised (Proverbs 31:30).

~I declare that You heal the brokenhearted and bind up my wounds (Psalm 147:3).

~I declare that I can be strong and courageous because You go with me and will never leave me or forsake me (Deuteronomy 31:6).

~I declare that God sets the lonely in families (Psalm 68:6).

~I declare that if I take delight in You, Lord, if I experience joy in Your presence, You will give me the desires of my heart (Psalm 37:4).

~I declare that You will never let me be tempted beyond what I can bear. When I am tempted, You will always provide a way out so that I can endure it (1 Corinthians 10:13).

~I declare that in Christ, I have been brought to fullness. I am complete in Christ (Colossians 2:10).

~I declare that now is not a time for me to wallow in pity. I declare that I am God's handiwork, created in Christ Jesus to do good works, which You prepared in advance for me to do (Ephesians 2:10).

~I declare that when I'm unmarried, I can live a life of undivided devotion to You. But a married woman is also concerned about how she can please her husband (1 Corinthians 7:34–35).

NOTES

Answer Key

NOTES

Lesson 2, Day One

1. Saint Paul was exasperated at the sight of the city full of idols.
2. He began with a compliment, observing that they were very religious, rather than launching into an indictment of all that he saw was wrong about them.
3. Saint Paul found one altar inscribed "to an Unknown God," and then set out to explain that God to his listeners.
4. The one true God does not live in sanctuaries made by human hands the way the Greek idols did. In addition, the God Paul was speaking of is not "like an image fashioned from gold, silver, or stone by human art and imagination."
5. God doesn't require our service; He doesn't need anything from us. Rather, all of life comes from and is sustained by Him. He orders the seasons and the boundaries so that people might seek Him. He is not far from any one of us. In God, we live and move and have our being. He demands that all people everywhere repent of sin because judgment will come one day.
6. Saint Paul said that we are transformed by the renewing of our minds.

Lesson 2, Day Two

1. **A.** In the past, God spoke in partial and various ways through the prophets, but in these last days He's spoken to us through a son.
   B. God spoke to the prophets through a burning bush; a still, small voice; visions and dreams; and sometimes face-to-face, plainly.
2. **A.** He is described as the the heir of all things, through whom God created the universe.
   B. All things came to be through Jesus, and without Him, nothing came to be.
   C. Jesus is given the nations as His inheritance, the ends of the earth as His possession.
3. We learn that Jesus reflects the glory of God, bears the exact imprint of His nature, sustains everything by His powerful Word, and sat down at the right hand of God after making purification for our sins.
4. He sat down at the right hand of the majesty on high.
5. Jesus is superior to the angels.
6. **A.** In this verse, wisdom is described as the reflection of eternal light, the spotless mirror of the power of God, the image of His goodness.
   B. Answers will vary.

Lesson 2, Day Three

1. **Daniel 10:4–15** The angel was like chrysolite (or topaz, a yellowish precious stone) and his face shone like lightning. His eyes were like fiery torches and his arms and feet looked like burnished bronze. The sound of his voice was like the roar of a multitude. Only Daniel saw the vision, but just the unseen presence of the angel caused the people with Daniel to run and hide themselves. Daniel himself was without strength, turned the color of death, and was powerless. The angel's voice caused him to fall forward, unconscious. The angel came as a messenger, sent to help Daniel by telling him the future. It's also interesting to note that Daniel's prayer was heard by God the minute he "made up his mind to acquire understanding and humble himself before God" (vs. 12). At that time, God began to answer his prayer by sending this angel. What comes next is a fascinating description of the unseen spiritual world that is far more real than what we see with our

human eyes. On his way to Daniel, the angel was detained by the Prince of Persia, who stood in his way. The archangel Michael came to help him, and continued to battle the prince while the angel in this passage traveled on to Daniel.

Isaiah 6:2–3, Revelation 5:11–12 The angels continually praise and worship God.

Acts 7:38, 53 An angel spoke to Moses on Mount Sinai, giving him "living utterances to hand on to" God's people. Acts 7:53 reveals that the Israelites believed that the law was transmitted to them by angels.

Psalm 34:8 (NAB), 91:11–12 Angels minister to and protect God's children.

Matthew 1:19–24; Luke 1:26–38, 2:9–12 The angel of the Lord announced the birth of Jesus.

2. Answers will vary.
3. The angels are never called "the Son."
4. God's promise to King David was fulfilled when Jesus was born, a descendant of David, who redeemed Israel and sits on its throne—not as an earthly king but as an eternal one.
5. **Hebrews 1:6 and CCC 333** The angels worship, adore, protect, serve, and strengthen Jesus. They will be present at Christ's return, to serve at His judgment.

   Luke 2:8–14 The angels worshipped Jesus when they announced His birth to the shepherds.
6. Answers will vary.

Lesson 2, Day Four

1. The angels are described as winds and fiery flames.
2. **A.** Your throne, a righteous scepter, being anointed.

   B. Jesus loves justice and hates wickedness.
3. Answers will vary.
4. **A.** To the Jewish believers who were suffering for their faith, it would have been comforting to remember that Jesus was there at the very beginning, establishing the earth. He isn't some new fad. He always was, and is, and always will be. "They will perish but you remain" reminded the readers that Jesus would be there for them forever—unchanging and faithful. Knowing that Jesus is "the same, and [His] years will have no end" would remind them that no matter what they might face in the future, Jesus would be there.

   B. Answers will vary.
5. Answers will vary.

Lesson 2, Day Five

1. God will be victorious. He foils the plans of the nations and thwarts the purposes of people who try to work their evil plans. His plans stand firm forever—from generation to generation. God is *always* in control.
2. **Philippians 2:10–11** One day, every knee (even those of His enemies) will bend at the name of Jesus, and every tongue will confess that He is Lord.

   1 Corinthians 15:24–25 At the end of time (the climax of history) Jesus will hand over the kingdom to God the Father, after He has destroyed every sovereignty and authority and power. Jesus will reign until He has put all enemies under His feet. This is a picture of Jesus destroying all sin, death, and evil on earth.

3. They are sent to serve those who are to inherit salvation. That's us.
4. Answers will vary.
5. According to CCC 331, the angels belong to Christ because He is at the center of their world. "They belong to him still more because he has made them messengers of his saving plan."

Lesson 3, Day One

1. We are to "attend all the more to what we have heard" so that we don't get carried away.
2. **A.** It's described as forsaking your first love.
   B. Answers will vary.
3. **A.** Answers will vary.
   B. The Jewish people believed that the law was delivered to Moses by the hands of angels.
   C. Saint Paul says that the time will come when people will not tolerate sound doctrine, but will follow their own desires and insatiable curiosity and will accumulate teachers who say what they want to hear. They will stop listening to the truth and will be diverted to myths.
4. **A.** In Hebrews 2:3, we see that the message was "declared through the Lord" (Jesus Himself). In verse 4, we see that it was "attested to us by those who heard him." This is a reference to the apostles passing down to others what they heard directly from Jesus. Also in verse 4, we see that the message was communicated by "testimony by signs and wonders and various miracles and by gifts of the Holy Spirit."
   B. The Holy Spirit is described as a spirit of adoption, who helps us cry out to God as our Abba, Father. The Holy Spirit confirms in our hearts (bears witness) that we are children of God.
5. **A.** Jesus, the anchor of our soul, will keep us firm.
   B. We will be anchored in our faith if we love the Lord God with all our heart, being, and strength. We should take to heart God's words and keep repeating them. Repeating them to ourselves and to our children will anchor them in our hearts. We are to recite them when we are at home and when we are away, when we lie down and when we get up. We are to write them on our arms and foreheads as a sign, and on the doorposts of our houses and on our gates.

Lesson 3, Day Two

1. God has not subjected the world to come to the angels.
2. **A.** The psalmist is contemplating the night sky, the cosmos. He's amazed by what God has planned for man—that He has made us "little less than a god, crowned him with glory and honor." He's amazed that God has given man rule over creation, putting all things at man's feet—animals, birds, and fish and more.
   B. Answers will vary.
   C. Yet at present we do not see "all things subject to him."
   D. We don't see "all things subject to him" but we do see Jesus "crowned with glory and honor."
3. Jesus is crowned with glory and honor because He suffered death, that by the grace of God He might taste death for everyone.

4. **Romans 5:17** Adam's trespass ushered death into our lives, and Jesus' death ushers in our reign.
   2 Timothy 2:12 We are promised in 2 Timothy 2:12 that if we endure, we will reign with Christ.
5. "We are God's children now; what we shall be has not yet been revealed. We do know that when it is revealed we shall be like him, for we shall see him as he is."

Lesson 3, Day Three

1. Everything has been created by Him and for Him.
2. **A.** The act is making the author and founder of our salvation (Jesus) perfect through suffering.
   B. Many children are brought to glory.
3. It was a stumbling block to the Jewish people and foolish to the Greeks.
4. **Hebrews 4:15** Although Jesus was tempted in all things, He was without sin.
5. **1 Peter 1:18–19** Jesus was like a lamb, unblemished and spotless.
   1 John 3:5 Jesus appeared in order to take away sins, but He was without sin.
6. **A. Romans 8:18** Our present suffering is not worth comparing with the glory that will be revealed in us because of our mature response to it.
   2 Corinthians 4:17 Our light and momentary troubles are achieving for us an eternal glory that far surpasses the current pain.
   B. Answers will vary.

Lesson 3, Day Four

1. **A.** Jesus is not ashamed to call us brothers (or sisters).
   B. Jesus is the radiance of God's glory and the exact representation of His being. He sustains everything by the power of His word. That He would acknowledge us as brothers and sisters and say that we have the same origin (we all descend from Adam) is truly amazing.
   C. Answers will vary.
2. Jesus proclaimed God's name to His brethren. He praised God in the assembly.
3. Isaiah 7:14 is where we first hear Jesus referred to as Emmanuel, seen in Matthew 1:23 as meaning "God with us."
4. **A.** Jesus destroys the one who has the power of death—the devil.
   B. They are described as people who, through fear of death, have been subject to slavery all their lives.
   C. People fear death because they fear pain, separation from those they love, the unknown, nonbeing, and punishment.[113]
   D. Answers will vary.
5. **Romans 8:35–37** Nothing can separate us from the love of Christ—not life, not angels, principalities, present things, future things, powers, height, depth, or any other creature. Nothing can separate us from Jesus.
   1 Corinthians 15:55, 57 Death has lost its victory and sting because we are given victory over it through Jesus.

---

[113] Healy, *Hebrews*, 77.

2 Corinthians 5:21 Our hearts can calm as we think of one day meeting God face-to-face if we have been a part of the "Divine Exchange," in which our sin was given to Christ and He gave us His righteousness in return.

Revelation 1:17–18 Jesus, our merciful Savior and hero–big brother, holds the keys to death and the netherworld.

Lesson 3, Day Five

1. Jesus had to become like His brothers in every way. He needed to do this so that He could be our merciful and faithful high priest before God to expiate our sins.
2. **A.** He's a merciful and faithful high priest.
   B. Answers will vary.
3. **A.** He expiates the sins of the people.
   B. **Romans 1:18** God's wrath is revealed from heaven against every impiety and the wickedness of those who suppress the truth with their wickedness.

   Revelation 19:15 Out of His mouth came a sharp sword to strike the nations. He will rule them with an iron rod, and He Himself will tread out in the wine press the wine of the fury and wrath of God the Almighty.

   Romans 3:23 *All* have sinned and fall short of the glory of God. We all need to be forgiven.
4. **A.** "Justification is not only the remission of sins, but also the sanctification and renewal of the interior man" (CCC 1989). "Justification detaches man from sin . . . It reconciles man with God. It frees from the enslavement to sin, and it heals" (CCC 1990).
   B. Justification is conferred in baptism.

   It conforms us to the righteousness of God, who makes us inwardly just by the power of His mercy.

   The purpose is for God and Jesus to be glorified, and for us to be given the gift of eternal life.
5. Jesus was tested and suffered; as a result, He is able to help those who are being tested.

Lesson 4, Day One

1. He calls the readers "holy 'brothers,' sharing in a heavenly calling."
2. **CCC 1227** "Through the Holy Spirit, Baptism is a bath that purifies, justifies, and sanctifies."

   Titus 3:3–5 Once we were foolish, disobedient, deluded, and enslaved to sin, but the kindness and generous love of Jesus came and changed everything. He saved us; it was all His doing—we can't take any credit for it. He cleansed us in baptism and completely renewed us in the Holy Spirit.

   1 Corinthians 6:11 We have been washed, sanctified, and justified (made holy) through baptism.

   CCC 1695 The Holy Spirit (1) teaches us to pray to the Father, (2) prompts us to live in such a way that people see "love in action" in us, (3) heals the wounds of sin and renews us internally through spiritual transformation, and (4) enlightens and strengths us to live as "children of light."

3. **A.** We are to cleanse ourselves of things that are evil. We're to turn from youthful desires and pursue righteousness, faith, love, and peace. We're to avoid foolish and ignorant debates that lead to quarreling. If we do these things and dedicate ourselves to God, then we'll be ready for "every good work."

   B. We are not to slip back into old patterns of sin, habits from when we didn't know better. It's time to apply what we know and allow our lives to be shaped by the choices God has told us are the best ones. He is to be our example in everything.

4. **A.** We are to reflect on Jesus.

   B. It begins with desire.

   C. Concentration requires discipline like that of an athlete.

   D. It requires an act of the will and time.

   E. Answers will vary.

Lesson 4, Day Two

1. He is described as the apostle and high priest of our confession.

2. Answers will vary.

3. **A.** Both were faithful.

   B. **Exodus 3:1–10** Moses was chosen for the epic task of delivering the Israelite people from slavery in Egypt. God, the I AM, appeared to him and ordained him for this task at the burning bush.

   Numbers 12:3 Moses was more humble than anyone else on earth.

   Deuteronomy 34:10–12 There had never been a prophet like Moses, who experienced intimacy with God that no one since Adam (pre-fall) had experienced. He performed signs and wonders before Pharaoh. God displayed His power through Moses.

4. He says that Moses was faithful as a *servant* in the house, but Christ was faithful as a *son*.

5. **A.** Christ ransomed us from the curse of the law by becoming a curse for us.

   B. Jesus was mocked and crucified so that we could be saved.

Lesson 4, Day Three

1. "The house" In Hebrews 3:3–6 is a reference to the Church—the people of God. We, as God's people, are being held together and are a dwelling place of God in the Spirit (Ephesians 2:21). According to 1 Peter 2:5, we are living stones being built into a spiritual house.

2. **A.** The fruits that should be planted in our hearts to make them a beautiful dwelling place for God are love, joy, peace, patience, kindness, goodness, faithfulness, gentleness, and self-control.

   B. Answers will vary.

   C. Answers will vary.

3. Hebrews 3:6 says that we need to "hold fast our confidence and pride in our hope" if we are to be God's house.

4. **CCC 1831** and **CCC 1837** Fortitude is a gift of the Holy Spirit that ensures firmness in difficulties and constancy in pursuit of the good.

Lesson 4, Day Four

1. They hardened their hearts and put God to the test.
2. They went astray in their hearts and did not know God's ways.
3. **A.** The Israelites began to complain. They questioned God's goodness and protection with the words, "Why is the LORD bringing us into this land only to have us fall by the sword? Our wives and little ones will be taken as spoil . . . Let us appoint a leader and go back to Egypt" (Numbers 14:3–4). Joshua and Caleb tried to convince them to trust in the Lord, but the people threatened to stone them.
   B. All the adults (twenty years and up) who fell into fear instead of trusting God would wander for forty years in the wilderness and never set foot in the Promised Land. Only Joshua and Caleb would be allowed into the Promised Land.
4. **A.** Answers will vary.
   B. Answers will vary.
5. This verse tells us that perfect love casts out fear.

Lesson 4, Day Five

1. **A.** We are told to take care not to have an evil and unfaithful heart and to forsake God as a result.
   B. An unfaithful heart is one that hears the Word initially and receives it with great joy, but because it has no root, it doesn't persevere under fire. When persecution or trials come, the unfaithful heart turns or drifts away from God.
   C. Answers will vary.
2. **A.** We are to encourage ourselves daily so that we don't grow hardened by the deceit of sin.
   B. Answers will vary.
3. Answers will vary.
4. **A.** The people who rebelled were the same ones who came out of Egypt under Moses.
   B. He was provoked with those who had sinned, whose corpses fell in the desert.
   C. He swore that those who were disobedient would not enter His rest.
   D. The author wants the reader to see that although the Israelites began well, they didn't end well. God was disappointed that even though they had seen the miracles of the exodus, they didn't believe God would come through for them this time. Their disbelief led to action—to disobedience.

Lesson 6, Day One

1. **A.** We are to be on guard so that we don't fail to enter into the promised rest.
   B. "Let us know, let us strive to know the Lord; as certain as the dawn is his coming. He will come to us like the rain, like spring rain that waters the earth." (Hosea 6:3)
2. **A.** We all have received the good news.
   B. Answers will vary.
   C. The word they heard didn't profit them because they were not united in faith with those who listened.
3. **A.** Answers will vary.
   B. Answers will vary.
   C. Answers will vary.

D. Answers will vary.

Lesson 6, Day Two

1. **A.** God's works were accomplished at the foundation of the world. He rested on the seventh day from all His works.
   B. Answers will vary.
2. **Lamentations 3:22–23** God's compassion never fails. He continues to act in mercy, offering it anew every day.
   Psalm 68:20–21 God continues to carry us and save us.
   John 5:17 God the Father is at work, and Jesus the Son is at work.
   Philippians 2:13 God is at work within us to help us want to obey, and gives us all we need to follow His will.
3. **A.** We are to remain in Christ and He is to remain in us. We are like a branch and He is the vine. We need to stay attached to Him, letting the sap of the Holy Spirit run from Him to us. Apart from Him, we can do nothing.
   B. Answers will vary.
4. The word *today* is repeated twice in Hebrews 4:7.

Lesson 6, Day Three

1. Joshua was one of the spies sent to check out the Promised Land. He was one of only two spies who had faith that God could bring them the needed victory. (Joshua and Caleb were the only people from that generation who were ultimately allowed to go into the Promised Land. This was God's reward to them for their faith in Him.) Joshua replaced Moses as the leader of the Israelites when Moses died, and led the people into the Promised Land.
2. **A.** Joshua and the Israelites did not conquer all the territory that God had given them. God had promised them the victory, but they did not fully possess what He had offered them.
   B. The generation of Israelites who had faithfully followed Joshua and claimed much of the Promised Land failed to pass their faith on to their children. That next generation "did not know the LORD or the work he had done for Israel, the Israelites did what was evil in the sight of the LORD. They served the Baals" (Judges 2:10–11).
   C. Answers will vary.
3. Sabbath rest still remains for the people of God.
4. **A.** It's described as God's rest—a rest from our work just as God rested from His.
   B. God has created us to do specific works while here on earth, but He does not expect us to do them in our own strength. He is at work within us to do what He has called us to. He will give us rest, even as we work, because He is shouldering the *responsibility* of the load being carried.
   C. Answers will vary.
5. We are told to strive to enter into that rest, so that we don't fall into the same example of disobedience.

Lesson 6, Day Four

1. The Word of God is living and effective, sharper than any two-edged sword, penetrating even between soul and spirit, joints and marrow, and able to discern reflections and thoughts of the heart.

2. When God's Word goes out, it does not return to Him empty, but does what pleases God, always achieving the end for which He sent it (Isaiah 55:10–11). God's Word is living and abiding. The grass withers and the flower wilts, but the Word of the Lord remains forever (1 Peter 1:23–24).

3. **A.** Answers will vary.
   B. Answers will vary.

4. We should be doers of the Word, not just hearers. He describes the Word of God as "the perfect law of freedom." If we are doers of the Word, we'll be blessed in what we do.

5. **Hebrews 4:13** We can't hide from God. Nothing is concealed from Him. Everything is naked and exposed to His eyes. Ultimately, we must render an account to Him of the way we have lived our lives.

6. Answers will vary.

Lesson 6, Day Five

1. **A.** We should hold fast to our confession of faith because we have a great high priest who has passed through the heavens.
   B. He sympathizes with our weaknesses because He was tested in every way.
   C. Answers will vary.

2. **A.** Jesus never submitted to the temptation. Unlike us, He was without sin.
   B. When we are weak, this is an ideal opportunity for the power of God to be seen in us and for grace to triumph in our lives.
   C. When Jesus offers Himself, He offers us. He sympathizes with our weaknesses in order to free us from the hold they have on us.
   D. Isaiah 6:1–5 Isaiah had a vision of God seated on a high and lofty throne. The train of His garment filled the temple. Seraphim were stationed above Him and cried out, "Holy, holy, holy is the Lord of hosts! All the earth is filled with his glory!" When that sound was heard, the frame of the door to the temple shook and the house was filled with smoke. Seeing God on His throne caused Isaiah to say, "Woe is me; I am doomed!"

   Revelation 4:2–11 Saint John had a vision of God on His throne. God's appearance sparkled like jasper and carnelian. Around the throne there was a halo as brilliant as an emerald. Twenty-four other thrones surrounded God's. Flashes of lightning, rumblings, and peals of thunder came from the throne, and seven flaming torches burned in front of it, where there was also something that resembled a sea of crystal.

3. **A.** We are to approach the throne of grace with confidence.
   B. We will receive mercy and grace for timely help.
   C. In CCC 2278, *parrhesia* is described as straightforward simplicity, filial trust, joyous assurance, humble boldness, and the certainty of being loved.
   D. Answers will vary.

Lesson 7, Day One

1. Every high priest is taken from among men and represents them before God, offering gifts and sacrifices for sin.
2. A high priest could deal patiently with the ignorant and erring because he was beset by weakness, too. He understood their plight based on his own experience of weakness.
3. **A.** He made an offering first for his own sins, and then for the sins of the people.
   B. Aaron approached the altar and slaughtered a calf. The blood from the calf was presented to him by his sons (fellow priests), and he dipped his finger in the blood and placed it on the horns of the altar. He poured the rest of the blood at the base of the altar.
4. **A.** The one mediator between God and the human race is Jesus Christ. Jesus was fully man (thus proving His solidarity) and had to overcome human weakness in order to obey (proving His sympathy).
   B. The priesthood of the old covenant was powerless to bring about salvation. It needed to repeat its sacrifices ceaselessly and was unable to achieve a definitive sanctification (which is the process of being made holy).
5. Answers will vary.

Lesson 7, Day Two

1. A high priest had to be called by God. No one could take that honor on themselves.
2. **Numbers 16:28–33** The Lord made a chasm, the ground opened its mouth, and Korah and all who belonged to him were swallowed up, going down alive to Sheol. The earth closed over them, and they disappeared.
   1 Samuel 13:10–14 God took the kingship away from Saul and gave it to someone else, "a man after his own heart" (King David). Saul lost his leadership position over this.
   2 Chronicles 26:16–21 After King Uzziah became strong, he became arrogant and entered the temple to make an offering on the altar of incense. The priests stood up to him, reminding him that this was not his right or role. King Uzziah became angry instead of repenting of his sin, and immediately became leprous. He remained a leper until his death.
3. He didn't glorify or exalt Himself. The One who said, "You are my son, this day I have begotten you," glorified Christ. It was the Father who glorified Christ.
4. "You are a priest forever according to the order of Melchizedek."
5. According to Genesis 14:18, Melchizedek was both King of Salem and priest of God most high.
6. Answers will vary.
   Jeremiah 29:11 "For I know well the plans I have in mind for you—oracle of the LORD—plans for your welfare and not for woe, so as to give you a future of hope."

Lesson 7, Day Three

1. He offered prayers and supplications with loud cries and tears.
2. **A.** Luke 22:39–44 is a description of Jesus' agony in the Garden of Gethsemane. Jesus begged God to take the cup of suffering away from Him, but affirmed that He wanted God the Father's will more than His own. His suffering and prayer were so intense that His sweat became like drops of blood falling on the ground.

B. "God made him who knew no sin to be sin for our sake, so that in him we might become the righteousness of God." (2 Corinthians 5:21)

3. Jesus was heard because of His reverence. It seems that His prayer was not answered affirmatively, because Jesus wasn't spared from death. But it was ultimately answered because He was raised from death to life in the Resurrection. In the words of Mary Healy, "Saint Thomas Aquinas observes [that] God did indeed 'save him from death,' not by sparing him the experience of dying but by raising him from death to indestructible life."[114]

4. Answers will vary.
   Answers will vary.
   Answers will vary.

Lesson 7, Day Four

1. He learned obedience through what He suffered.
   Answers will vary.

2. When Jesus was made perfect, He became the source of eternal salvation for all who obey Him.

3. We need to obey Him. Jesus is more than a good example for us to follow—He is the Son of God. So our response to Him needs to be more than honoring or respecting Him. We are to obey and acknowledge His authority over us.

4. Answers will vary.

5. God designated Jesus to be high priest in the order of Melchizedek.

Lesson 7, Day Five

1. He describes them as "sluggish in hearing," people who "should be teachers by this time" but instead "need to have someone teach [them] again the basic elements of the utterances of God." He described them as still needing milk, not being ready for solid food. They were lacking "experience of the word of righteousness" because they were still spiritual children.

2. If we are "fleshy people," then we are infants in Christ, unable to take in spiritually solid food. Being of the flesh means that we behave in an ordinary, human way. Symptoms of arrested spiritual development are jealousy, rivalry, and divisions in the community.

3. He wants to see a level of maturity in which their "faculties are trained by practice to discern good and evil."

4. Answers will vary.

5. Answers will vary.

Lesson 8, Day One

1. **A.** He's challenging us to leave behind the basic teachings and advance to maturity.
   B. Answers will vary.

2. The six basic teachings are repentance from dead works, faith in God, baptism, laying on of hands, the resurrection of the dead, and eternal judgment.

---

[114] Ibid., 108.

3. **A.** Interior repentance or conversion of heart is a "radical reorientation of our whole life, a return" to God. It means turning toward God with all our heart and turning away from evil. True interior repentance or conversion will entail the desire and resolution to change one's life, with the help of God's grace.

   B. Our good works matter because "faith without works is dead" (James 2:17).

   C. Answers will vary.

4. **A. John 14:16–17** The Holy Spirit is our advocate. He remains with us and is in us.
   Acts 1:8 We receive power.
   Romans 5:5 The love of God is poured out into our hearts through the Holy Spirit.
   2 Corinthians 3:17 Where the Spirit of the Lord is, there is freedom.

   B. Answers will vary.

5. The remaining basic teachings that refer to "the last things" are the resurrection of the dead and eternal judgment.
   John 11:25 Jesus is the resurrection and the life. Those who believe in Him will live eternally.
   2 Corinthians 5:10 We all will appear before the judgment seat of Christ, so that we each receive recompense according to what we have done and how we have lived.

Lesson 8, Day Two

1. Apostasy is "the total repudiation of the Christian faith."

2. He or she is enlightened, tastes the heavenly gift, shares in the Holy Spirit, tastes the good Word of God, and tastes the powers of the age to come.

3. **A. 1 Peter 2:9** says that we are "a chosen race, a royal priesthood, a holy nation, a people of his own" who have been called out of darkness into God's wonderful light.

   B. We are filled with hope that belongs to His call, we have riches of glory in our inheritance, and we are filled with the surpassing greatness of His resurrection power.

   C. As Christians, we experience power in our inner selves through the indwelling Holy Spirit. Christ dwells in our hearts through the Holy Spirit, and roots and grounds us in love. The presence of the Holy Spirit should continually remind us that we are loved with a love that surpasses knowledge.

   D. Answers will vary.

4. **A.** Answers will vary.

   B. "For human beings it is impossible, but not for God. All things are possible for God." (Mark 10:27)

Lesson 8, Day Three

1. He is sure of better things than apostasy regarding his readers' salvation. He knows God won't overlook their work and the love they've demonstrated for His name by having served and continuing to serve the holy ones.

2. **A.** They were publicly exposed to abuse and affliction and associated themselves with those who were treated that way, and they joined in the sufferings of those in prison and joyfully accepted the confiscation of their property, knowing they had a better and more lasting possession.

   B. Answers will vary.

C. He sees whatever we do for anyone to be a way in which we minister to Him. In helping others, we are helping God.

3. Jesus said that we'll know a true follower of Christ by his or her fruit. Good trees bear good fruit, and a rotten tree bears rotten fruit. Not everyone who says, "Lord, Lord," will enter, but only the person who does God's will.

4. **A.** The author wants to see eagerness or diligence *until the end*. He wants them to finish well—to run the race so as to win the prize.

   B. Saint Paul describes his life as being "poured out like a libation." As he reflects on the way he's lived, he's satisfied to say that he competed well, he finished the race, he kept the faith. At the end of his life, he looked forward to the crown of righteousness awaiting him in heaven. That crown is waiting for us as well, if we finish our race.

   C. 1 Corinthians 15:10 The secret to finishing the race well is allowing God's grace to work within us. It's depending on God and keeping our eyes on Him.

   2 Corinthians 1:9 Instead of trusting in ourselves, we are to trust in God, who raises the dead.

   2 Corinthians 12:9–10 Our weaknesses are actually our strengths if they cause us to rely on God instead of ourselves.

5. **A.** We are to avoid becoming sluggish.

   B. Answers will vary.

   C. We are to be imitators of those who are faithful and patient and are inheriting the promises of God.

   D. Answers will vary.

Lesson 8, Day Four

1. We are led to Abraham, who was promised that God would bless and multiply him.

2. **A.** God had Abraham bring a three-year-old heifer, a three-year-old female goat, a three-year-old ram, a turtledove, and a young pigeon. He then had Abraham cut them in half and place each half opposite the other.

B. Genesis 15:17 When it was dark, a smoking fire pot and a flaming torch appeared, and passed between those pieces.

   C. Answers will vary.

3. **A.** A human swears an oath by someone greater than themselves. It serves as an end to the argument.

   B. There is no one greater than God, so He could only swear an oath by Himself.

4. The two immutable things are the word of His promise and His oath.

5. **Exodus 14:14** The Lord will fight for me. I need only to keep still.

   Isaiah 30:15 By waiting and by being calm I will be saved, in quiet and in trust shall be my strength.

   Isaiah 43:1–2 I do not need to fear, because God has redeemed me. He has called me by name. I belong to Him. When I pass through waters, He will be with me. When I pass through rivers, I will not be swept away. When I walk through fire, I will not be burned or consumed by the flames.

Lesson 8, Day Five

1. **A.** We, who have taken refuge in Christ, are strongly encouraged to hold fast to the hope that lies before us.

   B. **Become aware** Answers will vary.

   Seek to understand Answers will vary.

   Take action Answers will vary.

2. Our hope is described as an anchor for the soul.

3. Our anchor is "into the interior behind the veil."

4. No matter where we go, God's hand will guide us; His right hand will hold us fast. We don't need to fear, because God is with us. When we lose our grasp, He will uphold us with His victorious right hand.

5. **A.** He entered as our forerunner.

   B. Jesus has given us the message that in His Father's house there are many dwelling places, and He has gone to prepare a place for us. He is preparing it now, and will come back and take us to Himself, so that we can be where He is.

   C. He intercedes for us.

Lesson 10, Day One

1. **A.** Melchizedek is described as the King of Salem and priest of God Most High. His name means "righteous king" and "king of peace."

   B. Melchizedek blessed Abraham. Abraham gave Melchizedek "a tenth of everything."

   C. The greater person blesses the lesser person.

2. Melchizedek brought out bread and wine. According to CCC 1333, this prefigures the Eucharistic celebration.

3. We learn that he didn't have a father, mother, or ancestry. He didn't have beginning of days or end of life. In this, he resembles the Son of God. His priesthood remains forever.

4. **A.** The descendants of Levi who received the priestly office were to take tithes from the people.

   B. Although Melchizedek wasn't a priest from the Levite tribe, Abraham still gave him a tithe.

5. Levi was "still in the loins of his ancestor," Abraham, when Melchizedek met him.

6. Answers will vary.

Lesson 10, Day Two

1. No. According to Hebrews 7:11, perfection did not come through the Levitical priesthood.

2. There's the order of Melchizedek and the order of Aaron.

3. **A.** A change of priesthood necessitates a change of law.

   B. The law would be in their minds and written on their hearts.

4. Jesus came from the tribe of Judah, which placed Him in the lineage of kings.

5. His qualification was based on the power of a life that cannot be destroyed.

6. Answers will vary.

Lesson 10, Day Three

1. The former commandment was annulled because of its weakness and uselessness, and because it brought nothing to perfection.
2. Because of Jesus, we are introduced to hope. This allows us to draw near to God.
3. Jesus has become the guarantee of an even better covenant.
4. **A.** The people who approach God *through Jesus* are saved.
   B. There is no salvation except through Jesus.
5. **Hebrews 7:25** He lives forever to make intercession for us.
   2 Corinthians 5:21 "For our sake he made him to be sin who did not know sin, so that we might become the righteousness of God in him."

Lesson 10, Day Four

1. **A.** He is always able to save those who approach God through Him.
   B. Answers will vary.
2. Jesus lives forever *to make intercession* for those who have turned to Him for salvation.
3. It's described as "the judgment of the last day." The "conduct of each one and the secrets of hearts" will be brought to light. "The culpable unbelief that counted the offer of God's grace as nothing" will "be condemned."
4. **A.** The wages of sin is death, but the gift of God is eternal life in Christ Jesus.
   B. No, God did not say that sin doesn't matter or that no payment needed to be made. Jesus died for us, in our place. He paid the wages of sin on our behalf.
   C. I need to confess with my mouth that Jesus is Lord and believe in my heart that God raised Him from the dead. I am to "call on the name of the Lord." We are saved by grace through faith. For our faith to be genuine, it must be seen by the fruit of our lives. According to James 2:17, faith without works is dead.
5. **Romans 8:34** Jesus is at the right hand of God, interceding for us.
   Romans 8:35–39 Nothing can separate us from the love of Christ—not anguish, distress, persecution, famine, nakedness, peril, or the sword. We conquer overwhelmingly through Him who loved us. Neither death, life, angels, principalities, present things, future things, powers, height, depth, nor any other creature can separate us from the love of God in Christ Jesus.
   1 John 2:1 If we sin, we have an advocate with the Father, Christ Jesus the righteous One.

Lesson 10, Day Five

1. **A.** He is holy, innocent, undefiled, separated from sinners, and higher than the heavens.
   B. He was holy, innocent, undefiled, and free from sin, so He did not have to offer a sacrifice for Himself. When He offered Himself, it was such a complete sacrifice that no other sacrifice was needed.
2. If we confess our sins, God will forgive them and cleanse us from unrighteousness. He does this because of His faithful and just character.
3. Answers will vary.
4. There is nothing noble about suffering for doing wrong, but if you suffer for doing right, know you have God's approval. We have been called to suffer redemptively because this is the example Christ gave us. We are to follow in in His footsteps. When He suffered,

He did not sin. He didn't revile in return, retaliate, or threaten. Instead, He entrusted Himself to the One (our heavenly Father) who judges justly. Jesus bore our sins, and by His wounds, we are healed.

Lesson 11, Day One

1. The main point is that "we have such a high priest": Jesus.
2. **A.** Jesus has taken His seat at the right hand of the throne of the majesty in heaven.
   B. Answers will vary.
   C. Romans 8:17 You are a joint heir with Christ. If you suffer with Him, you will also be glorified with Him.
   2 Corinthians 5:17 You are a new creation in Christ. The old has gone; the new has come.
   1 Thessalonians 5:5 You are a child of the light, not of darkness.
   1 Peter 2:9 You are a chosen race, a royal priesthood, a holy nation, a people of His own. You have been called to come into the light.
   Answers will vary.
3. Jesus is "a minister of the sanctuary and of the true tabernacle that the Lord, not man, set up" (Hebrews 8:2).
4. He encourages us to not be discouraged even when our bodies waste away and we experience afflictions. All that we faithful endure and learn from is "producing for us an eternal weight of glory beyond all comparison." This happens as we "look not to what is seen but to what is unseen; for what is seen is transitory, but what is unseen is eternal."

Lesson 11, Day Two

1. He is appointed to offer gifts and sacrifices.
2. **A.** The high priest was to offer animal sacrifices, killing the animal and then sprinkling the blood on the ark of the covenant.
   B. Jesus offered His own body and blood.
3. **Leviticus 1:3** The animal (the offering) needed to be a male without blemish.
   Leviticus 1:4 The person offering the sacrifice was to put his hand on the head of the animal, so it would be acceptable to make atonement for the one who offers it.
   Leviticus 1:5 The bull was slaughtered and then the blood was offered.
   Leviticus 1:9b The priest was to burn all of it on the altar. It was to be totally consumed.
4. **Hebrews 4:15** Jesus was without blemish—without sin.
   2 Corinthians 5:17 God made Him who knew no sin to be sin for us. In a sense, we put our hands on His head, and our sins were transferred to Jesus. He made atonement for us, suffering in our place. His life was the price paid to ransom us.
   1 Peter 1:18–19 We were ransomed by the precious blood of Jesus, as of a spotless, unblemished lamb.
   John 13:1 Jesus loved us to the end. He was totally consumed with love for us and held nothing back.
5. Jesus is the bread that comes down from heaven and gives us life. If we eat of Him, we will never hunger or thirst. God provides for us with His presence in the Eucharist. Jesus was the grain of wheat that fell to the ground and died, but much fruit was produced because of His sacrifice.

6. We are to continually offer God a sacrifice of praise and confess His name, giving Him credit for the good in our lives.

Lesson 11, Day Three

1. **A.** They worship and serve in a copy and shadow of the heavenly sanctuary.
   B. God told Moses to make everything according to the pattern that was shown to him on the mountain. Moses entered the cloud of the Lord's presence and went up on the mountain for forty days and forty nights.
2. The new covenant was enacted on better promises than the old one.
3. **A.** In ancient cultures, covenants were a means to forge and maintain relationships between individuals, families, tribes, and even nations.
   B. The Bible records the various ways "God has drawn humanity into a familial relationship with himself through divine oaths."
   C. The Bible is divided into two parts, based on two covenants, the old and the new.
   D. A covenant involves the exchange of persons.
   E. He called on God or the gods to inflict death or some other grave penalty on him should he fail to keep the obligations of the covenant.
4. The people who actually broke God's law should have been cursed. But instead, Jesus became a curse for us.

Lesson 11, Day Four

1. **Exodus 19:5–6** God said that if the Israelites would obey Him completely and keep His commandments, they would be His treasured possession among all the peoples, a kingdom of priests, a holy nation.
   Exodus 19:7–8 Moses explained the terms of the covenant to the Israelite people and they responded with promises to do all that God had asked.
   Jeremiah 31:32 The people broke the covenant. (There are so many verses in the Old Testament that tell this same story. In Hosea 6:7, breaking the covenant is described as violating it, and in doing so, betraying God.)
   It's the people, not God, who are at fault.
2. **A.** God ignored them.
   B. No. The Lord called them back. For a brief moment He abandoned them, but then with great tenderness He took them back. In an outburst of wrath, for a moment, God hid His face from them, but with enduring love He took pity on them and redeemed them.
3. God would write His Word on their hearts and put His law in their minds.
4. Ezekiel prophesied that we would be given a new heart and a new spirit, that our stony hearts would be taken out and we'd be given hearts of flesh. These new hearts would help us to obey God's law.

Lesson 11, Day Five

1. **Hebrews 8:10** The law will be placed into people's minds and written on their hearts.
   Hebrews 8:11 People will know God, from least to greatest.
   Hebrews 8:12 God will forgive His people's evildoing and remember their sins no more.

2. **A.** There is no one like God, who removes guilt and pardons sin. He doesn't persist in anger forever, but delights in mercy. He has compassion, over and over, and treads our iniquities underfoot. He casts our sins into the depths of the sea.

   B. God transcends human fatherhood and motherhood, although He is their origin and standard: No one is father as God is Father.

   C. In Christ, I am chosen and destined, according to God's will.

   D. Answers will vary.

3. Answers will vary.

   Answers will vary.

   Answers will vary.

   Answers will vary.

   Answers will vary.

4. **A.** Jesus identified the New Covenant as His blood, poured out for us.

   B. Answers will vary.

Lesson 12, Day One

1. The first covenant had regulations for worship and an earthly sanctuary.

2. **A.** The lampstand, the table, and the bread of offering were found in the Holy Place.

   B. The lamp was kept burning regularly with clear oil of crushed olives. It was set up outside the veil. Aaron (the high priest) was to set it up to burn from evening until morning. The lamps were to be of the pure gold menorah.

   C. On every Sabbath day, the old loaves were to be eaten by the priests and fresh loaves were to be put on the table.

   D. We are being transformed in that moment, being made more like Christ.

3. **A.** The area behind the second veil of the tabernacle was called the Holy of Holies. This was where the gold altar of incense and the ark of the covenant were located.

   B. The gold jar containing manna, the staff of Aaron that had sprouted, and the tablets of the covenant (the Ten Commandments).

   C. This is where God met with the people. It symbolized His presence.

4. **A.** The cherubim of glory stretched above the ark of the covenant.

   B. God is seated, or enthroned, on the cherubim.

5. The cherubim overshadowed the place of expiation. Also called the "mercy seat," it was the place where God met with man.

Lesson 12, Day Two

1. **Exodus 27:20–21** They tended to the menorah, keeping the lamps burning always.

   Exodus 30:7–8 They burned incense every morning and at twilight.

   Leviticus 24:8–9 They replaced the old show bread with freshly baked bread and ate the old bread in a sacred space.

2. **A.** The high priest would go into the inner room (the Holy of Holies) offering blood for himself and for the sins of the people. He was not allowed to go in whenever he pleased, lest he die. To enter, the high priest had to wear the right clothing, be bathed, and have obtained the proper animals for the purification and burnt offering. When he went into the Holy of Holies after slaughtering the animals, he was to take a censer full of glowing embers from the altar and some incense and bring them inside

the veil. After putting incense on the fire, he was to sprinkle the blood of the bull and the goat on top of the ark's cover and in front of it.

    B. The ceremony that followed involved a scapegoat. A live goat was brought forward, and the high priest laid both hands on its head while confessing the sins of the Israelites, symbolically putting them on the goat's head. The scapegoat was then led into the wilderness, carrying off all the iniquities to an isolated region.

3. The Holy Spirit was showing that the way into the sanctuary had not yet been revealed, while the outer tabernacle still had its place.

4. The gifts and sacrifices are unable to "perfect the worshiper in conscience" (Heb 9:9).

5. Answers will vary.

Lesson 12, Day Three

1. Jesus passed through the greater and more perfect tabernacle not made by human hands.

2. **A.** The veil separated the Holy Place from the Holy of Holies.

    B. The veil was woven of violet, purple, and scarlet yarn and of fine linen. Cherubim were embroidered on it.

3. **A.** Jesus entered the sanctuary with His own blood and obtained eternal redemption.

    B. Jesus obtained eternal redemption *for us* through His blood.

    C. Answers will vary.

4. The flesh was cleansed by the "blood of goats and bulls and the sprinkling of a heifer's ashes."

5. The blood of Christ cleanses the conscience from dead works to worship the living God.

Lesson 12, Day Four

1. **A.** One who links or reconciles separate or opposing parties.

    B. The two separate or opposing parties are God and the human race.

    C. It gained us access to God's saving grace for humanity.

2. This verse refers to sins committed under the first covenant.

3. **A.** There needs to be a death.

    B. The first covenant was inaugurated with blood.

    C. The death of animals was required for the Israelites to receive forgiveness.

4. After proclaiming every commandment to the people, Moses sprinkled the book of the law, the people, the tabernacle, and all the vessels of worship with blood.

5. **A.** It purifies.

    B. Without the shedding of blood, there is no forgiveness.

Lesson 12, Day Five

1. **A.** They were purified by animal blood.

    B. They would need to be purified by a better sacrifice than animal blood.

2. **A.** Jesus entered heaven to appear before God on our behalf.

    B. He sits at the right hand of God and intercedes for us. Jesus is our advocate in heaven. He speaks to the Father in our defense.

3. No. Jesus offered His life once, for all. It is finished. No other sacrifice is needed.

4. **A.** After death, we face the judgment.

    B. Death marks the end of man's earthly pilgrimage, of the time when he can accept God's grace and mercy. His response to that offer of grace and mercy decides his ultimate destiny. There are no second chances after death, and there is no reincarnation.

5. Jesus will return to earth a second time, not to take away sin, but to bring us to salvation (Hebrews 9:28). At His second coming, He will return the way He ascended—through the clouds in the sky (Acts 1:11). The sound of trumpets and the voice of an archangel will announce that Jesus is returning, and He'll come down from heaven (1 Thessalonians 4:16). Jesus will come upon the clouds of heaven with power and great glory, He'll send out His angels with a trumpet blast, and they'll gather His elect from one end of the heavens to the other (Matthew 24:30–31).

Lesson 14, Day One

1. The law is described as "only a shadow of the good things to come, not the very image of them." It is unable to make the people perfect who are coming to worship.
2. **A.** In the sacrifices, there is only a remembrance of sin.
    B. In Jeremiah 31:34, God said that He would forgive His people's sins and remember them no longer.
    C. Isaiah 1:18 says that though our sins are like scarlet, they'll become white as snow; though they are red like crimson, they'll become white as wool. Isaiah 43:45 says that God wipes out our sins and remembers them no more. Psalm 103:12 says that God removes our sins from us as far as the east is from the west.
3. God did not want sacrifice and offering. Instead, He wanted someone willing to do His will.
4. Answers will vary.
5. We are consecrated through the offering of Christ's body, once for all.

Lesson 14, Day Two

1. **A.** Every priest stands daily at his ministry, offering frequently those same sacrifices that can never take away sins.
    B. Jesus offered one sacrifice for sins and took His seat forever at the right hand of God.
2. Jesus accomplished on earth the work that His Father gave Him to do. Because of that, He can say, "It is finished."
3. **A.** Jesus is waiting until His enemies are made His footstool.
    B. The Lord is waiting to fulfill His promises because He is patient with mankind. He doesn't want a single one of us to spend eternity apart from Him but instead wants us all to accept His offer of grace (2 Peter 3:9). He is waiting to be gracious to us; His desire is to show us mercy (Isaiah 30:18).
    C. Answers will vary.
4. With His one offering He has made perfect forever those who are being consecrated.
5. The prophet Jeremiah said that God would put His laws in our hearts and write them upon our minds. He also said that God would not remember our sins and evildoing.

Lesson 14, Day Three

1. **A.** We are confident that we can enter the sanctuary, and this confidence is based on what the blood of Jesus does for us.
   B. *Parrhesia* (confidence) is straightforward simplicity, filial trust, joyous assurance, humble boldness, and the certainty of being loved.
   C. Answers will vary.
2. **A.** The veil of the tabernacle is equated with Christ's flesh.
   B. The veil of the sanctuary was torn in two from top to bottom.
   C. Jesus is the way, the truth, and the life. No one comes to the Father except through Him. He is the "new and living way" to the Father.
3. **A.** We should have a sincere heart and we should approach in absolute trust, with our hearts sprinkled clean and our bodies washed in pure water.
   B. According to Titus 3:4–5, when the kindness and generous love of God our Savior appeared, not because of any righteous deeds we had done but because of His mercy, He saved us through the bath of rebirth and renewal by the Holy Spirit.
4. **A.** We are to firmly grasp hold of our confession that gives us hope. We should do this because He who promised is trustworthy.
   B. The One who has called us is faithful, and He will also accomplish it. It's not all up to us, and it doesn't depend on other people in our lives fulfilling their promises. We can utterly count on God (1 Thessalonians 5:24). The Lord is faithful; He will strengthen us and guard us from the evil one (2 Thessalonians 3:3). Jesus is coming for us, and His name is faithful and true (Revelation 19:11).
   C. It describes hope as "placing our trust in Christ's promises and relying not on our own strength, but on the help of the grace of the Holy Spirit."
   D. Answers will vary.
5. **A.** We are to rouse each other to love and good works, and not stay away from our assembly (neglecting community) but instead, encourage each other.
   B. Answers will vary.

Lesson 14, Day Four

1. **A.** If we sin deliberately after receiving knowledge of the truth, there won't be a sacrifice for sin to cover us. We'll just be left with a fearful prospect of judgment and a flaming fire.
   B. A time will come when people won't tolerate sound doctrine and will instead follow their own desires. They'll still want to be taught, but they'll gather teachers around them who say what they want to hear. They'll stop listening to the truth and will be diverted by what sounds more appealing. 2 Timothy 4:3–4 connects with Hebrews 10:26, because if we walk away from the truth and from God, we walk toward judgment. There's much evidence of this happening today: Teachers abound who tickle our ears, telling us that we can be the center of our universe, that truth is relative, that if it feels good, it must be good.
2. A person who rejected the law of Moses was to be put to death, without pity, on the testimony of two or three witnesses.

3. **A.** The author described this rejection of Christ as having contempt for the Son of God, considering unclean the covenant blood by which He was consecrated, and insulting the spirit of grace.

   B. **James 5:16** We can confess our sins to each other and pray for one another, so that we all can be healed. We can try to live righteously, because the "fervent prayer of a righteous person is very powerful."

   1 Peter 4:8 We love sacrificially and extravagantly, because "love covers a multitude of sins."

   Answers will vary.

4. It's a fearful thing to fall into the hands of the living God.

5. Answers will vary.

Lesson 14, Day Five

1. **A.** The readers of Hebrews had endured a great contest of suffering, being publicly exposed to abuse and affliction and standing with people who were experiencing the same. They joined in the sufferings of those in prison and gladly accepted the confiscation of their property. What helped them to persevere through these losses was knowing that they had a better and lasting possession.

   B. Our momentary and light afflictions are producing for us an eternal weight of glory beyond all comparison.

   C. We need to look not to what is seen but to what is unseen. We need to focus not on the temporary and transitory, but on eternity.

2. **Philippians 4:6–7** We are to go to God with our needs and make our requests known, but we are to do it *with thanksgiving*. Thanking God for something within the situation will help bring joy to the surface in our hearts.

   James 1:2–3 It helps us to choose joy when we focus on what we gain through the trial. We are growing in strength, in our ability to persevere.

   Matthew 16:27, Revelation 22:12 We will be rewarded in heaven for how we live on earth.

3. **A.** We'll need endurance.

   B. Knowing that Christ is returning should motivate us.

   C. If we draw back instead of living by faith, God takes no pleasure in us.

   Answers will vary.

4. **A.** Saint Paul tells us that God's grace is sufficient for us. His power is made perfect in weakness. Christ's power dwells with me, and my weaknesses make room for His power. When I am weak, in Christ I am strong.

   B. We remember who we are. We remember who is inside us. He who is in us is stronger than he who is in the world.

   C. We are to trust in the Lord with all our heart, and not lean on our own understanding. We are to acknowledge Him in all our pursuits, and He will make the path straight.

   D. Answers will vary.

Lesson 15, Day One

1. **A.** Hebrews 11:1 says that "faith is the realization of what is hoped for and evidence of things not seen."

   B. Answers will vary.

2. **Titus 2:13** We can hope for Christ's return, the second coming.

   1 John 3:2–3 We are going to be changed. What we shall be has not yet been revealed, but one day we shall be like Jesus and will see Him as He is.

   2 Timothy 2:12 If we persevere, we will reign with Him.

   Revelation 22:4–5 We will look upon the face of Jesus, and His name will be on our foreheads. Night will be no more, and we won't need light from lamp or sun, because God will give us light, and we will reign with Him forever and ever.

3. We know by faith that the universe was ordered by the Word of God, so that what is visible came into being through the invisible.

4. Answers will vary.

Lesson 15, Day Two

1. **A.** Through faith, Abel offered a sacrifice greater than Cain's.

   B. God sees into the heart (1 Samuel 16:7), and there was something He observed in Cain that didn't please Him. God told him that if he acted rightly, he'd be accepted, so there was something in his action that was not righteous.

   C. Answers will vary.

2. **A.** Enoch was taken up into heaven and didn't die. Hebrews tells us this happened because he pleased God.

   B. Answers will vary.

3. **A.** To please God, we need faith. When we approach Him, we should believe that He exists and that He rewards those who seek Him.

   B. Answers will vary.

4. **A.** He built the ark, following God's command, despite the fact that he didn't live near the sea. He also warned others of God's coming judgment, regardless of ridicule and discomfort.

   B. Those who follow Christ are often considered fools, and their reputations as educated, open-minded, and tolerant people may be sacrificed.

   C. Answers will vary.

5. **A.** He was looking forward to the city with foundations, whose architect and maker is God.

   B. Answers will vary.

Lesson 15, Day Three

1. **A.** They all finished well and "died in faith." They didn't receive what had been promised but saw and greeted it from afar. They acknowledged that they were strangers and aliens on earth.

   B. "I have competed well; I have finished the race; I have kept the faith. From now on the crown of righteousness awaits me, which the Lord, the just judge, will award to me on that day, and not only to me, but to all who have longed for his appearance."

2. **A.** They were seeking a better homeland, a heavenly one.

B. Because they sought a better homeland, God was not ashamed to be called their God, because He had prepared a city for them.

C. We aren't strangers and aliens; we are fellow citizens with the saints and members of the household of God. Our citizenship is in heaven.

3. **A.** Abraham believed God's promise of descendants, and knew those descendants were to come through Isaac. We see evidence that Abraham believed that somehow God would provide or that He would bring Isaac back to life when he said, "I and the boy will come back to you" (Genesis 22:5).

B. Answers will vary.

4. When Abraham was asked to sacrifice the son God had given him, it was considered "a final stage in the purification of his faith." When Abraham's faith did not weaken, he was "conformed to the likeness of the Father who [did] not spare his own Son but [delivered] him up for us all" (CCC 2572).

5. By faith, Isaac blessed his sons Jacob and Esau in regard to their future; Jacob, when he was dying, blessed each of Joseph's sons; and Joseph, when he was dying, spoke about the exodus and the fact that he wanted his bones buried in the Promised Land when his people eventually left Egypt.

Lesson 15, Day Four

1. **A.** Moses' parents saw he was a beautiful child, and "they were not afraid of the kings' edict."

B. She hid him in a papyrus basket and put it among the reeds on the bank of the Nile. Moses' sister, Miriam, stood watch. One of Pharaoh's daughters discovered him, and decided to adopt him and raise him in Pharaoh's household.

C. When we baptize infants, it is the faith of the parents that brings the child to the font of grace. We are under penalty of death, but through the waters of baptism, we are born again to new life. We go into the water as slaves to sin but come out free in Christ.

D. Luke 10:19 We have been given authority to "tread on serpents and scorpions and upon the full force of the enemy." I'm not suggesting that we invite interaction with demonic beings or purposely step on a serpent. But this verse indicates that there is a source of power available to us that most of us do not tap into. We have this authority because of our baptism. It's rooted in our baptismal identity as beloved daughters of God, the priest, prophet, and king.

2 Timothy 1:7 God has placed the Holy Spirit in our hearts, and the Spirit is not one of cowardice, but of power, love, and self-control. We can draw on the courage of the Holy Spirit when we are afraid.

1 John 4:18 Perfect love casts out fear. When we know we are recklessly loved by a God who loves perfectly, our trust in Him grows, casting out our fear.

2. **A.** He associated himself with "the people of God" even though associating himself with Pharaoh's household guaranteed him fleeting pleasures. He considered those fleeting pleasures to be sinful, so he walked away from them. He had his eye fixed on a heavenly reward. "He persevered as if seeing the one who is invisible" (Hebrews 11:27).

B. Answers will vary.

3. **A.** Moses needed personal faith to keep the Passover and sprinkle the blood on the doorsteps, and strong leadership skills to convince the Hebrew people to do likewise. He also needed faith and leadership skills to step out into the Red Sea, trusting that it would become dry, and to convince the Hebrew people to follow.

   B. Psalm 78:72 A good leader shepherds with a pure heart and skilled hands.

   Philippians 2:3–4 A good leader doesn't take action out of selfishness or vanity, rather humbly regards others as more important than him- or herself, looking out for others' interests.

   1 Timothy 4:12 Good leaders set an example for others by their beliefs, speech, conduct, love, faith, and purity.

4. **A.** God told the Israelites that instead of laying siege to the walls of Jericho and engaging in traditional battle, they were to march around the city one time each day while blowing horns, for six consecutive days. It appeared senseless and foolish. But on the seventh day, God had them march around Jericho seven times. The seventh time, they blew the horns and the walls came tumbling down.

   B. This appearance of either an angel of superior rank or the Lord Himself reminded Joshua that he was not fighting this battle alone. God was with him.

5. Even though it meant betraying her own people, Rahab hid the Israelite spies and helped them escape when they came to scout out Jericho. Her faith was made evident in her actions and also her words: "I know that the Lord has given you the land, and that a dread of you has come upon us, and that all the inhabitants of the land tremble with fear because of you. . . . We heard, and our hearts melted within us; everyone is utterly dispirited because of you, since the LORD, your God, is God in heaven above and on earth below" (Joshua 2:9, 11).

Lesson 15, Day Five

1. **A.** The heroes of Hebrews 11:32 (Gideon, Barak, Samson, Jephthah, David, Samuel, and the prophets) conquered kingdoms, did what was righteous, obtained the promises, closed the mouths of lions, put out raging fires, escaped the devouring sword, became strong in battle, and turned back foreign invaders.

   B. Out of weakness, they were made powerful. The same is true for us. As Saint Paul wrote in 2 Corinthians 12:9, God's grace is sufficient for us, and His power is made perfect in weakness.

   C. Answers will vary.

2. "The passage talks about her womanly heart and her manly courage. She seems to be a whole person who can be both compassionate and strong, who can agonize over the death of her sons but can also face the same tune that had been played for them. Her courage comes from her hope in God, a hope that does not depend on rosy results for her sons or for her: Her hope is in God who has the power to create, and then eternally offers mercy."[115]

---

[115] "The Mother of the Maccabees," in *Little Rock Catholic Study Bible,* ed. Catherine Upchurch (Little Rock, AR: Liturgical Press, 2011), 914.

3. They endured mockery; scourging; chains and imprisonment; being stoned, sawed in two, and put to death at sword point; went about in skins of sheep or goats; and were needed, afflicted, and tormented.

4. **A.** The world was not worthy of them.

   B. We are challenged to remain faithful until death, and God will give us the crown of life.

5. God had foreseen something better for us: the grace of believing in His Son, Jesus, "the pioneer and perfecter of our faith."

Lesson 16, Day One

1. **A.** A great cloud of witnesses surrounds us as we run the race of faith.

   B. The "cloud of witnesses" are those who have preceded us into the kingdom, especially those whom the Church recognizes as saints. They contemplate God, praise Him, and constantly care for those whom they have left on earth. According to Matthew 25:21, they have been put in charge of many things. Their intercession for us is their most exalted service. They offer us help in this way, and we can and should ask them to intercede for us and for the whole world.

   C. Answers will vary.

2. **A.** We need to get rid of every burden and sin that clings to us. Specifically, we need to get rid of the works of darkness, the old self, falsehood, anger and gossip, moral impurity, malice, deceit, insincerity, and slander.

   B. Answers will vary.
   Answers will vary.
   Answers will vary.
   Answers will vary.

3. **A.** Our eyes should be fixed on Jesus, the leader and perfecter of faith.

   B. He fixed His eyes for the sake of the joy that lay before Him.

   C. Saint Paul said he considered all the things that the world says matter most to be "refuse," worthless compared to winning Christ.

4. We should consider how Jesus endured such opposition from sinners.

5. **A.** In the readers' struggle against sin, they haven't yet resisted to the point of shedding blood.

   B. Answers will vary.

Lesson 16, Day Two

1. We are not to forget that we were exhorted to not disdain the Lord's discipline or lose heart when He reproves us. This is because God disciplines those He loves and scourges every son He acknowledges.

2. **Job 38:1–13** This passage reminds us of the greatness of God and the limits of man. God, as our Creator, has the right to call the shots. But He doesn't just have the right, He has the foreknowledge and wisdom to know the best course of action.

   James 4:7 and Luke 22:42 When we recognize God's greatness and that He is in control, we are to submit our will to His. We are to seek His will above our own.

   Romans 5:8 God's love for us was proven on the cross. While we were still sinners, utterly undeserving of mercy and grace, Jesus died for us.

Luke 10:25–28 What matters most to God is that we would spend eternity with Him. Our salvation and spiritual healing are His primary concern.

Revelation 21:3–5 This passage is speaking of heaven. That is where we will experience total healing—not earth. In heaven, God will wipe every tear from our eyes and there will be no more death, mourning, wailing, or pain. There, God will make all things new.

3. We are to view our trials as discipline because God is treating us as His children. Good parents discipline their children, and it is always for the children's benefit. God disciplines us so that we can grow in holiness.

4. **A.** Discipline is painful at the time, but later it brings the peaceful fruit of righteousness. This doesn't come automatically, though. It is reserved for those who are trained by it.

   B. Answers will vary.

5. **A.** We are to strengthen our drooping hands and our weak knees. We are to make straight paths for our feet, so that what is lame may not be dislocated but may instead be healed.

   B. Answers will vary.

Lesson 16, Day Three

1. **A.** We are to strive for peace with everyone, and for holiness. We are to make sure that no one is deprived of the grace of God and that no bitter root springs up and causes trouble. We are to avoid immorality and godlessness.

   B. Without holiness, no one will see the Lord.

   C. Answers will vary.

   D. Answers will vary.

2. The atmosphere was dark, gloomy, and stormy. There was a blazing fire (Exodus 19:18). God's voice sounded like a trumpet blast (Exodus 19:16, 18–19) and it caused the people to tremble. The overriding emotional response of the people was fear.

3. Countless angels are there in festal gathering, and the assembly of the firstborn enrolled in heaven. God is there as the judge of all, and the spirits of the just are there. Jesus is also there, as the mediator of the new covenant.

4. The lesser case was the warning that God gave the Israelites on Mount Sinai (when His voice shook the earth). The greater case is the warning we are now receiving from God.

5. **A.** We are receiving the unshakable kingdom. We should respond with gratitude and then offer worship pleasing to God in reverence and awe.

   B. We are to respond with gratitude and worship because God is a consuming fire.

Lesson 16, Day Four

1. **A.** We are to continue in mutual love. We are not to neglect hospitality because through it some have unknowingly entertained angels.

   B. Answers will vary.

2. We should be mindful of prisoners as if we were sharing their imprisonment, and of the ill-treated, because we are also in the body.

3. **A.** Marriage should be honored among all and the marriage bed should be kept undefiled. We are warned that God will judge the immoral and adulterers.

B. Our lives are to be free of love of money because God will never abandon us. We don't need to be afraid or buy more and more to create a sense of security. God is our helper and He will never forsake us.

4. **A.** We are to remember our leaders and imitate them.
   B. Answers will vary.

5. Jesus Christ is the same yesterday, today, and forever.

Lesson 16, Day Five

1. **A.** We are warned not to let ourselves be carried away by all kinds of strange teachings.
   B. We are no longer to be spiritual infants, tossed by waves and swept along by every wind of teaching arising from human trickery.
   C. He was likely talking about rules regarding food.

2. The altar of the new covenant is the Lord's cross, from which the sacraments of the Paschal mystery flow.

3. **A.** The bodies of the animal sacrifices were burned outside the camp, and Jesus suffered outside the gate.
   B. We are to go to Him outside the camp, bearing the reproach that He bore. We do this because here we have no lasting city, but we seek the one that is to come.

4. **A.** We are to continually offer God a sacrifice of praise, the fruit of lips that confess His name. We are also to do good and to share what we have. Those sacrifices please Him, too.
   B. Answers will vary.

5. **A.** We are to be obedient to our leaders and defer to them. We are also to pray for them.
   B. Answers will vary.

Prayer Pages

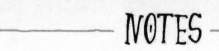

NOTES

walking with purpose

Dear Jesus,

You are the radiance of God's glory and the exact representation of His being. You sustain all things by Your powerful Word. May You increase in my mind and heart as I come to know You better through this study of Hebrews.

May I pay careful attention to what I learn so that I don't drift away. Please keep my heart tender and teachable—never hardened.

May I fix my eyes on You. As I come to recognize Your all-sufficiency, may I stop hustling for my worth, and instead make every effort to enter the rest You offer.

May I come to love Scripture more and more, recognizing it as alive and active, sharper than any double-edged sword, penetrating even to dividing soul and spirit, joints and marrow, and judging the thoughts and attitudes of the heart. May I be a doer of the Word, not just a hearer.

May I draw near to the throne of grace with confidence and find mercy and grace there in my time of need.

May I learn obedience from what I suffer and move beyond a desire for comfort to a desire for spiritual maturity.

May I grab hold of the hope set before me and be greatly encouraged. May my hope in You be an anchor for my soul, firm and secure.

Since I am surrounded by such a great cloud of witnesses, may I throw off everything that hinders and the sin that so easily entangles. May I run with perseverance the race marked out for me, fixing my eyes on You alone.

Amen.

Prayer Requests

Date:

Date:

Prayer Requests

Date:

Date:

Prayer Requests

Date:

Date:

Prayer Requests

Date:

Date:

Prayer Requests

Date:

Date:

Prayer Requests

Date:

Date:

Prayer Requests

Date:

Date:

Prayer Requests

Date:

Date:

Prayer Requests

Date:

Date:

"For to the one who has, more will be given"
Matthew 13:12

CHRIST'S LOVE IS ENDLESS.

And the journey doesn't end here.

Walking With Purpose is more than a Bible study, it's a supportive community of women seeking lasting transformation of the heart. And you are invited.

Walking With Purpose believes that change happens in the hearts of women – and, by extension, in their families and beyond – through Bible study and community. We welcome all women, irrespective of faith background, age, or marital status.

Connect with us online for regular inspiration and to join the conversation. There you'll find insightful blog posts, Scriptures, and downloads.

For a daily dose of spiritual nourishment, join our community on Facebook, Twitter, Pinterest and Instagram.

And if you're so moved to start a Walking With Purpose study group at home or in your parish, take a look at our website for more information.

walkingwithpurpose.com
The Modern Woman's Guide to the Bible.

walking with purpose

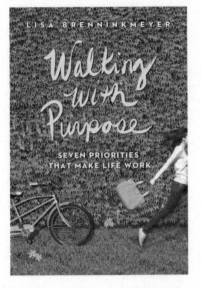

❋ DEEPEN YOUR FAITH ❋ OPEN YOUR ARMS ❋ BROADEN YOUR CIRCLE ❋

When your heart opens, and your love for Christ deepens, you may be moved to bring Walking With Purpose to your friends or parish. It's rewarding experience for many women who, in doing so, learn to rely on God's grace while serving Him.

If leading a group seems like a leap of faith, consider that you already have all the skills you need to share the Lord's Word:

- Personal commitment to Christ
- Desire to share the love of Christ
- Belief in the power of authentic, transparent community

The Walking With Purpose community supports you with:

- Training
- Mentoring
- Bible study materials
- Promotional materials

Few things stretch and grow our faith like stepping out of our comfort zone and asking God to work through us. Say YES, soon you'll see the mysterious and unpredictable ways He works through imperfect women devoted to Him.

Remember that if you humbly offer Him what you can, He promises to do the rest.

"See to it that no one misses the grace of God" Hebrews 12:15

**Learn more about bringing Walking with Purpose to your parish.
Visit us at walkingwithpurpose.com
The Modern Woman's Guide To The Bible.**

INTRODUCING 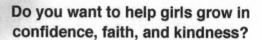 **THE MODERN GIRL'S GUIDE TO THE BIBLE.**

Do you want to help girls grow in confidence, faith, and kindness?

The Lord is calling for women like you to speak truth into the hearts of young girls – girls who are understandably confused about their true worth and beauty. Blaze is a fun and engaging program developed especially for 7th and 8th grade girls to counteract the cultural forces that drive them to question their value, purpose, and faith.

Like Walking With Purpose, Blaze makes the wisdom of the Bible relevant to today's challenges. Blaze teaches girls to recognize the difference between the loving, affirming voice of their heavenly Father and the voices that tell them they aren't good enough.

Would you like to be a positive influence on the girls you know? Start a Blaze program in in your parish or community.

It's easy and convenient to share God's word with a Leader's Guide and Blaze kit that includes:

- Blaze Prayer Journals
- Truth vs. Lie Cards
- Fun gifts for the girls
- Facebook and Instagram messaging to maintain connection and amplify the message

Additional resources to nurture girls' spiritual growth:

- Discovering My Purpose – a 6-session Bible study that leads girls on an exploration of their own spiritual gifts
- Between You & Me – a 40-day conversation guide for mothers and daughters

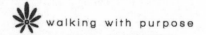

For more spiritual inspiration or to learn more about Blaze and Walking With Purpose, visit us at walkingwithpurpose.com/BLAZE

You're also invited to join our community on Facebook, Twitter, Pinterest and Instagram.

"Be who God meant you to be and you will set the world on fire." - Saint Catherine of Siena

THE GUIDED TOUR OF GOD'S LOVE BEGINS HERE.

Opening Your Heart: The Starting Point begins a woman's exploration of her Catholic faith and enhances her relationship with Jesus Christ. This Bible study is designed to inspire thoughtful consideration of the fundamental questions of living a life in the Lord. More than anything, it's a weekly practice of opening your heart to the only One who can heal and transform lives.

Explore these topics and more:

- What is the role of the Holy Spirit in my life?
- What does the Eucharist have to do with my friendship with Christ?
- What are the limits of Christ's forgiveness?
- Why and how should I pray?
- What is the purpose of suffering?
- What challenges will I face in my efforts to follow Jesus more closely?
- How can fear be overcome?

A companion DVD series complements this journey with practical insights and spiritual support.

Opening Your Heart is a foundational 22-week Bible study that serves any woman who seeks to grow closer to God. It's an ideal starting point for women who are new to Walking with Purpose, and those with prior practice in Bible study, too.

To share Walking with Purpose with the women in your parish, contact us at walkingwithpurpose.com/start.

Walking With Purpose
The modern woman's guide to the Bible.
walkingwithpurpose.com

walking with purpose

walking with purpose

These transformative full-length Bible studies are created to help women deepen their personal relationship with Christ. Each study includes many lessons that explore core themes and challenges of modern life through the ancient wisdom of the Bible and the Catholic Church.

INTRODUCTORY LEVEL

Opening Your Heart

A thoughtful consideration of the fundamental questions of faith – from why and how to pray to the role of the Holy Spirit in our lives and the purpose of suffering.

Living In the Father's Love

Gain a deeper understanding of how God's unconditional love transforms your relationship with others, with yourself, and most dearly, with Him.

INTERMEDIATE LEVEL

Keeping in Balance

Discover how the wisdom of the Old and New Testaments can help you live a blessed lifestyle of calm, health, and holiness.

Touching the Divine

These thoughtful studies draw you closer to Jesus and deepen your faith, trust, and understanding of what it means to be God's beloved daughter.

ADVANCED LEVEL

Discovering Our Dignity
Modern-day insight directly from women of the Bible presented as a tender, honest, and loving conversation—woman to woman.

Beholding His Glory
Old Testament Scripture leads us directly to our Redeemer, Jesus Christ. Page after page, God's awe-inspiring majesty is a treasure to behold.

Beholding Your King
This study of King David and several Old Testament prophets offers a fresh perspective of how all Scripture points to the glorious coming of Christ.

Grounded In Hope
Anchor yourself in the truth found in the New Testament book of Hebrews, and gain practical insight to help you run your race with perseverance.

Fearless and Free
This study is for any woman confronting the reality that life isn't easy through six compassionate lessons to flourish in Christ's love.

Walking With Purpose is a supportive community of women seeking lasting transformation of the heart through Bible study. We welcome all women, irrespective of faith, background, age, or marital status. For a daily dose of spiritual nourishment, join our community on Facebook, Twitter, Pinterest and Instagram.

walkingwithpurpose.com

walking with purpose

 **Mission**

Walking with Purpose transforms the hearts
and lives of women by providing Bible studies
that enable women to know Christ
through Scripture and the teachings of the
Roman Catholic Church.

 Vision

To enable every Catholic woman
in America to experience our life-changing
Bible study, *Opening Your Heart.*

Join us in transforming the hearts and lives of women.
Make a gift to Walking with Purpose today!

walkingwithpurpose.com/donate